**Public Participation
in Planning**

Public Participation in Planning

Edited by

W. R. DERRICK SEWELL

Department of Geography
University of Victoria

and

J. T. COPPOCK
Department of Geography
University of Edinburgh

JOHN WILEY & SONS

London · New York · Sydney · Toronto

Library of Congress Cataloging in Publication Data:
Main entry under title:

Public participation in planning.

   Includes index.
   1. Cities and towns – Planning – Citizen participation – Addresses, essays, lectures. 2. Regional
planning – Citizen participation – Addresses, essays,
lectures. I. Sewell, W. R. Derrick, II. Coppock,
John Terence.
HT166.P8   309.2'12   76–56800

ISBN 0 471 99474 X

Typeset in IBM Press Roman by Preface Ltd., Salisbury, Wilts.
Printed in Great Britain by Unwin Brothers Ltd.,
The Gresham Press, Old Woking, Surrey.

List of Contributors

J. T. COPPOCK

Department of Geography, University of Edinburgh, High School Yards, Edinburgh EH1 1NR, Scotland.

NORMAN DENNIS

Department of Social Studies, University of Newcastle on Tyne, Newcastle, England.

WILLIAM HAMPTON

Senior Lecturer, Department of Extramural Studies, University of Sheffield, Sheffield, England.

JOHN C. HENDEE

Division of Legal Affairs, U.S. Forest Service, Washington, D.C. 20250

HELEN INGRAM AND SCOTT J. ULLERY

Department of Government, University of Arizona, Tucson, Arizona 85721, U.S.A.

ROGER KASPERSON

Graduate School of Geography, Clark University, Worcester, Mass. 01610, U.S.A.

JOHN P. MACKINTOSH M.P.

House of Commons, London SW1A 0AA, England.

W. S. MUTCH

School of Forestry and Natural Resources, University of Edinburgh, Kings Buildings, Edinburgh, Scotland.

TIMOTHY O'RIORDAN

School of Environmental Sciences, University of East Anglia, Norwich, Norfolk, England.

STEVEN SCHATZOW

Office of General Counsel, U.S. Environmental Protection Agency, Washington, D.C., U.S.A.

W. R. DERRICK SEWELL

Department of Geography, University of Victoria, Victoria V8W 2 Y2, B.C. Canada.

MARGARET SINCLAIR

728 Avenue Road, Toronto, Ontario, Canada.

J. M. THOMSON

European Inter-City Transport Study, OECD, 2 Rue Andre Pascal, 75775 Paris CEDEX 16, France

COLIN WOOD

Department of Geography, University of Victoria, Victoria V8W 2Y2, B.C. Canada.

Contents

Preface

In the period since the Second World War, there appears to have been increasing disillusionment with both central and local government. In part, this reflects a wider reaction against authority in various forms, expressed in demands for a greater say in decisions which affect people's lives and in direct action to ensure that these demands are met. Whether willingly or otherwise, the need for greater involvement by those affected has been increasingly recognized by administrators and politicians and a variety of mechanisms have been tried with varying success. Much of this concern has been focused on changes in the character and extent of the built environment and on those man-made environmental changes which affect, whether obviously or subtly, the quality of human life for both present and future generations.

The theme of public participation therefore seemed a very appropriate one for a joint seminar sponsored by the School of the Built Environment and the Centre for Human Ecology in the University of Edinburgh, a seminar which was the genesis of this book. The School of the Built Environment is a loose federation of the Departments of Architecture, Civil and Fire Engineering, Geography and Urban Design and Regional Planning, and holds an annual seminar which embraces the interests of the constituent departments and has indeed ranged widely over the environmental and social sciences. The Centre of Human Ecology attempts to encompass an even wider span of interests, ranging from divinity, through the social and natural sciences, to medicine and law. The seminar, held in Edinburgh in May 1973, was attended by fifty invited contributors and discussants, including elected members and officials from central and local government and academics from a wide range of disciplines. Some twenty-three papers were precirculated and formed the basis for lively workshops and discussions. Inevitably, those attending were mainly British, but the movement towards public participation is probably more strongly developed in North America. While it seemed that a selection of the papers presented could usefully form the basis of chapters in a book on public participation, the editors felt that it would be advantageous to readers on both sides of the Atlantic if they achieved a better balance by inviting further contributions

x

from those who had investigated a variety of aspects of public participation in the United States and Canada. The present volume is the result, and it is interesting to note that, while the chapters relating to the United Kingdom are conceived within the framework of statutory planning, most of those which deal with North American examples are concerned with broader environmental issues (a reflection perhaps of the lesser development of effective legislation and machinery to control land—use change, urban development and pollution, and also perhaps of different attitudes towards government). Whatever the causes, the examination of the variety of ways of securing public participation in different legal and cultural environments should be of value to all who believe that 'planning is for people'.

W. R. DERRICK SEWELL
J. T. COPPOCK

Tables

Figures

1
A Perspective on Public Participation in Planning

W. R. Derrick Sewell and J. T. Coppock

Planning in the 1970s faces a critical challenge: how to accommodate a mounting demand for a greater degree of public participation. It emerged initially in connection with problems relating to cities, such as urban renewal, the location of noxious facilities and the development of transport networks. Recently it has become even more widespread, embracing such matters as poverty, education and the protection of the environment. While this challenge is not new, it has become increasingly intense in the past decade and is being experienced in the United Kingdom, in North America and elsewhere.

Roots of the Mounting Pressure

Pressure for an expanded role for the public in planning is rooted in both philosophical and pragmatic considerations. The former is related primarily to the general belief in democratic societies that the individual has the right to be informed and consulted and to express his views on matters which affect him personally. In modern representative government reliance is placed upon elected representatives, who provide a channel of communication between the governors and the governed, and upon various traditional techniques such as the ballot box, public inquiries and letters to officials or to newspapers. This system works well when the interests can be identified, when those affected can articulate their views and when channels of communication are well-known to the individuals involved. It works less well when it is difficult to determine precisely whose interests would be affected and when people do not have to convey their views. In recent years there has been growing concern that the public — or at least significant segments of it — has developed an increasing feeling of alienation towards governmental decision-making. Sometimes there are no channels of communication for the transmission of information or the expression of views, and even where they exist, the public may not know about them or they may seem ineffectual. In some instances a profound distrust of the entire system has developed. The problem has been especially acute in matters that affect minorities, but it now involves issues which concern a large proportion of the population of particular areas, notably issues relating to modifications of the environment (Wengert, 1971a; Marshall *et al.*, 1972).

Pragmatic considerations cover chiefly the failure of plans or decisions to identify public preferences correctly, and it is in these circumstances that the questioning of the present system has been particularly intense. Schemes which have been drawn up by planners and promoted by politicians have subsequently failed to obtain public support, either at the ballot box or after implementation. There are numerous illustrations in both the urban field and in the development of natural resources, notably in urban redevelopment (for example, when relocation disrupts social interrelationships or intensifies alienation, as in high-rise dwellings), the construction of highway networks, and in projects for water development, such as various reservoirs for urban water supply in the United Kingdom (Eversley, 1973; Dennis, 1972; Meyerson & Banfield, 1955; Gregory, 1972). This failure may reflect an incorrect identification of goals or of preferred means, but whatever the cause, it has sometimes proved very costly, in both economic and social terms. For example, some $64 million was spent on the Spadina Expressway in Toronto before construction was finally halted.

The growing dissatisfaction with existing means of consulting the public has been demonstrated in a variety of ways. Perhaps the most significant has been the dramatic increase in the number of pressure groups seeking to influence planning and policy-making. Not only have traditional groups grown markedly in size but there has also been a large increase in the number of new groups, especially those concerned with urban and environmental problems (Bell & Held, 1969; Pross, 1975; Scott, 1957). These trends are characteristic of many countries (Pross, 1975; Hendee, 1969, Draper, 1975).

This growth has been accompanied by some important changes in the nature and composition of groups, the goals they seek and the strategies they employ. Thus membership of the environmental groups is not confined to well-meaning middle-class citizens (Dunlap & Gale, 1972; Allaby, 1971) nor to those whose sole concern is the preservation of wildlife habitats or scenic amenities (Hendee, 1969). Urban action groups increasingly include the affected as well as the benevolent (Bell & Held, 1969). Furthermore, while many groups use traditional strategies in seeking influence, such as establishing contacts with planners and politicians, preparing briefs for hearings or writing letters, other strategies have also been tried, ranging from the formation of workshops and the holding of public meetings to the staging of demonstrations (Allaby, 1971; Dunlap & Gale, 1972).

Responses to the Growing Demands

Governments and government agencies have responded to varying degrees and in a variety of ways to the growing demands for more public participation. These responses have included the initiation of studies to assess the nature and significance of the demands, the mounting of experiments to determine the effectiveness of various methods of involving the public, and the passage of legislation and the alteration of administrative structures to provide for some future participation. Several governmental and academic investigations relating to public participation have been undertaken on both sides of the Atlantic, some of which examine the question as it affects a broad range of areas of government interest (Canada, Task Force on Government Information, 1969; Ministry of Housing and Local Government, 1969), others as it concerns a particular area of interest, such as urban problems (Mogulof, 1970; Spiegel, 1968; Lynch, 1972; Ontario Select Committee on the Ontario Municipal Board, 1972; Ontario Committee on Government Productivity, 1972), poverty (Moynihan, 1969), or problems of resource management (Canada, Canadian Council of Resources and Environment Ministers, 1973).

Associated with these studies have been several in-depth studies and experiments, aimed at assessing the effectiveness of particular avenues of participation. Some of these have included attempts to involve members of the public in the broad issue of urban planning; for example, the New York City Regional Plan Association adopted a programme of mailed questionnaires, television broadcasts, public meetings and conferences, and more than 5000 people became involved in the discussions (Robshaw, 1969). Some attempts have concerned planning for water resources development (Bishop, 1971; Chevalier & Cartwright, 1971; Borton et al., 1970; Vindasius, 1974). Others have sought to assess the effectiveness of various avenues of participation in structure planning, as Hampton describes later in this volume in relation to England and Wales. In Canada, an attempt was made on a national basis to determine public views about problems affecting natural resources, through a Man and Resources Conference, organized in successive steps from neighbourhood and local meetings, provincial meetings, and finally a national meeting (Canada, Canadian Council of Resources and Environmental Ministers, 1973).

The results of these various studies seem to indicate that no one technique is adequate and that a combination of several is usually required. A recent review by Vindasius (1974) shows that each technique has advantages and disadvantages (Figure 1.1). The techniques presently in use include the following:

1. Public opinion polls and other surveys;
2. Referenda;
3. The ballot box;
4. Public hearings;
5. Advocacy planning;
6. Letters to editors or public officials;
7. Representations of pressure groups;
8. Protests and demonstrations;
9. Court actions;
10. Public meetings;
11. Workshops or seminars;
12. Task forces.

While these might be ordered in several different ways, as listed here they seem to indicate a gradual increase in commitment of time of those involved and increasing

Type of public involvement mechanism	Descriptive dimensions				
	Focus		Degree of two-way communication	Level of public activity required	Agency staff time. requirements
	Scope	Specificity			
Informal local contacts	low	high	high	medium	medium
Mass media (including use of newspapers, radio and TV)	high	low	low	low	low
Publications	high	medium	low	low	medium
Surveys, questionnaires	medium	high	low	medium	medium
Workshops	low	high	high	high	high
Advisory committees	low	high	high	high	high
Public hearings	medium	low	low	high	medium
Public meetings	medium	low	medium	medium	medium
Public inquiry	high	low	low	high	high
Special task forces	low	high	high	high	high
Gaming simulation	low	high	high	high	high

Legend: • low ● medium ⬤ high

Figure 1.1 Descriptive dimensions of public involvement mechanisms

possibilities for interaction between planners and the public, and hence increasing opportunities for mutual education as to perspectives. Several of the experiments conducted to date (Vindasius, 1974) suggest that the introduction of public meetings, workshops and seminars, and task forces has been especially helpful in establishing maintaining credibility and confidence. They are not, however, a panacea.

Governmental responses have also included the passage or modification of legislation and/or alteration of existing administrative structures to permit a greater degree of public participation. While in some instances (as in the Canada Water Act) participation is encouraged but not required, in others there are specific requirements for such participation. In England and Wales, for example, the Town and Country Planning Acts of 1968 and 1969 require public participation in the formulation of structure plans (Robshaw, 1969). In the United States the slogan 'maximum feasible participation', coined by Daniel Moynihan, was first given expression in the anti-poverty legislation (the Economic Opportunity Act), and later in the Model Cities Programme of urban renewal and the environmental protection legislation (National Environmental Policy Act, 1969). Specific guide-lines have been drawn up, describing procedures for obtaining inputs from the public.

In several countries new administrative organizations have been established, often staffed by specialists, who have included psychologists, sociologists and geographers, to organize or co-ordinate programmes of public participation. Such organizations have been set up by government departments in some parts of the United States (Mogulof, 1970), Canada (Sewell, 1975), France (Tenière-Buchot), and the United Kingdom, on either an experimental or a permanent basis.

Results of Programmes for Increasing Public Participation

This movement towards greater public participation is still at an early stage in most countries and it is not possible to reach firm conclusions on how far it will go or what its final form will be. In some instances an enlarged role for the public in planning and policy-making has been both accepted and encouraged by the public, government officials and politicians. In some cities it has provided the spark for action where other attempts had failed, as in planning in New York (Robshaw, 1969) and San Francisco (Schoop & Hinten, 1971). Public participation pro-grammes of the U.S. Corps of Engineers have received enthusiastic responses in several parts of the United States (Mazmanian & Nienaber, 1974), as have programmes in various parts of Canada. Involvement in structure planning in the United Kingdom has also attracted favourable comment.

The experience, however, has not been universally good and there has been a steady stream of reports by participants, administrators and observers pointing to negative results. In some instances programmes seem to have foundered because too much was expected of them: they did not immediately deliver the Promised Land, or they did not achieve the political change which some of the participants wished to accomplish (Bell & Held, 1969). In others they failed because they seemed merely to furnish a means of endorsing what the planners or the politicians had already decided, a charge which has frequently been made in connection with urban renewal programmes in the United States, programmes for highway or airport construction, and policy-making with respect to pollution control.

In some instances planners, administrators and politicians have enthusiastically welcomed greater interaction with the public, especially where this seemed to be a means of assessing more accurately public views, obtaining additional expertise, or furnishing greater opportunities to gain public understanding of proposed policies. On the whole, however, a generally cautious view seems to have been adopted, resulting in rather small, incremental changes in existing mechanisms for involving the public. The reasons given include the fact that greater involvement inevitably means that more time is taken in reaching a decision, and that the costs of planning increase (especially where long, drawn-out public hearings are involved). Perhaps there is also an underlying concern that increased public participation will result in a reduction of power and prestige for the planner, the administrator or the politician.

This attitude of caution, coupled with a number of negative experiences, has led some observers to suggest that the movement towards group public participation may already be on the wane and that it may soon die out. Mazmanian and Nienaber (1974), for example, have noted that history is replete with instances of enthusiasm for more direct involvement in participation, followed by distrust and even opposition. They suggest that this can be explained partly by the 'free rider problem', i.e., the fact that members of the public are apathetic and unconcerned about most issues and are content to let representatives decide on their behalf, reflecting a belief that the costs of participation are more than the individual gains; and partly by the fact that government officials are resistant to change (and tend to be satisfied with traditional procedures and to be unwilling to alter them unless it is clear that improvements in efficiency, power and prestige will follow). Hence, unless the public sees clearly demonstrable gains from increased participation over the long term, and unless officials and decision-makers are convinced that the process will be improved, relatively little change may be expected.

These views seem to be endorsed by Anthony Downs's (1972) theory of the 'issue—attention cycle' which, he suggests, strongly influences public attitudes and behaviour concerning most domestic problems. Downs identifies five stages in the evolution of and attention to political issues, namely: (1) pre-problem; (2) alarmed discovery and euphoric enthusiasm; (3) realization of the cost of significant progress; (4) gradual decline of intense public interest; (5) post-problem stage (see Figure 1.2). In other words, problems tend to leap suddenly into prominence, remain there for a short time and, although perhaps unresolved, fade away, to be replaced by other problems which are perceived as more urgent. If present participation in environmental affairs is appraised in terms of the five-stage cycle, it may now be passing from Stage 2 to Stage 3 and is hence not yet a dying issue. Whenever that stage is reached, it may result in a declining amount of public involvement. Legislation and changes in administrative structures and public policies, however, will ensure that a somewhat higher level of such participation will prevail than before the present movement began.

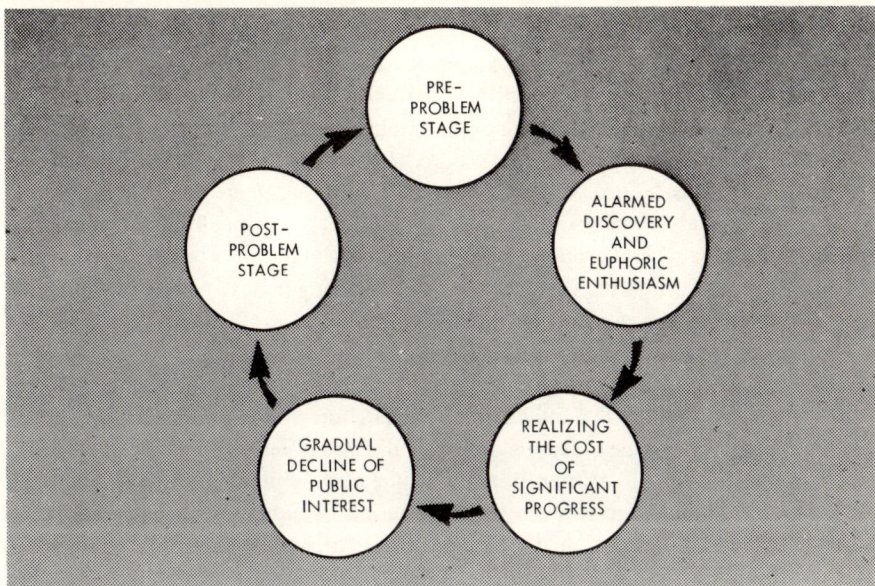

Figure 1.2 The issue-attention cycle

Emerging Problems

The level and the form of public participation will hinge in part on the answers to six critical questions, identified by Wengert (1971c).

(i) Who should participate?

Ideally the process of decision-making should take into account the views of all those who have a legitimate interest in the matter at issue. Sometimes it is clear who such individuals are, particularly where both those who will gain and those who will pay can be identified. The provision of a new access road to a recreational area, paid for by the owners of summer cottages who would use it, is an illustration. There are many issues, however, where it is very difficult to identify all the legitimate interests, as in urban renewal or problems of environmental preservation.

Typically, reliance is placed upon interest groups and concerned individuals making their views known through such channels as contacts with officials, letters to newspapers, or appearances at public meetings or hearings. Recent experience has shown, however, that there may be substantial minorities, notably the poor and other racial groups, who fail to make their views known, for one reason or another. It has also shown that some individuals oppose policies or institutions in principle, without necessarily having a personal interest in them themselves. The dilemma of deciding who has a 'legitimate' interest in particular environmental issues has sometimes pitted those who believe they do not need to have a direct personal stake in a given issue in order to express their views, against officials who define 'legitimate interest' in terms of 'identified legitimate interests'.

(ii) Who is likely *to participate?*

As has already been noted, the public tend to be apathetic about most policy issues unless they are clearly and directly affected, and unless they are convinced that personal involvement in planning or policy-making is likely to make some difference. Most issues are 'routine' (Sewell & Wood, 1971) and can be left to responsible officials to take care of them. A few are 'strategic', and these tend to capture the attention of existing interest groups: occasionally they spark the formation of new *ad hoc* groups composed of individuals who feel threatened and who see in group action the opportunity of influencing policy in their favour (or at least minimizing the harm they might experience).

Planning and policy-making tend to be in the hands of relatively small elites of officials and politicians, who are influenced to some extent by various interest groups, though these involve only a small proportion of the public. In the United States, for example, some sixty per cent of all citizens belong to an interest group, interpreted as all kinds of interest groups (including church groups) (Almond & Verba, 1963). Similar figures seem to characterize the situation in Canada but the proportion is much lower in many European countries (Curtis, 1971). If account is taken of those involved in various forms of *political* activity, however. it is probable that less than seven per cent of the electorate in most countries is involved on a continuous basis. Beyond this, some issues receive comparatively little attention from interest groups. Hendee (1969) suggests, for example, that conservation issues are the focus of attention of no more than one per cent of American citizens.

Equally important is the fact that those involved tend to be drawn from the ranks of the better educated, better paid and more politically aware members of the public (Babchuck & Booth, 1969). Even where membership of iterest groups or community action programmes extends to other social classes, leadership and advice are often provided by those in the middle and upper classes (Bell & Held, 1969).

Continuous participation rests, of course, on indications that some useful purpose is being served. Members of the public involved in planning, for example, need to feel that they are participating in something that is likely to have tangible results; the same is true of those who try to influence policy formulation. When such confidence declines, so also does the motivation for involvement. Hence, while the birth rate of environmental interest groups was phenomenal in the early 1970s, a large proportion of them died; some members joined other groups but many have become disenchanted and are no longer involved in any kind of interest group activity.

(iii) How much participation is possible and desirable?

It is neither useful nor possible to consult every individual on every issue that may interest him: the challenge is to find the array of issues where inputs from 'legitimate interests' would lead to higher levels of social satisfaction. As Wengert (1971a) has suggested, progressively higher levels of participation may not necessarily lead to progressively higher levels of social satisfaction or more democratic decision-making, nor may it necessarily result in a reduction of alienation. He goes on to point out that there has been a tendency to get caught up in the rhetoric – 'Enthralled with moralisms and honorary stances, many who have written on the subject have not undertaken the analyses nor the empirical work necessary to support their many premises'. The central question of how far it is possible (or desirable) to move from the present system of representative democracy to a system of participatory democracy remains.

(iv) On what issues and at what stages in decision-making is public participation desirable?

There are numerous issues that compete for public attention. 'Routine' matters require little or no direct inputs from the public in decisions about them, but 'strategic' matters typically involve conflicts between interests (as in the use of a natural resource or a decision whether or not to relocate a given community), and hence there is a need to consult the interests involved. A major difficulty, however, is that of identifying 'strategic' issues and providing the necessary machinery to deal with them when no avenues of communication have previously existed (Sewell & Wood, 1971).

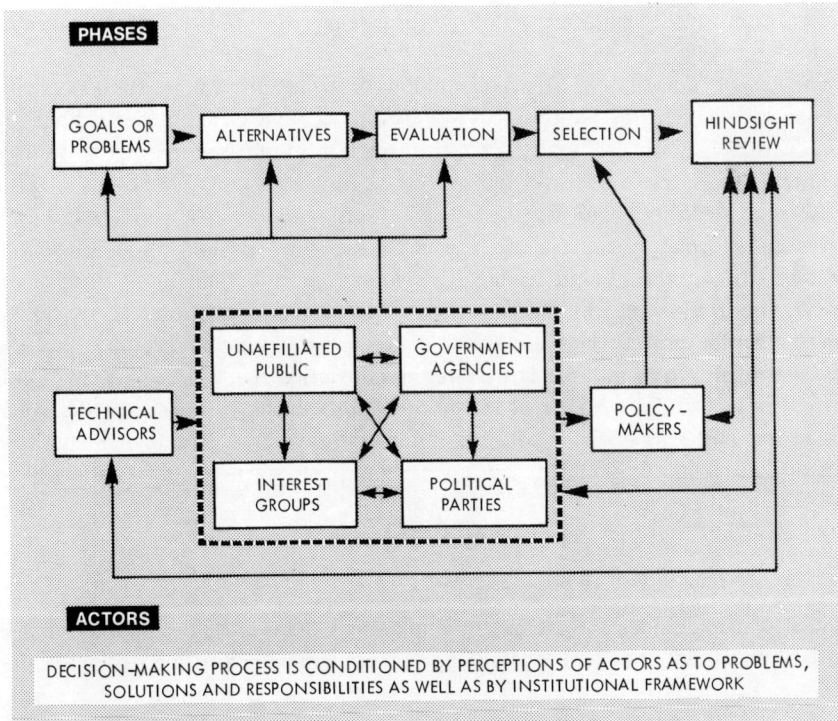

Figure 1.3 The process of Policy-Making and the roles of actors

Decision-making consists of a number of stages or phases which are linked through several channels of communication. Various interests can bring influence to bear at each of these stages, either through planning agencies or through decision-makers (Figure 1.3). Many of those who have argued in favour of an expanded role for the public, have suggested that members of the public should be involved at all stages; others have suggested that public inputs are more critical at some stages than at others, notably in identifying goals and criteria, drawing up lists of alternative strategies and isolating the potential impacts of the latter.

There are other dilemmas as to whether the same people should be involved at all stages, and if not, which groups should be involved at which points. A further problem is how to maintain interest, especially when the planning process is long and no definite commitment has been made to take any action.

(v) What weight should be attached to the views of well-organized, articulate interest groups as against the views of the unorganized public?

The results of public participation may appear in various forms — letters, comments at meetings, responses to questionnaires — and the problem arises how these should be compared. Various questions present themselves as a result.

Should, for example, all opinions be given equal weight, irrespective of knowledge of the respondents; and should one letter indicative of interest and concern rank equally with answers to a questionnaire from a reluctant, randomly selected respondent?

Whether or not such a general appraisal of 'what the public thinks' can be produced, there remains the problem of deciding what weight such views should be given. This decision is essentially a political one for, at one extreme, the process of consultation can play a decisive role in the selection of alternatives, by-passing the elected representatives, while at the other extreme, public participation can be no more than a formal procedure, undertaken to satisfy a legal obligation or to avoid more difficult conflicts, and having little weight in the final decision. Even if planners, politicians and administrators are prepared to accept a role as providers of what the public wants, there are major problems of reconciling the interests and objectives of different groups. The degree of conviction that public participation is worthwhile is also likely to affect attitudes towards the cost of participation, for it must be recognized that public consultation is costly, whether in actual expenditure or in time, particularly if it is to be undertaken in ways which allow confidence to be placed on the results.

(vi) How can meaningful views on regional and national issues be obtained?

Much of the discussion relating to planning and the role of the public in it has focused upon cities and local areas. Here, it seems, members of the public are able to relate directly to the problem, and to interact on a continuous basis with planners and officials. The difficulty of obtaining well-informed public views tends to increase rapidly as the locus of the topic of concern moves from the local to the regional level, and then to the national level; the difficulty is even greater where international questions are involved. Yet many of the problems which now face society are at least regional if not national in character; for example, whether or not there should be accelerated or decelerated economic growth, where the elements of a national highway or airport system or (as in Scotland) oil production facilities should be sited. Even when the various views have been obtained, the task of reconciling them remains. That, as John Mackintosh suggests in Chapter 13, is both the dilemma and the responsibility of the elected representative.

The chapters which follow shed some light on these questions, derived in some instances from the philosophies of the authors and in others from the experience of actual programmes of public participation. They underline the fact that, although there seems to have developed a growing acceptance of the ideology of public participation, there remain considerable difficulties in putting it into practice.

References

References marked with an asterisk are additional to those cited in the text and provide fuller coverage of the field.

Allaby, Michael, 1971. *The Eco-Activists: Youth Fights for the Human Environment*, London: Charles Knight.
Almond, G. A. & S. Verba, 1963. *The Civic Culture*, Princeton: Princeton University Press.
*Arvill, Robert, 1969. *Man and Environment: Crisis and the Strategy of Choice*, Harmondsworth, Middlesex: Penguin Books.
Babchuck, N. & A. Booth, 1969. 'Voluntary Association Membership: A Longitudinal Analysis', *American Sociological Review*, **34**(1), 31—45.
Bell, Daniel & Virginia Held, 1969. 'The Community Revolution', *The Public Interest*, Summer, 142—177.
Bishop, A. Bruce, 1971. *Public Participation in Water Resource Planning*, Springfield, Va.: Federal Scientific and Technical Information Clearinghouse, December.
Borton, Thomas E. *et al.*, 1970. *The Susquehanna Communication—Participation Study: Selected Approaches to Public Involvement in Water Resources Planning*, Springfield, Va.: Federal Scientific and Technical Information Clearinghouse, December.
Canada, Task Force on Government Information, 1969. *To Know and Be Known*, Ottawa: Queen's Printer, 2 vols.
*Canada—British Columbia Okanagan Basin Agreement, 1971, 1972, 1973. *Annual Reports*, Victoria, B.C.
Chevalier, M. & T. L. Cartwright, 1971. 'Public Involvement in Planning: The Delaware Case', in W. R. Derrick Sewell & Ian Burton (eds.), *Perceptions and Attitudes in Resources Management*, Ottawa: Information Canada, pp. 111—120.
*Curran, T, P., 1971. 'Water Resources Management in the Public Interest', *Water Resources Bulletin*, February, 33—39.
Curtis, James A., 1971. 'Canada as a Nation of Joiners', in *Social Process and Institution*, James Gallagher & Ronald D. Lambert (eds,), Holt, Rinehart & Winston, pp.147—164.
*Damar, Sean & Cliff Hague, 1971. 'Public Participation in Planning: A Review', *Town Planning Review*, **42** (3), July, 217—232.

Dennis, Norman, 1972. *Public Participation and Planners' Blight*, London: Faber & Faber.

Downs, Anthony, 1972. 'Up and Down with Ecology – The Issue Attention Cycle', *The Public Interest,* **29**, Summer, 38–50.

Draper, Dianne, 1975. 'Environmental Interest Groups and Institutional Arrange-ments in B.C. Water Management Issues', in Bruce Mitchell (ed.), *Institutional Arrangements for Water Management: Canadian Experiences*, University of Waterloo, Department of Geography Monograph Series No. 5.

Dunlap, Riley E. & Richard P. Gale, 1972. 'Politics and Ecology: A Political Profile of Student Eco-Activists', *Youth and Society*, June, 379–397.

Eversley, David, 1973. *The Planner in Society: The Changing Role of a Profession*, London: Faber & Faber.

*Gale, Richard P., 1972. 'From Sit-in to Hike-in: A Comparison of The Civil Rights and Environmental Movements', in W. M. Burch *et al.* (eds.), *Social Behaviour: Natural Resources and the Environment*, New York: Harper & Row, pp. 280–305.

*Great Britain, Department of Environment, 1973. *Public Participation in General Improvement Areas*, London: Her Majesty's Stationery Office.

Great Britain, Ministry of Housing and Local Government, 1969. *People and Planning*, Report of the Committee on Public Participation in Planning (Skeffington Committee), London: Her Majesty's Stationery Office.

Gregory, Roy, 1972. *The Price of Amenity* London: Macmillan.

Hendee, John C., 1969. 'Conservation, Politics, and Democracy', *Journal of Soil and Water Conservation*, November–December, 213–215.

*Hendee, John C. *et al.*, 1974. *Public Involvement and the Forest Service: Experience, Effectiveness, and Suggested Direction*, Washington, D.C.: U.S, Forest Service.

*Kasperson, Roger E. & Berna Breitbast, 1974. *Participation, Decentralization, and Advocacy Planning*, Association of American Geographers Resource Paper No. 25, Washington, D.C.

*Krause, Elliott, 1969. 'Functions of a Bureaucratic Ideology: Citizen Preparation', *Social Problems*, Summer, 129–143.

*Lyden, Fremont James, 1969. 'Citizen Participation in Policy-Making: A Study of a Community Action Program', *Social Science Quarterly*, December, 631–642.

Lynch, Thomas D. (ed.), 1972. 'Symposium on Neighborhoods and Citizen Involvement', *Public Administration Review*, May–June.

Marshall, Dale Rogers *et al.*, 1972. *Minority Perspectives*, Baltimore: Johns Hopkins Press.

*May, Judith V., 1971. *Citizen Participation: A Review of the Literature*, Davis, California: University of California, Institute of Governmental Affairs.

Mazmanian, Daniel A. & Jeanne Nienaber, 1974. *Citizen Participation in Agency Decision-Making: Can it Survive?*, paper presented at a meeting of the.Public Choice Society, Newhaven, Conn., March 21–23.

Meyerson, Martin & E. G. Banfield, 1955. *Politics, Planning and the Public Interest: The Case of Public Housing in Chicago*, New York: The Free Press.

*Miller, Delbert C., 1972. 'The Allocation of Priorities to Urban and Environmental Problems by Powerful leaders and Organizations', in W. M. Burch *et al.* (eds.), *Social Behaviour: Natural Resources and the Environment*, New York: Harper & Row, pp. 306–327.

Mogulof, Melvin B., 1970. *Citizen Participation: A Review and Commentary of Federal Policies and Practices.* The Urban Institute, Washington D.C.

*Morley, G. (ed.), 1973. *Ask the People*, Winnipeg: Agassiz Centre for Water Studies.

*Morley, G. G., 1973. *Canada's Environment: The Law on Trial*, Winnipeg: Agassiz Centre for Water Studies.

Moynihan, Daniel P., 1969. *Maximum Feasible Misunderstanding: Community Action in the War on Poverty*, New York: The Free Press.

*Nicholson, Simon & Barbara K. Schreiner, 1973. *Community Participation in City Decision-Making*, Watton Hall, Milton Keynes, the Open University.

*Nowlan, David & Nadine Nowlan, 1970. *The Bad Trip: The Untold Story of the Spadina Expressway*, Toronto: House of Anansi.

Ontario Committee on Government Productivity, 1972. *Citizen Involvement*, Toronto: Queen's Printer.

Ontario, Select Committee on the Ontario Municipal Board, 1972. *Final Report*, Toronto.

Pross, A. Paul (ed.), 1975. *Pressure Group Behaviour in Canadian Politics*, Scarborough, Ontario: McGraw-Hill Ryerson.

Robshaw, Peter, 1969. *Public Participation in Urban Planning*, Ditchley Park, Oxfordshire: The Ditchley Foundation.

Schoop, E. Jack & John E. Hinten, 1971. 'The San Francisco Bay Plan: Combining Policy with Police Power', *Journal of the American Institute of Planners*, January, 2–10.

Scott, John C., 1937. 'Membership and Participation in Voluntary Associations', *American Sociological Review*, June, 315–357.

*Sewell, W. R. Derrick, 1971 'Integrating Public Views in Planning and Policy-Making', in W. R. Derrick Sewell & Ian Burton (eds.), *Perceptions and Attitudes in Resources Management*, Ottawa: Information Canada, pp. 125–132.

*Sewell, W. R. Derrick, 1974. 'Perceptions, Attitudes and Public Participation in Countryside Management in Scotland', *Journal of Environmental Management*, 2, 235–258.

Sewell, W. R. Derrick, 1975. 'Public Involvement', in *Comprehensive River Basin Planning*, Ottawa: Canada, Dept. of Environment, Water Resources Service.

Sewell, W. R. Derrick & Colin Wood, 1971. *Environmental Decision-Making and Environmental Stress*, paper presented at Annual Meeting of the Canadian Association of Geographers, Waterloo, Ontario.

Spiegel, Hans B. C. (ed.), 1968. *Citizen Participation and Urban Development*, Washington, D.C.: Center for Community Affairs, NTL Institute for Behavioural Science, National Education Association, 2 vols.

*Starrs, Catherine & Gail Stewart, 1972. *Gone Today and Here Tomorrow*, report prepared for the Committee on Government Productivity Ontario, Toronto: Queen's Printer.

*Szablowski, George J., 1972. *Public Bureaucracy and the Possibility of Citizen Involvement in the Government of Ontario*, report prepared for the Committee on Government Productivity Ontario, Toronto: Queen's Printer.

Teniére-Buchot, P. F., 1976. 'The Role of the Public in Water Management Decisions in France', *Natural Resources Journal*, 16, 1, 159–176.

*Thayer, Frederick C., 1972. *Participation and Liberal Democratic Government*, report prepared for the Committee on Government Productivity Ontario, Toronto: Queen's Printer.

*U.S. Environmental Protection Agency, 1972. 'Citizen Action Can Get Results', *EPA Citizens' Bulletin*, Washington, D.C.

Vindasius, Dana. *Public Participation Techniques and Methodologies: A Resumé.* Ottawa: Information Canada, 1974

Wengert, N., 1971a. 'Public Participation in Water Planning' A Critique of Theory, Doctrine and Practice', *Water Resources Bulletin*, February, 26–32.

*Wengert, N., 1971b. 'Political and Social Accommodation: The Political Process

14

and Environmental Preservation', *Natural Resources Journal*, **11** (3), July, 437–446.

Wengert, N., 1971c. *Where Can We Go with Public Participation in the Planning Process?*, paper presented at a Symposium on Social and Economic Aspects of Water Development, Cornell University.

*Willeke, Gene, 1974. 'Theory and Practice of Public Participation in Planning', Proceedings of the American Society of Civil Engineers, *Journal of the Irrigation and Drainage Division*, March, 75–86.

*Wolpert, Julian & Anthony I. Mumphrey, 1971. 'A Decision-Model for Locating Controversial Facilities', *Journal of the American Institute of Planners*, November, 397–402.

*Wolpert, Julian, Anthony Mumphrey & John Seley, 1972. *Metropolitan Neighborhoods: Participation and Conflict over Change*, Association of American Geographers, Commission on College Geography Resource Paper No. 16, Washington, D.C.

2

In Dispraise of Political Trust

NORMAN DENNIS

Political Trust

In political sociology a person's trust is his assessment of the probability that, without his having to do anything at all himself, the orders and policies of his rulers will be beneficial to him and to others he cares about. In diagram form, trust can be shown as four circles encompassing his satisfaction with the results of political decisions (Figure 2.1).

The first is his trust in the current incumbents of office, who produce the decisions which affect him. The second circle contains the political institutions of the society or group – the system of offices which the incumbents occupy, the procedures of election and appointment which must be followed to have the offices duly filled, and the operating rules (as Easton calls them) which constitute the ways in which members of a system are expected to behave as officers and members of the rank-and-file (Easton, 1965). It is possible to be dissatisfied with a particular set of decisions, abhor and despise the current holders of political and administrative office, expecting nothing but still more harm to flow from their use of power, and yet have confidence that the system as it stands is one which, on the whole, will produce the best results. Faith in the institutions of the group or community may, of course, be lost and this is much more serious for the system than loss of faith in the particular incumbents of office at a particular period of time.

Thirdly, there is the political culture. The culture is the set of ideas about, and moral judgements on, human nature and history which sustain any particular set of social arrangements. For example, the idea or feeling that people develop best when discipline is imposed upon them, as contrasted with the idea or feeling that people develop best when they are freely left to their own devices. Power ennobles: power destroys the power wielder. Human nature is the same the world over: racial, national, religious and other differences are deep and ineradicable. Men are fundamentally equal in their abilities, as contrasted with the idea that men are fundamentally and immutably unequal in their abilities. Inequality is a disgrace, as contrasted with the idea that inequality is a blessing. Progress is inevitable: progress is unlikely or impossible. Social change ought to be fostered: social change ought to be suppressed. The community has a life of its own, separate from and superior to the lives of the individuals who compose it, as contrasted with the idea that the

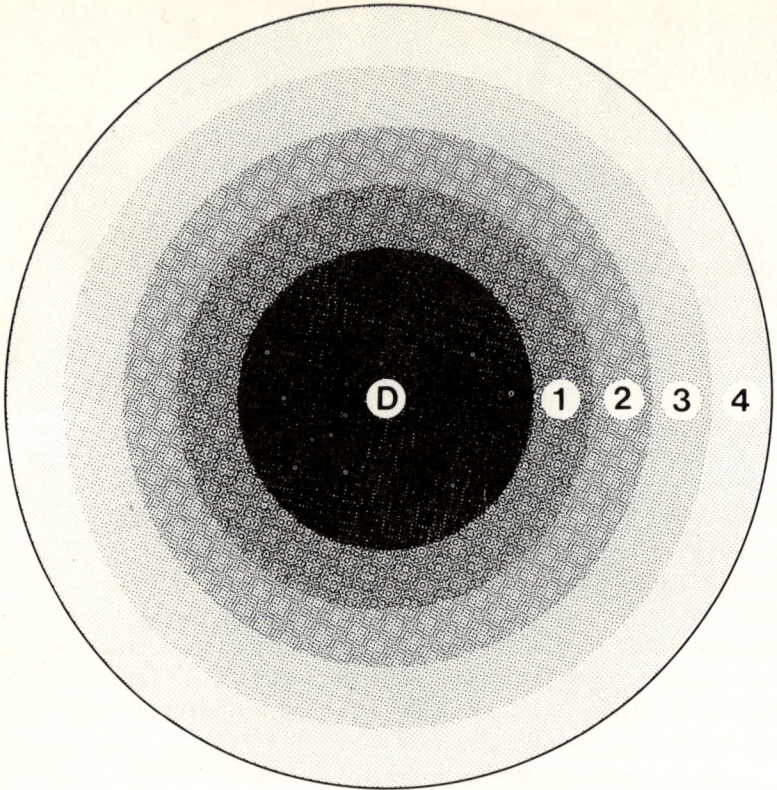

D ········ DECISIONS AND COMMANDS
1 ········ INCUMBENTS IN OFFICE
2 ········ POLITICAL INSTITUTIONS
3 ········ POLITICAL CULTURE
4 ········ THE POLITICAL COMMUNITY

Figure 2.1 Circles of trust

community has no existence except as the relations between individuals, and these relations can have no purpose except to secure the well-being of discrete persons — and so forth.

Fourthly and finally there is the circle of trust which encloses decisions, incumbents, institutions and culture, namely, trust in the political community, whether the political community is the state or a group within it. A citizen may feel that decisions are damaging to him, believe that without his intervention the likelihood is that the current holders of office will issue commands which will be to his disadvantage, that the system and the political culture as they stand will continue to throw up such holders of office, and yet believe that the community of which he is a member will eventually produce a culture, institutions and political personnel who will act as the agents of his welfare and the welfare of those he holds dear.

As Walter Bagehot said in discussing the dignified and efficient parts of the English constitution in the nineteenth century, 'every institution must first win the loyalty and confidence of mankind and then employ that homage in the work of government'. Trust — the willingness of the rank-and-file to let the authorities get on with the job of producing decisions undisturbed — can be seen as a stock which accumulates or diminishes in response to the citizen's experiences of decisions and commands. (The rank-and-filer's level of trust and the authority's level of discretion are thus two sides of the same coin.) Freedom from interference and challenge is a highly valuable political resource, but it is a resource which must be constantly recouped and augmented. As Talcott Parsons says, one of the most important 'returns' on the 'expenditure' of power is trust. It directly affects the leadership's capacity to make further commitments without undue expenditure of effort in mobilizing prior approval or in controlling dissension (Parsons *et al.*, 1961).

Power, from the point of view of the holders of *de jure*, constitutional positions in any group or society, is 'the capacity to mobilize the resources of the society for the attainment of goals for which a general "public" commitment has been made or may be made' (Parsons, 1960). It belongs with an office, or better still, to the system of which the office or position forms a specialized part. The mobilization of resources of a complex group or society is characteristically accomplished by, and in the view of many cannot be accomplished without, some (unknown degree of) concentration of power (Hawley, 1963).

Were established authorities able to meet the felt needs of all the governed, if they always did so, and if the rank-and-file were satisfied with this state of affairs, trust would be absolute and there would be no problem of participation. There would be no politics: political institutions, to use famous phrases, would 'wither away', and 'the administration of things would replace the government of men'. But in this world discontent is endemic and, from the vantage point of the established authorities a crucial problem is the management of conflict. Authorities are the managers of the conflicts which arise between members of the rank-and-file — as umpires and controllers above and outside these conflicts. But authorities are also managers of conflicts between the rank-and-file and themselves: managers of challenges to their own decisions, actions and ways of doing things. Their interest in controlling challenges to their own authority is in keeping the cost of their decisions cheap, principally by establishing and maintaining trust at a high level.

In the study of large-scale organizations, sociologists have paid particular attention to the modification of the professed aims of the organization from what it is supposed to be doing for the benefit of others, in the direction of what better suits the interests of the organization's own personnel. Sociologists have been particularly interested in the modification of goals due to the ties of influence among members of the organization as they tend to concentrate power in the hands of officials, and the displacement of the officials' motives through routinization and other processes (Selznick, 1943). From a standpoint outside the organization, it may appear as a disembodied abstraction, and that sight has been lost of the people it 'serves'. From the standpoint of people in one part of the organization, another part of the organization may similarly look remote and hostile. In other words, trust may have evaporated. The most recent writer on the subject, Alan Fox, expresses the view that relationships which depend on a high level of trust are not within the reach of societies based on an elaborate division of labour.[1] Instabilities, the measures power-holders adopt to deal with them, and rank-and-file resistance to those measures constitute, in Fox's (1974) view, a severe threat to all the traditional Western rights and liberal freedoms.

Authorities, then, are not able to produce results which always satisfy the rank-and-file. Nor are they always able to prevent this dissatisfaction being generalized into distrust. This is so for a variety of reasons. Suitably *motivated* staff may be unavailable (even when otherwise well-trained). Dissatisfaction is a matter of *relative* deprivation. One may object today to a shared telephone line as strongly or more strongly as one objected only a few years ago to a shared toilet, or be more upset because there is a small leak in the central heating system than one was when the only tap in the dwelling froze in the backyard in the winter. With the virtues of extravagance and self-indulgence replacing the virtues of thrift and self-control, authorities today may be finding it more and more difficult, not easier, to produce satisfying results and retain confidence, even where the scope of their formal powers and the resources at their disposal have immeasurably increased. And authorities, unlike nature, can be blamed.

In a closed system, with complete internal control of communications by the authorities, so that only their versions of facts, events, laws and values are available, what is lost in trustfulness by the lack of results satisfactory to the rank-and-file can be counterbalanced by lies. But to the extent that the system is open to outside influences, and communications within the system allow dissenting versions to compete with those of the authorities, unsatisfying results may lead to a decline in trust on the part of the rank-and-file. This makes it more expensive for the authorities to get their own way and less certain that they will be able to do so.

At the other end of the 'trust' scale to 'complete confidence' in the incumbents of office, in the institutional arrangements, in the values which underlie them and in the integrity of the group or community, is 'alienation'. Alienation from the incumbents describes the attitudes of the member of the rank-and-file who believes that the authorities, left to themselves, not only do not serve his interests; he believes they are sacrificing his interests to serve their own (Lane, 1962). Alienated from the operating rules, he believes they are rigged to keep out of office those who would be friendly to him. Given the system, throwing the rascals out only means making room for another set of rascals: 'the conductor changes, the music is the same'. Alienated from the group's culture, he dismisses its noblest aspirations as the piety of frauds and buffoons, the purpose of which is to veil the system's faults and distracts and bemuse its critics. Alienated from decisions, incumbents, institutions and philosophy, he may despair of the group altogether and contemplate on an individual basis resignation, apostasy, treason, desertion, voluntary exile or, on a group basis, devolution or secession.[2]

Induced Trust

In the relations between authorities and the rank-and-file, trust is not a datum. It is not a sort of Forties nor Fisk field, capable of yielding power galore to whoever can float out his rig and sink a well. It is, nevertheless, a political resource in all groups which is at the same time valued, potent, staple and abused.

Authorities keep the confidence of the rank-and-file, where it is not deserved, first, by insulation. The rank-and-file is insulated from knowledge which would indicate that their interests are being neglected and their needs unfulfilled. This is achieved by erecting barriers to the disclosure of information; through the doctrine of confidentiality; by the specification of 'proper channels'; by selective entry to positions of authority, so that irresponsible elements will not gain access to dangerous truths; by selective exit (the expulsion of harmless dissidents, 'kicking upstairs' for dissidents who have beans to spill, but who will take a reasonable view of them, and vilification, abuse and discredit for those dissidents who will not); by rewards (promotion, power, prestige), punishments and socialization for newcomers to membership and to positions of authority to ensure that as far as possible an orthodox view is adopted about the appropriate relationship between officials and members.

The corollary of controlled hindrances to access is, secondly, the controlled disclosure of information. A public relations exercise may put a gloss on a particular bad decision. Those not adversely affected by it may be persuaded that the bad decision was a good one. In favourable circumstances of isolation and fragmentation in a population (see strategy five, below), a high proportion of the victims of a bad decision may be led to believe that most others affected by it have benefited and their own case is a rare and unlucky abnormality. Elements potentially hostile to a decision may be co-opted as a means of (a) ensuring the protest vents itself within a situation controlled by the authorities, and, in particular, one insulated from the rank-and-file; and (b) ensuring that the most dangerous of the protesters express their view to the authorities but only by permitting themselves to be opened to persuasion by the authorities. The classic study of co-optation as a method of syphoning-off leaders of the rank-and-file and emasculating protest is Philip Selznick's *T.V.A. and the Grass Roots* (1953).

Verba, writing before the participation mania of the American poverty programmes of the 1960's (whose faint contagion was to appear in this country in officially sponsored 'public participation', especially in town planning and the social services), concluded that it was, in most cases, a matter of 'member endorsement'. In much of the small-group literature (he wrote) 'participatory democratic leadership' referred not to a technique of rank-and-file decision-taking, but to a technique of persuasion by the authorities (Verba, 1961).

In addition to insulation the authorities may use the rather two-edged technique of complication. Harold Macmillan, in a television interview, was once asked about the embarrassment of the Profumo affair. He remarked that if a scandal hit the administration it was really rather better from the point of view of maintaining public trust that there should be more than one. The public's attention, he said, could always be distracted from one to the other. Scandals can become so complicated that the members of the rank-and-file lose track of what has happened and may bolt back into the safe hole of trust. This more or less wilful complication of issues takes place within a context of already complex situations. It has been pointed out that the Ten Commandments (well-known directives from the authorities to the rank-and-file) contain 297 words. The American Declaration of Independence, setting out certain self-evident truths about the relationships between the authorities and rank-and-file, contains 300 words. The E.E.C. directive on the import of caramels and caramel products contains 26,911 words.[3] Whatever may be said about Leviticus, it never goes into such detail. At contemporary levels of complication, where may the rank-and-file go except into trust of the experts who (they believe) are masters of these rules?

Thirdly, the authorities put the best construction available on the higher levels of activity and thought, even where it is admitted that there may be some defects at the lower levels. We may read, for example, that once the British public administrator's crust of apparent disillusion has been pierced, 'you will find a man who feels with the fiercest intensity for those things . . . which a lifetime of experience has impressed on him as matters which are of vital concern for the well-being of the community'. His life – that is, the institutions within which he works – makes him not only an idealist, but 'above all, a realist' (Bridges, 1950). According to Anthony Crosland, British civil servants see their duty as putting politician's proposals to tests of 'logic' and 'feasibility' (Kogan, 1971). The traditional values of the British paid public servant, it is said, are 'accountability' and 'answerability', by which they are required to have a clear base of authority provided by the decisions and legislation of elected politicians. There is a strong concern, we are told, with the uniformity of provision of public services (in strong contrast to the American value of pluralism and local autonomy) (Kogan, 1974). The post-war expansion of governmental services at both national and local authority level is leading to less stress being laid publicly on 'simple dutifulness and accountability', and more on 'entrepreneurial values', suited to a more 'dynamic' role.[4]

Where such high-flown definitions of reality fail to allay discontent and distrust, authorities may adopt strategies to discourage tendencies for the rank-and-file to generalize their dissatisfaction with descisions to the point of becoming dissatisfied with he incumbents of office, and discourage tendencies for them to generalize their distrust of incumbents to institutions, social values and the integrity of the group or community itself. Disputes are therefore defined, where possible, as reflecting agreement on principles, disagreement only on the application of the principles, The history and the setting of decisions are de-emphasized. The adoption of this strategy means that each bad decision is presented on its own, and not as one of a series of bad decisions or as part of a complex of present problematical decisions. Stripped of history and context, incumbents of office can more plausibly hold out to the rank-and-file the prospect of 'better things to come'. Similarly, what Smelser (1963) terms 'norm-oriented' distrust, which challenges only the institutional *methods* of pursuing the society's goals, is less threatening to a system than 'value-oriented' distrust, which challenges the validity of the goals themselves. There is a vast difference between on the one hand the American Progressives (such as LaFollette), whose aim was to 'cure the ills of democracy with more democracy', by the use of the initiative, the referendum, etc., or the N.A.A.C.P. in the Brown case, whose aim was equality of opportunity in the strictly traditional American sense, and on the other hand the black and white radical movements of the late 1960's which not only repudiated existing institutions but reviled conventional American culture.

The fourth strategy adopted by authorities to secure, protect or heighten trustful feelings on the part of the rank-and-file is that of defining their own power to bring about outcomes they prefer (for self-regarding or other-regarding purposes, out of selfishness or altruism, preferred by them for whatever reason) as being different in essence to the power of members of the rank-and-file to bring about outcomes. the members of the rank-and-file prefer. The power of authorities, it is said, is wielded on behalf of the system as a whole (as in the definitions given by Parsons and Hawley quoted previously — as well as, of course, some of the very greatest philosophers in the history of mankind). The power of authorities is 'legitimate'. Legitimacy, it is said, is what gives their decisions 'authority' as distinct from being decisions which depend for their application on naked force. Implicitly, and very frequently explicitly too, the power of the legitimate authorities is sacred, other power profane.

The fifth and final strategy is the encapsulation of individual malcontents. Participation itself can be a potent device in the hands of the authorities with which to weaken or destroy 'pluralistic' situations and to create or encourage the growth of 'mass' situations. Group responses to the authorities' decisions and information, as distinct from the responses of isolated and unorganized individuals, are belittled, blocked and attacked. Official participation 'exercises' are instituted in which as far as can be arranged and assured information is conveyed to and representations are considered from individuals only. In the tradition of political studies stemming from de Tocqueville, tendencies towards pluralism, or on the contrary towards social fragmentation, and the consequences of social fragmentations for freedom and political oppression, have been taken as crucial to the understanding of modern societies.[5]

But in so far as they succeed by these strategies in inducing trust in the rank-and-file (with the many benefits of trust for the economical exercise of power) they also succeed in removing themselves from knowledge of the actual effects of their decisions and commands — an important drawback. Especially with the fourth strategy, the tremendously useful one of the sanctification of established authority, there is not only the defect of blocking information-feedback from the rank-and-file. Even when sanctification is used as a rational technique (used 'cynically'), there is the ever-present danger that the authorities themselves may come to believe that authority as such actually does halo and transfigure their perception, their knowledge and their judgement, and allows rules of evidence to be relaxed for them or held in abeyance. That is at any rate one aspect of the generalization 'all power tends to corrupt'.

The Political Resources of the Rank-and-file

Theories which put authority, legitimate power, into a class of its own (not simply because it does have distinctive and important qualities, but as a phenomenon *sui generis*) exist for the sake of social control, not as sound social science.

Power, all social power, is simply a probability that one actor within a social relationship will be in a position to carry out his will despite resistence (Weber, 1947). Power, as Lasswell and Kaplan (1950) put it, is distributive, and the aim of politics is – they mean ought to be – to determine how and on what basis it is distributed. To speak of 'society' as a power wielder is 'to miss the whole point of political analysis'. Polsby (1963), following in the Yale tradition (he had worked under Robert Dahl in the celebrated study of 'who governs' New Haven), argues that the question of power is wide open, and is not to be deduced from a knowledge of the formal structure of authority. One cannot tell whether or not someone is powerful 'unless some sequence of events, competently observed, attests to his power'.

When the rank-and-file are discontented with the result of their authority's policies and the implementation of the policies, and disenchantment has seeped into the institutional system and the culture, what will the rank-and-file do to draw attention to their discontent and distrust? It may be an apathetic or an active response (Lipset, 1960). But what *can* the rank-and-file do if they want to be active?

The power of the rank-and-file is on occasion authoritative, as when their votes decisively determine who among a number of contenders shall hold elective office or when they cast their votes on resolutions at general meetings, annual conferences etc.[6] But the rank-and-file's power is most frequently not authoritative. It is limited to influence. Influence is power minus authority.

A person's or group's influences depends on their 'resources'. Resources in this context are those things which when properly applied in sufficient quantities will improve the chance that a decision favoured by the influencer will be made. Resources may be applied to alter the decision-taker's *situation*, bringing about new intentions because the situation had changed. Resources may be applied, alternatively, only to change the decision-taker's intentions by *persuasion*, given the existing situation (Parsons, 1963).

Situational resources may be either negative or positive. The negative situational resources of the rank-and-file are those available to be added to the situation as disadvantages for the leadership. Some of these are generally applicable to all authorities – for example, the withdrawal of labour, peaceful civil disobedience, and 'the dangerous drug of violence'. Others are applicable to some authorities only, for example, some form of blackmail (concessions or rewards in exchange for not disclosing something which discredits the authorities). Some resources are readily available, for example, petition signatures. Other resources are to a greater or lesser degree difficult to muster, depending on the issue, the population, the principal actors and the situation generally, for example changes in traditional party loyalties in terms of votes and demonstrators who are willing to defy the forces of law and order.

Positive situational resources are those which are added to the situation as inducements to the decision-taker to alter his intention to favour the influencer: votes, money, praise etc.

Influence which depends not on altering the context of an authority's decision in these senses, but merely on persuading the authority that it has its facts wrong, or has misinterpreted the law, or neglected certain values, or overlooked the claims of certain groups (altering 'the context' in this limited sense) hinges on the availability to the rank-and-file of the following three resources. The first resource is the rank-and-fiiers' confidence in the validity of their own perception of the situation (trust in themselves). Secondly, skills in writing and speaking, especially skills in writing and speaking to hostile or indifferent authorities. Thirdly, access to the communications media. In modern society communications flow to and are disseminated from a few central points. If an event or an opinion does not get into these channels of communication, then, so far as influence is concerned, it might as well not have occurred, it could have remained unexpressed. At every point along the communication paths of newspapers, radio, T.V., journals, books, public meetings and lectures, 'gatekeepers' stand. These are the people who have the right to say whether the message shall be received, to what extent it shall be altered, and whether it shall be retransmitted at all. Characteristically, members of the rank-and-file in groups and communities lack all these resources.

The Dysfunctionality of Trust and the Indispensability of Free, Pluralistic Participation

Co-operative effort, under conditions of an increasing number and specialization of functions (the division of labour) requires, it means, delegation. Of the activities related to the goods and services any individual consumes, an ever-decreasing proportion are the activities of the individual himself. In many spheres of life he must act through agents. Delegation, the relationship of principal and agent, creates a tendency towards what Selznick terms the 'bifurcation of interests'. In modern society these activities cease to be carried out by individuals and small groups such as the family and the village. They are replaced as the producers of goods and services by large-scale organizations, in industry, in commerce, in education, in science, in the state. What is more, these large-scale organizations tend more and more to be monopolistic or monopsonistic. Those taking decisions, and those either benefiting or suffering from the decisions, show an increasing tendency to be different people. The consequences of policy are therefore progressively more remote from those who have devised and those who execute policy. In a word, the decision-taker becomes divorced from reality. By 'reality' I do not have in mind any arcane philosophical point about the long, slow swell of European thought, rising to this or that view of physical or human nature – as concrete, unmistakable, and universally apprehensible, or as always requiring heavy doses of subjective organization by devisers of the measuring rods a society will choose to wield. I mean that there either is or is not a light in the backlane of a named street in an identified location; that a form of words is either recorded in a specified document or it is not so recorded. I mean 'the world' as it is perceived and experienced by citizens in modern communities when they are handling those parts of it which have consequences for themselves: broadly, that is, the world which (to use William James's phrase) a pungent sense of reality creates in the common sense of individuals and groups.

Because of the rank-and filers' propensity to reside confidence in them; because of the authorities' ability to build trust where, to a rational man with full knowledge of all the relevant facts, trust would appear to be misplaced; and because of the paucity of resources at the disposal of the members of the rank-and-file to bring the relevant facts as they have seen, heard and felt them to their attention, such authorities are not well-equipped to be aware of realities, and are in constant danger of relating to images of their own invention, with no existence except in their own heads. Protected by their institutional position from the rigours of the world they create for others, they themselves may experience no discomfort. But, in the absence of effective pluralistic participation free from the authorities' control, the members of the rank-and-file, on whose behalf and for whose benefit they purport to act, may and too often do find themselves with parts in the hallucinations of people who have the power to make them play out the roles allotted to them, as painful as they are fantastic.

Notes

1. Fox is dealing mainly, however, with authorities and rank-and-filers in *work* relationships. More attention is paid to trust in some other types of organization, notably those containing a group of specialist 'politicians'.
2. Between the extremes of complete confidence and absolute distrust is neutrality. This is the attitude that if I do nothing the chances that the outcome of the authority's decisions and actions will correspond to what I wish for myself or others, are fifty-fifty.
3. This fact is reported, and the contrast drawn, in the *Sunday Times*, 2 June 1974.
4. The process of redefinition of the values of the national civil service can be seen in 'Professional Standards in the Public Service', a Report of a Subcommittee of the First Division Association, *Public Administration*, **50**, 1972. For the process of redefinition at the local authority level, see *The New Local Authorities: Management and Structure*, (The Bain's Report), London: HMSO, 1972. See also D. V. Donnison, 'Committees and Committee Men', *New Society*, 18 April 1968; H. Thomas, *Crisis in the Civil Service*, London: Blond, 1968; Lewis A. Gunn, 'Politicians and Officials – Who is "Answerable"?' *Political Quarterly*, **43**, 1972, 253–260; R. A. Chapman & A. Dunsire, *Style in Administration*, London: Allen & Unwin, 1971.
5. See Alexis de Tocqueville, *Democracy in America*, ed. R. D. Heffner, New York: Mentor, 1956, especially 'What Sort of Despotism Democratic Nations have to

Fear', p. 303. A succinct characterization of a 'mass society' and a 'pluralistic society' is given in C. Wright Mills, 'Mass Society and Liberal Education', 1954, in *Power, Politics and People*, ed. I. R. Horowitz, New York: Oxford University Press, 1963, pp. 353–373.

6. What makes a decision-maker the 'legitimate authority' is – what makes a decision-maker the legitimate authority. 'Legitimacy' is what a group or society makes into 'legitimacy' – for example, 'it's the way it's always been done' (tradition); 'it's what the rule book says' (rational–legality); 'it's the word of this marvellous man' (charisma). H. H. Gerth & C. Wright Mills, *From Max Weber*, London: Routledge & Kegan Paul, 1948.

References

Bridges, Sir Edward, 1950. *Portrait of a Profession*, Reid Lecture, Cambridge University Press.

Easton, David, 1965. *A Systems Analysis of Political Life*. New York: John Wiley.

Fox, Alan, 1974. *Beyond Contract: Work, Power and Trust Relations*. London: Faber & Faber.

Hawley, Amos H., 1963. 'Community Power and Urban Renewal Processes', *American Journal of Sociology*, **68**, 422–431.

Kogan, Maurice *et al.*, 1971. *Politics of Education*, Harmondsworth: Penguin Books.

Kogan, Maurice, 1974. 'Social Policy and Public Organizational Values', *Journal of Social Policy*, **3**, 103–104.

Lane, Robert E., 1962. *Political Ideology*, New York: Free Press.

Lasswell, Harold D. and Abraham Kaplan. 1950. *Power and Society*, New Haven: Yale University Press.

Lipset, Seymour M., 1960. *Political Man.* London: Heinemann.

Parsons, Talcott, 1960. *Structure and Process in Modern Societies*. New York: Free Press.

Parsons, Talcott, 1963. 'On the Concept of Influence', *Public Opinion Quarterly*, **27**, 42–43.

Parsons, Talcott, *et al.*, 1961. *Theories of Society*, New York: Free Press.

Polsby, Nelson W. 1963. *Community Power and Political Theory*, New Haven: Yale University Press.

Selznick, Philip, 1943. 'An Approach to a Theory of Bureaucracy', *American Sociological Review*, **8**, 47–54.

Selznick, Philip, 1953. *T.V.A. and the Grass Roots*, Berkeley: University of California Press.

Smelser, Neil J., 1963. *Theory of Collective Behavior*, New York: Free Press.

Verba, Sidney, 1961. *Small Groups and Political Behaviour,* Princeton: Princeton University Press.

Weber, Max, 1947. *The Theory of Social and Economic Organization*, Oxford: Oxford University Press.

3

Research into Public Participation in Structure Planning

WILLIAM HAMPTON

> ... the diner — not the cook — will be the best judge of the
> feast (Book III, Ch. XI, 3.14).
>
> ... when there are so many who contribute to the process of
> deliberation, each can bring his share of goodness and moral
> prudence (Book III, Ch. XI, 5.2).
>
> Aristotle, *The Politics*

Public participation is an integral part of the planning procedure adopted in England and Wales since 1968,[1] and may be considered in some respects as a counterbalance to the withdrawal by the Secretary of State from control over the details of local plans. Local plans may now be adopted by resolution of the local planning authority as long as they conform to a structure plan prepared by the county planning authority and approved by the Secretary of State. The public are entitled to be informed of planning proposals at both structure and local planning levels and they must be given an opportunity to make representations on such matters. These provisions have created a new environment within which planners and public must interact. The public, of course, are frequently concerned at the impact of decisions contained in local plans and their opinions are made known through a variety of local activities, but greater involvement by the public in the preparation of local plans is not sufficient to ensure a full discussion of the development plan. The structure plan will contain the broad strategic policies within which local planning will be constrained. Efforts must be made to engage the public in the discussion of long-term policy.

The Town and Country Planning Act, 1968, in common with most other legislation, did not give guidance on the methods by which its precepts might be observed. A committee was set up, therefore, under the chairmanship of the Joint Parliamentary Secretary of the Ministry of Housing and Local Government (Mr. Arthur Skeffington, M.P., to formulate advice on these questions. The committee reported in 1969 (Great Britain, Ministry of Housing and Local Government), and began by defining certain key words in their terms of reference. Such definitions have no statutory effect but they are clearly very persuasive as a guide both to local planning authorities and to ministers when they consider public participation programmes.

The Skeffington Committee defined participation as the act of sharing in the formulation of policies and proposals; the public are no longer simply asked to judge a finished or near-finished product. In this respect the Committee would no doubt prefer the second of the two quotations from Aristotle which head this chapter. The public, to paraphrase Harry Truman, are being invited to share the heat in the kitchen of public policy discussions. The Committee defined publicity as the making of information — facts, arguments and explanations — available to the public. And the public were not only those who show themselves in organized groups; the Committee were equally concerned with individuals, including those who lack experience or initiative in presenting their views.

The Skeffington proposals placed heavy new responsibilities upon local authorities. The definitions outlined in the previous paragraph made it incumbent upon them to seek the participation of every member of the public in the discussion of planning matters. This was obviously a counsel of perfection; there was little experience of methods by which widespread public involvement could be achieved. Skeffington discussed a number of suggested techniques for public participation and invited local planning authorities to 'experiment in the techniques they employ, even at the risk of occasional failure'. The Committee, understandably, could not be more specific. In 1972 the Department of the Environment stated:

> So far there has not been sufficient opportunity to establish which methods for securing publicity and public participation will be most appropriate in practice to these different types of plan. This is particularly so with the newest type of plan, the structure plan. . . . Further, more needs to be known, not only about the methods and the techniques of publicity and public participation, but also about the degree of benefit obtained from them compared with the time taken to prepare and submit plans, and the cost and the calls on the time of the community and local government (Great Britain, Department of Environment, 1972).

A research programme was established to provide information on these questions and produced a series of interim reports on specific techniques in preparation for a full-length study of the subject.[2]

Objectives of Public Participation

The assessment of success or failure in public participation exercises obviously depends upon the reasons for which the exercises are undertaken. The Department of the Environment suggests:

> If the policies to be embodied in the plans are to be understood and generally accepted, and if the proposals in them are to be implemented successfully, the authorities must carry the public with them by formulating, for public

discussion, the aims and objectives of the policies and then the options for realising these aims and objectives. Giving the public the opportunity to participate in the formative stage will, when handled with skill and understanding, not only make the plan a better plan, but also do much to improve relationships between the planning authorities and the public. Participation is a two-way process (Great Britain, Department of Environment, 1972).

This approach emphasizes, quite naturally, the improvements in the planning process which may follow public participation. The first function of planners is to plan: meaningful participation is about enhancing this activity. However, the participants may be pursuing quite different objectives. Some may be concerned to increase their influence over the policies of the planning authority to an extent which is not contained within such phrases as 'carry the public with them' or 'improve relationships between the planning authorities and the public'. Others will pursue still more radical objectives, wishing to replace the existing representative system by some form of decentralized or even anarchistic decision-making structure.

These various approaches are not as easily distinguishable as we may sometimes suppose. We may easily identify the extremes, but this does not always help. Types of democracy lie along a continuum from representative to participatory in a manner which can be obscured by conventional bipolar analysis.[3] We do not have *either* representative democracy *or* participatory democracy; we have a system which in its complexity is a mixture of both. The introduction of public participation techniques into the planning process implies a movement along the continuum from representative to participatory democracy.

Such a development may have profound consequences for the roles which elected representatives, public servants and citizens are expected to play. At the very least there should be a much wider and more open public debate about policy issues, but this may proceed to a sharing of responsibility for decisions among a larger number of people.[4] The possibility of such changes is not always accepted — or even recognized — by those who continue to talk in purely planning terms. The resulting conflict between actors in a public participation programme who approach from different directions is frequently characterized by broadsides from established positions rather than by an actual engagement of minds.

Despite an appreciation of these wider philosophical considerations the present chapter is presented within a narrower context. We are concerned with the introduction of public participation in the structure planning process within a representative system of democracy which contains certain participatory elements. Within this system there are two major objectives which may be served by a development of public participation. First, the planning process may be improved by the dispersal and collection of information which both adds to the data available to the planners and enables the local authority to canvass support for the concept of planning to meet certain community needs. There is, of course, a fine line to be drawn between canvassing support in the sense of securing or enabling a consensus and manipulating consent in a Machiavellian manner: we assume goodwill with our eyes open.

Secondly, public participation may enhance citizenship by encouraging individuals or groups of individuals to play a more active part in the discussion and determination of public policy. Such an approach encompasses a wide range of possibilities from promoting consultative democracy through the involvement of major organizations to 'the improvement of the people themselves' (Mill, 1910). This second objective is a frequent source of rhetoric both for elected representatives and for active participants but its full implications are seldom explored. Planners — and councillors? — should perhaps have compulsory courses in political philosophy.

A Schema for Public Participation

For the present we remain with more mundane considerations. Public participation programmes include various techniques which may be subjected to a threefold classification. First, there are those techniques concerned with dispersing information; secondly, those concerned with collecting information; and thirdly, those concerned to promote an interaction between the planning authority and the public. These classifications may be related as subsidiary objectives to the two major objectives previously mentioned. An apparent congruity then appears between the dispersal and collection of information and the improvement of the planning process on the one hand, and between the promotion of interaction and the enhancement of the democratic process on the other. This appearance is only superficial, indicating a tendency rather than a firm division; the various techniques may be used to achieve various objectives: much will depend upon the manner in which they are used and the package of which they form part.[5]

The threefold classification may be further developed both by considering the substance of each broad approach and by the breadth of public involvement. The public is not a homogeneous mass; there are many different publics who need to be involved in any public participation programme. A schema is shown in Table 3.1 which illustrates one possible development of the analysis presented so far; a few comments may help to clarify the synopsis.

The further breakdown of the three subsidiary objectives by posing three 'what' questions and three 'who' questions gives nine possible approaches under each main heading. Obviously, it would be possible to refine the schema further but the Table is sufficiently detailed for purposes of illustration. Each set of three questions proceeds from a narrower to a wider approach. For example, from dispersing information about decisions already taken to making all information freely available; or from involving officers from major public bodies, such as nationalized concerns, to seeking the participation of individual members of the public. We may suppose that the adoption of a narrower approach will lead to demands for a movement along the continuum. The giving of some information, for example, will lead to a demand for more; the involvement of some groups will lead to demands from others for the same facilities. Further, it will be impossible to adopt certain approaches from one section without adopting a suitable approach from another. For example, information about the attitudes and opinions of the general public

Table 3.1. A schema for public participation

1. *Dispersal of information*
   What information?
   (a) Information about decisions already taken: i.e. a single policy
   (b) Information about discussions taking place: i.e. alternative policies
   (c) Open government: i.e. all information freely available

   Who is informed?
   (a) Major elites: e.g. other public bodies or major commercial concerns
   (b) Minor elites: e.g. local interest groups
   (c) The general public as a collectivity of individuals

2. *Gathering information*
   What information?
   (a) Information about physical facts: i.e. census data, etc.
   (b) Information about decisions taken by other public or private bodies
   (c) Information about public attitudes and opinions

   Who is listened to?
   (a) Major elites: e.g. other public bodies or major commercial concerns
   (b) Minor elites: e.g. local interest groups
   (c) The general public as a collectivity of individuals

3. *Interaction between planning authority and public*
   What kind of interaction?
   (a) Through the widening of the debate: e.g. by the dispersal of more information
   (b) Through the involvement of elites: e.g. working parties for interest groups
   (c) Through the encouragement of the individual citizen

   Who are the public?
   (a) Major elites: e.g. other public bodies or major commercial concerns
   (b) Minor elites: e.g. local interest groups
   (c) The general public as a collectivity of individuals

will not be available unless information has been dispersed upon which such attitudes and opinions can be founded.

If we compress this approach into a simple diagram, with all the distortion which such compression brings, then we may consider the various approaches to be contained within three nesting boxes (Figure 3.1). The opening of a box implies revealing its contents, which may lead to demands for the use of approaches not previously favoured by the local authority. Similarly the attempt to gain access to an inner box involves opening the outside boxes. Only the most limited technical information can be gathered without informing some of the public of the reasons for its collection; the more information required then the more needs to be dispersed. Interaction between the planning authority and the public will naturally only take place on the basis of an exchange of information. If the analogy of a box has overtones of Pandora, then perhaps this is not entirely inappropriate.[6]

The analysis is further complicated by different actors in the participation

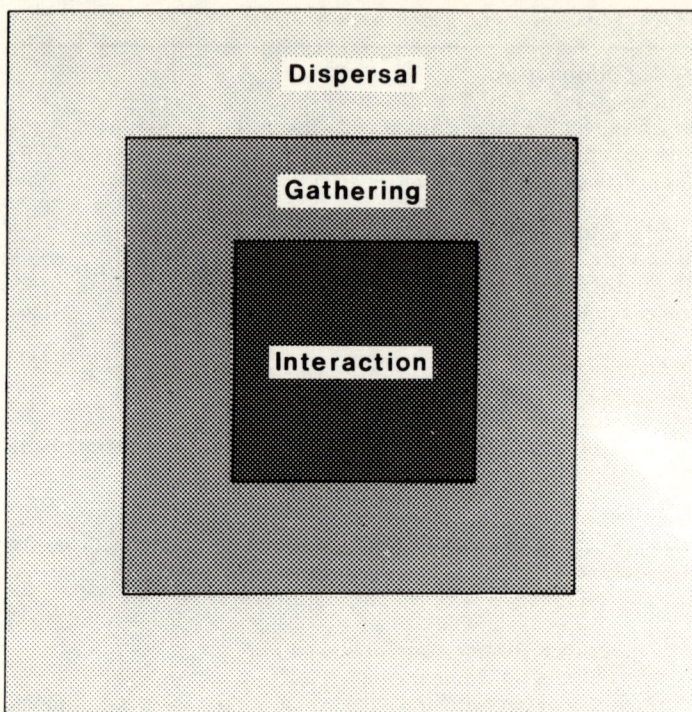

Figure 3.1 The public participation box

process seeking different major objectives through the use of the subsidiary objectives implied by the various approaches contained in the boxes. This complexity makes the concept of a ladder as used by Arnstein (1969) singularly inappropriate in a discussion of public participation in planning. A ladder inevitably implies an hierarchical relationship between its rungs, but we have seen that a public participation programme may contain elements from various parts of Arnstein's typology; and different actors in the process may be standing on different rungs. The resulting conflicts are part of the normal political process of reconciling the different objectives of those participating and make it difficult to place any particular participation programme within an hierarchical typology.

Models of Public Participation

With these reservations in mind, we may return to our schema for public participation. For illustrative purposes we have placed nine possible approaches within each box. Let us now construct a number of models of public participation which might be adopted by a local planning authority. To do this we shall take one of the nine approaches from each of the three boxes. An element shown by the letter (b) or (c) in Table 3.1 is assumed to subsume elements shown by earlier letters in the alphabet. It is difficult, as we have maintained, to retain the purity of any model in operation because different actors in the process may be working on the basis of different models, but the models may be useful in suggesting hypotheses to test.

Examples of public participation models are given below.

Model A

Elements: (a) Dispersing information about decisions already taken to major elites.
        (b) Gathering information about decisions taken by major elites.
        (c) Encouraging interaction between the planning authority and the public by widening the debate within major elites.

Model B

Elements: (a) Dispersing information about discussions taking place to minor elites.
        (b) Gathering information about public attitudes and opinions from minor elites.
        (c) Encouraging interaction between the planning authority and the public by involvement of minor elites through working parties.

Model C

Elements: (a) Opening government to the general public as a collectivity of individuals.
        (b) Gathering information about public attitudes and opinions from the general public as a collectivity of individuals.
        (c) Encouraging interaction between the planning authority and the public by approaching the general public as a collectivity of individuals.

These three cases exhibit different approaches to the breadth of public involvement which is desirable. Model A is not, perhaps, concerned with *public* participation at all, but with prudent decision-taking. Model B is the approach of the conscientious planner with limited resources, and of the cautious councillor who feels that mass participation is a chimera. Model C is an approach towards participatory democracy within a representative framework. Again, the wider models subsume the narrower and there is a tendency for public participation exercises to move towards more open stances. This tendency will derive partly from public demand and partly from the professional commitment of the officers directly concerned, especially if specialist posts are created within planning departments.

Although it is possible to construct a large number of models there are certain elements which are inconsistent with each other. The use of such models will cause difficulty.

Examples of inconsistent public participation models are given below.

Model D

Elements: (a) Dispersing information about decisions already taken to the general public as a collectivity of individuals.

(b) Gathering information about public attitudes and opinions from major elites.

(c) Encouraging interaction between the planning authority and the public by approaching the general public as a collectivity of individuals.

Model E

Elements: (a) Dispersing information about discussions taking place to the general public as a collectivity of individuals.

(b) Gathering information about physical facts from major elites.

(c) Encouraging interaction between the planning authority and the public by the involvement of minor elites through working parties.

In both these cases one aspect of the model is providing a greater incentive for the involvement of the public than other aspects. In Model D the planning authority is seeking interaction with individual members of the public while giving them information only about decisions already taken and showing interest only in the opinions and attitudes of major elites. In Model E the planning authority is dispersing information about discussions taking place, setting up working parties for minor elites, yet showing interest only in information obtained from major elites about physical facts within their compass. The consequence in both cases will be frustration on the part of those members of the public who become involved only to be met by a lack of interest or failure to consider their contribution to the discussions. The planners will then be accused of building a facade of public participation without any substantial structure.

The Techniques of Public Participation

The techniques of public participation may be related to the subsidiary objectives of information dispersal, information gathering and the promotion of interaction between the planning authority and the public. Naturally, some techniques will be useful in achieving more than one objective; and different actors in the process may have varying views about the purpose of a particular technique;

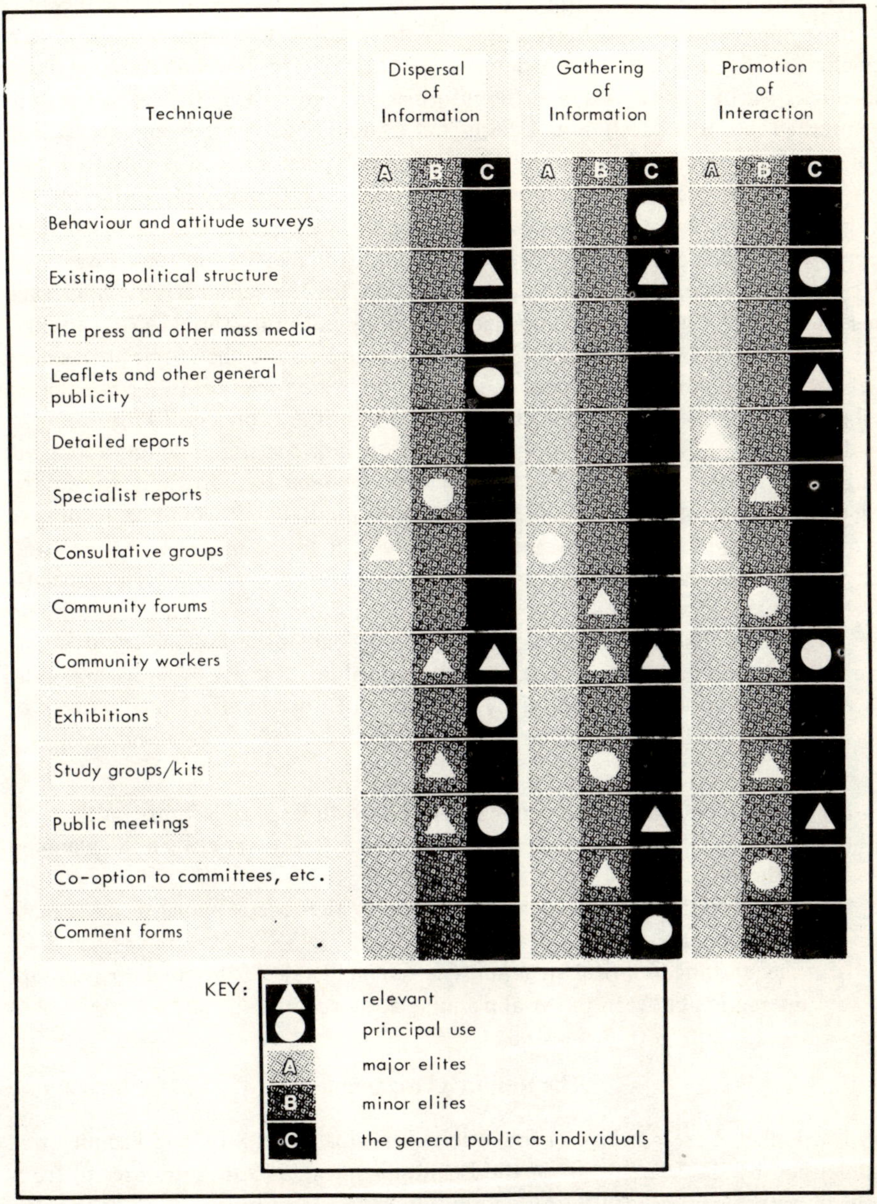

Technique	Dispersal of Information			Gathering of Information			Promotion of Interaction		
	A	B	C	A	B	C	A	B	C
Behaviour and attitude surveys						○			
Existing political structure			△			△			○
The press and other mass media			○						△
Leaflets and other general publicity			○						△
Detailed reports	○						△		
Specialist reports		○					△	○	
Consultative groups	△			○			△		
Community forums					△				○
Community workers		△	△		△	△		△	○
Exhibitions			○						
Study groups/kits						○			△
Public meetings		△	○		△				△
Co-option to committees, etc.					△			○	
Comment forms						○			

KEY:

△ relevant

○ principal use

A major elites

B minor elites

C the general public as individuals

Figure 3.2 The relationship of specific techniques to subsidiary objectives in public participation

but, equally, some techniques will be inappropriate in the context of specific models of public participation.

Let us discuss public meetings as an example. The usefulness of public meetings is most apparent as a vehicle for dispersing information to members of the general public. A meeting allows a variety of communication techniques to be used, including various visual aids, and the information conveyed by the speaker may be reinforced during a question and discussion session. In a large meeting it is difficult to receive information from the audience, and even more difficult to create opportunities for constructive interaction between the planning authority and the public. Nevertheless, some of those attending will seek to use a meeting for these purposes. A planning authority, while arranging their meetings in such a way as to facilitate the primary purpose, should also allow for the subsidiary purposes such meetings might serve. For example, the planning authority should make arrangements to record points made by the audience and ensure that some mechanism exists to take up individual complaints even if these are irrelevant to the main point of the meeting (Stringer & Ewens, 1974; Goldsmith & Saunders, 1976).

In Figure 3.2 an attempt has been made to link specific techniques and the various subsidiary objectives. The column headings refer back to Table 3.1 and the subcolumn headings to the 'who' subdivisions in that table. It would be possible to show a usefulness for most techniques with respect to the majority of objectives, but an attempt has been made to indicate those objectives for which a specific technique is most relevant and to isolate its principal use. From Figure 3.2 it should be possible to assemble a package of techniques suitable for a model of public participation assembled from the elements outlined in Table 3.1. What we are doing in effect is to produce a series of hypotheses which would affect the contents of such packages. Examples of such hypotheses include:

(a) Public meetings are most appropriately used to disperse information;
(b) If community workers are employed then interaction between the planning authority and local people will increase;
(c) If information is to be disseminated among the general public then the mass media should be used;
(d) The existing political structure (i.e. councillors) can be used to promote interaction between the local planning authority and the public.

The Research Programme

The Linked Research Project into Public Participation in Structure Planning was established by the Department of the Environment in 1973. Research teams from four universities proceeded by case study methods in five principal local authority areas. The total programme was co-ordinated to ensure a common approach where appropriate. Naturally, the local authorities concerned co-operated fully with the research teams and they were represented in the Department of the Environment steering and liaison arrangements. The purpose of the research was:

(a) To provide information on the merits and demerits of different approaches to public participation, which can be passed on in the form of advice to local authorities, and general information to the public-at-large;

(b) To provide guidance to the Department of the Environment in its ongoing contact with local authorities during plan preparation, and in its responsibility to assess submitted plans in the process of approval.

To meet these needs for practical guidance, the techniques of public participation are being studied in the planning process rather than in isolation. The context of a particular local authority may have an important influence on the effectiveness or otherwise of a technique and must be allowed for in any assessment. Such contextual factors include the socio-economic structure of the area; the political structure; the attitudes and conceptions of officials; the local authority organizational structure; the nature and strength of existing community organizations and groups; and the expectations of the public based on any previous experiences in public participation. There are obviously too many variables for these to be isolated, thus allowing the research to proceed by a series of controlled experiments; nor is such scientific rigour always acceptable in applied social science research. We should not run the risk of constraining a participation exercise simply to facilitate research.

The researchers pursued a threefold approach. First, there was a desk analysis of local authority documents and files and interviews with local authority personnel. This established details of the programme being adopted and of attitudes within the local authority towards the programme. Secondly, the researchers attended public meetings, exhibitions and other public participation events to observe the proceedings. Thirdly, participants were interviewed about their opinions and response to participation activities. By this threefold approach, the research has been able to point out incongruencies between the expectations of the organizers of the programme and the results achieved both 'objectively' as observed by the researchers and 'subjectively' as viewed by the participants. There is no possibility of defining an ideal programme of public participation against which to measure the practical examples being studied; the analysis of incongruities between expectations and achievements must therefore stand proxy for such an assessment.

The general lessons being learnt from the research seem obvious when stated, but the implications for future programmes are not easy to accept. Basically, local authorities need to spend more time in preparation of a public participation programme; and there needs to be an analytical approach which distinguishes between various objectives and various audiences and adopts appropriate techniques on the basis of this analysis. Research papers on particular techniques discuss the details of applying such an approach. The Interim Research Papers on public meetings have already been cited and others are concerned with consultation with organizations (Stringer & Plumridge, 1974; Boaden & Collins, 1975; Hampton and Beale, 1976) and with the public participation programme connected with the development of settlement policy in Cheshire (Goldsmith and Saunders, 1975). Other papers take up more general issues such as the considerations which affect a decision to employ outside consultants on public participation programmes (Hampton & Walker, 1975b), the method adopted by one local authority for handling the response to its programme (Hampton & Walker, 1975a), and the use of sample surveys in public participation programmes (Boaden & Walker, 1976). A further paper presents some guidelines for the preparation of publicity material which are drawn from an examination of a wide range of research findings in other fields (Stringer & Plumridge, 1975). Altogether some fourteen papers will be published.

Conclusion

As public participation programmes become more sophisticated the expense both in money terms and in staff time will increase. Specialized literature for particular audiences costs more money than a general leaflet; a large number of small meetings are more difficult to arrange than a few large ones; properly manned exhibitions can absorb thousands of man-hours. If public participation is to remain as part of the structure plan process, then such costs will have to be accepted. Attempts to provide only for more limited models of involvement may prove counter-productive as the public attack what they consider to be the insincerity of the local authority in erecting a facade of public participation. Fortunately, our evidence suggests that sections of the public are ready and able to discuss strategic issues if appropriate opportunities are made available: resources devoted to public participation will not be wasted if deployed in the proper manner.

Appendix

The Legislative Background to Public Participation in Structure Planning in England and Wales, 1968–1972

The Town and Country Planning Act, 1968, introduced a major change in the approach to local authority planning in England and Wales. The new concept of planning is based on a distinction between structure, i.e. strategic, planning and the local plans which will implement, in various ways, the broad policies contained in the structure plan. The 1968 Act has now been consolidated in the Town and Country Planning Act, 1971, together with major sections of a number of earlier statutes. These include the Town and Country Planning Act, 1962, the Civic Amenities Act, 1967, and the Control of Office and Industrial Development Act, 1965. The 1971 Act has been amended subsequently by the Town and Country Planning (Amendment) Act, 1972, which provides for examinations in public of structure plan submissions; and by the Local Government Act, 1972, which allocates the various planning functions between the new county and district councils. In view of this legislative complexity, a brief survey of the new process will illuminate the public participation procedures.

A structure plan formulates policy and general proposals for a county area. In preparing a structure plan the local planning authority will institute a survey to examine matters which may be expected to affect the development of the area. The survey should include description and analysis of census or other survey data relating to the principal physical and economic characteristics of the area; the size, composition and distribution of the population; the communications, transport and traffic systems; and other related matters, or matters specified by the Secretary of State.[7] The survey should be concerned with providing the factual basis to an understanding of the present and future problems and potential of the area with the intention of justifying the decisions in the plan.

The structure plan itself is a written statement which may contain or be accompanied by such diagrams, illustrations and descriptive matter as the local planning authority considers appropriate; it will not contain a map. The plan should formulate the local planning authority's policy and general proposals in repect of the development and other use of land in the area — including measures for the improvement of the physical environment and for the management of traffic — and such other matters as the Secretary of State may direct. The plan should also state the relationship of these proposals to the development proposals of neighbouring areas.[8]

Structure plans must be submitted to the Secretary of State. Before determining whether or not to approve a plan the Secretary of State must consider any objections made to him. He must also provide for an examination in public of such matters affecting his consideration of the plan as he considers ought to be examined. The Secretary of State may make regulations with respect to the procedure at such examinations, and he is not required to secure to any local planning authority or other person a right to be heard. The organizations and persons who may take part in a public examination are those whom the Secretary of State in his discretion invites to do so, or who are invited by the person holding the examination.[9]

A local planning authority in an area for which a structure plan has been prepared, or is in course of preparation, may prepare a local plan for any part of that area. A local plan must conform generally to the structure plan and may be accompanied by such diagrams, illustrations and descriptive matter as the local planning authority think appropriate. The plan will consist of a map and a written statement which formulated in appropriate detail the authority's proposals for the development and other use of land, including measures for the improvement of the environment and for the management of traffic; and such other matters as the Secretary of State may direct.[10] Under certain circumstances, the Secretary of State may direct a local planning authority to submit a local plan for his consideration, but normally the local authority will adopt the local plan by resolution.[11] Together with the structure plan, the local plans will then form the development plan for the area.

Local plans may be of three main types: district plans, action area plans and subject plans, but none of these may be adopted until the structure plan for the area has been approved. Before that stage is reached, however, the local authority may carry the preparation of local plans up to and including the point of public participation. A district plan is concerned with the whole range of planning matters for part of the area covered by a structure plan. Such areas may include the whole, or part, of an urban area or the rural parts of a county. Action area plans will guide the comprehensive planning of areas in which action is to commence within ten years. Because they express an order of priority in dealing with planning matters, the local planning authority must include a decision to prepare an action area plan in the structure plan, either on first submission or by amendment.

It is intended that most local planning matters should be dealt with as part of district or action area plans. This will enable planning issues to be treated comprehensively. However, there may be some issues requiring the development of detailed local policies and proposals which cannot be conveniently fitted into the timetable of district plans. In these circumstances, a subject plan may be prepared. Examples of issues which could be treated in this way include the reclamation of a number of sites left derelict by mineral workings, the conservation of several areas of architectural interest, and the recreational use of a river valley or a strip of coast.[12]

The Local Government Act, 1972, included an amendment to the Town and Country Planning Act, 1971. The amendment allocates planning responsibilities between the county and district councils created by the Act. Basically, the preparation of a survey and structure plan are functions exercisable by the county planning authority, while the preparation of a local plan is a function exercisable by a district planning authority, but this simple division of labour is complicated by two further provisions. First, a structure plan may provide for the preparation of local plans exclusively by the county planning authority. Secondly, the county planning authority, in consultation with the district planning authorities, has the responsibility for preparing a development plan scheme which both designates the authorities by whom local plans shall be produced and sets out a programme for their preparation.[13] The detailed allocation of planning functions between county and district councils has led to acrimonious debates in many parts of the country, particularly in the metropolitan areas.

When preparing a structure plan the local planning authority must, under the Town and Country Planning Acts, take such steps as will in their opinion secure adequate publicity for the Report of Survey and the matters which they propose to include in the plan. Further, they must provide adequate opportunities for people who may wish to make representations to the authority about such matters; and they must ensure that people know of these opportunities. The authority must consider any representations made to them within a prescribed period, and the structure plan when submitted to the Secretary of State must be publicly available. Objections to the submitted plan may be made to the Secretary of State by members of the public. When submitting a structure plan to the Secretary of State, the local authorities are required to include a statement of the steps taken to comply with these provisions for public participation. The Secretary of State must satisfy himself of the adequacy of the public participation programme before proceeding to consider the structure plan itself.[14] Similar provisions, with appropriate amendments, apply to the preparation of local plans.[15]

Notes

1. A survey of the complex legislative development will be found in the appendix to this chapter. Separate provisions for Scotland have followed the English legislation, but this chapter refers only to England and Wales.
2. Dr Noel Boaden, Michael Goldsmith and Peter Stringer share responsibility with me for directing this programme and I have benefited greatly from our discussions of the present paper. Another member of the team, Neil Collins, made some helpful criticisms of an earlier draft. I remain solely responsible for the final draft.
3. cf. Carole Pateman, *Participation and Democratic Theory*, (Cambridge: C.U.P., 1970), chapters 1 & 2; and William Hampton, 'Popular Participation in Local Democracy', in Stephen Hatch (ed.), *Towards Participation in Local Services* (London: Fabian Tract 419, Feb. 1973).
4. cf. William Hampton and Penelope Pike, '*The Open Council and Public Participation:* the Leichhardt Experience', *Policy and Politics*, Vol. 3, No. 1 (September 1974).
5. cf. Bernard Crick, 'Them and us', in his collection of essays, *Political Theory and Practice* (London: Allen Lane the Penguin Press, 1972).
6. 'Pandora's Box. The box in which Hope alone remained when by its rash opening all objects of desire were dispersed to play havoc among mankind'! *The Concise Oxford Dictionary.*
7. Town and Country Planning Act, 1971, Section 6.
8. Town and Country Planning Act, 1971, Section 7.
9. Town and Country Planning (Amendment) Act, 1972, Section 3.
10. Town and Country Planning Act, 1971, Section 11.
11. Town and Country Planning Act, 1971, Section 14.
12. This discussion of the types of local plans is based on *Development Plans: A Manual on Form and Content*, London: HMSO, 1970, pp. 47, 55 and 59.
13. Local Government Act, 1972, Section 183.
14. Town and Country Planning Act, 1971, Section 8.
15. Town and Country Planning Act, 1971, Section 12.

References

Arnstein, Sherry R., 1969 'A Ladder of Citizen Participation in the USA', *Journal of the American Institute of Planners*, **35** (4), 216–224.

Boaden, Noel & Neil Collins, 1975. *Consultation with Organisations in the Merseyside Structure Plan*, Interim Research Paper 6.

Boaden, Noel & Raymond Walker, 1976. *Sample Surveys and Public Participation*, Interim Research Paper 10.

Goldsmith, Michael & Peter Saunders, 1975. *The Tale of Lewis the Cat: Public Participation and Settlement Policy in Cheshire*, Interim Research Paper 8.

Goldsmith, Michael & Peter Saunders, 1976. *Participation through Public Meetings: the Case in Cheshire*, Interim Research Paper 9.

Great Britain, Department of the Environment, 1972. *Circular 52/72*, London: HMSO.

Great Britain, Ministry of Housing and Local Government, 1969. *People and Planning*, London: HMSO.

Hampton, William & Wendy Beale, 1976. *Methods of Approaching Groups in South Yorkshire*, Interim Research Paper 11.

Hampton, William & Raymond Walker, 1975a. *The Role of a Working Party in Considering the Public Response to a Draft Structure Plan: a Case Study from Teesside*, Interim Research Paper 4.

42

Hampton, William & Raymond Walker, 1975b. *The Role of Consultants in the Public Participation Process: the Teesside Experience*, Interim Research Paper 5.
Mill, John Stuart, 1910. *Representative Government*, London: Dent.
Stringer, Peter & Susan Ewens, 1974. *Participation through Public Meetings: the Case in North East Lancashire*, Interim Research Paper 2.
Stringer, Peter & Gillian Plumridge, 1974. *Consultation with Organisations on the North East Lancashire Advisory Plan*, Interim Research Paper 3.
Stringer, Peter & Gillian Plumridge, 1975. *Publicity Guidelines*, Interim Research Paper 7.

Note: Interim Research Papers are available from, Linked Research Project, Department of Extramural Studies, University of Sheffield, 85 Wilkinson Street, Sheffield S10 2GJ.

4

The Expansion of Turnhouse, Edinburgh Airport

WILLIAM E. S. MUTCH

The planning and devopment of airports in many countries have produced *causes célèbres* of environmental conflict and public participation. Kennedy Field in the United States and the massive Third London Airport Inquiry come immediately to mind, but the same issues are raised, just as sharply, in smaller airports, and, on the smaller scale, the tactics and principles may be seen more easily.

The account of the local public response to the planning proposal for the redevelopment of Edinburgh Airport is a case study of the denial of public participation in planning. The events revealed the inadequacy of the planning system in Scotland and its insensitivity to constructive criticism, beginning and ending with the rejection of people's environmental needs.

Turnhouse Airport lies to the west of Edinburgh, only seven kilometres from the city centre. It began as a grass airfield for the Royal Flying Corps in 1915, was used throughout the Second World War as a fighter station, and still has a small military role. Regular civil air transport began in 1947 when the airfield was taken over by the Ministry of Civil Aviation, and civil operations have continued to expand through successive changes in ownership: to the Air Ministry in 1956; to the Ministry of Aviation in 1960; in 1966 to the Board of Trade, subsequently the Department of Trade and Industry; and on 1 April 1971 to the British Airports Authority (BAA).

The first paved runway was built in 1939 on a bearing of 130–310° Mag. (SE–NW), and lengthened to 1830 metres in 1956. There is a secondary runway (80–260°) of 1053 metres which is too short for modern commercial aircraft. These runways are designated 13/31 and 08/26 respectively (Figure 4.1).

The usual 310° approach takes aircraft over the southern and southwestern parts of the city. This had virtually no significance until the local introduction of jet aircraft in 1972, since when noise pollution has increased intolerably (Figure 4.2).

Even in the early 1960s the limitations of Turnhouse were apparent. Not only had the main runway been built at right-angles to the prevailing wind, but it had been so sited that it could not be extended to take larger aircraft or to instal radio-electronic landing aids which need about 2350 m of runway length (BAA, 1971 –1). Diversions and cancellations due to crosswinds and poor visibility at

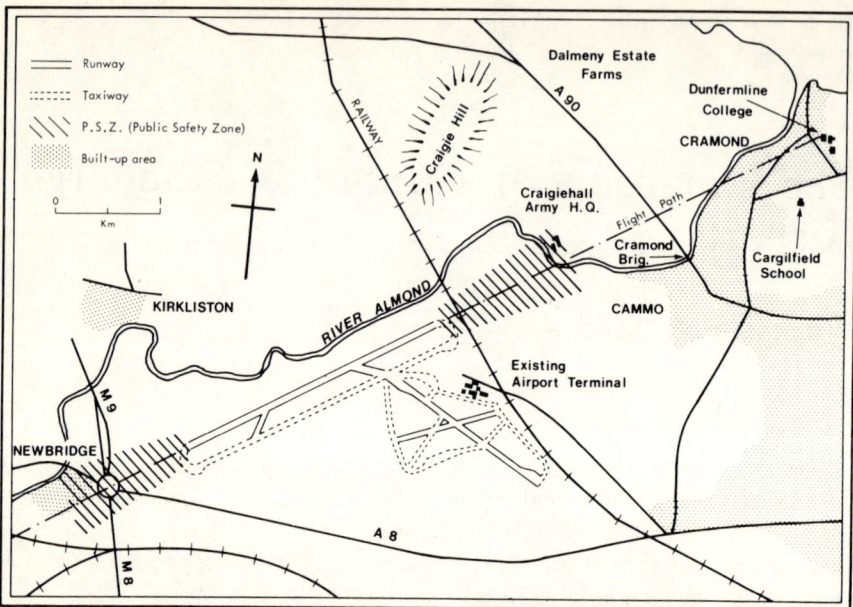

Figure 4.1 Edinburgh Airport: The BAA plan (now constructed) related to the old runways and terminal buildings. The northeast flight path crosses residential areas

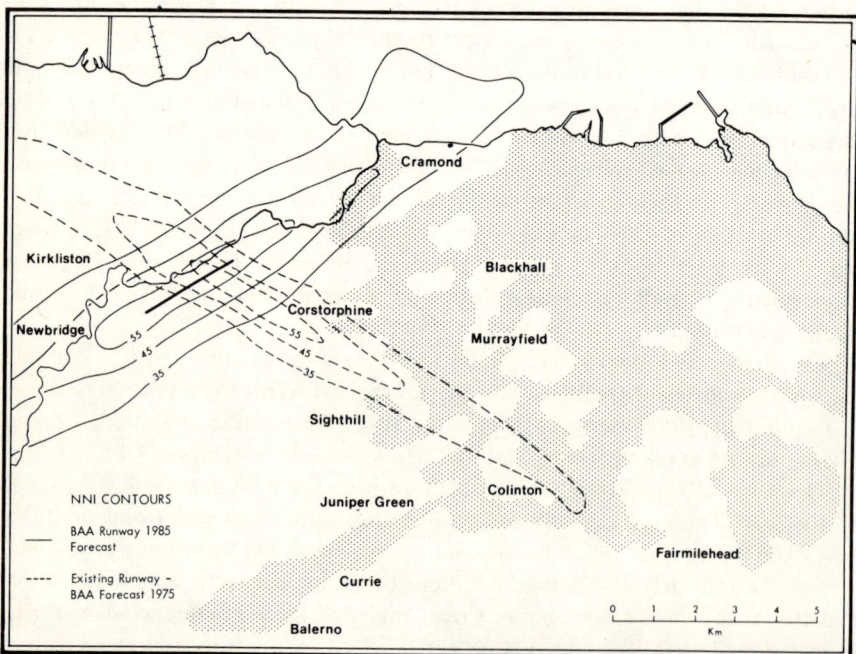

Figure 4.2 Edinburgh Airport: The 'noise footprint' of aircraft traffic using the old and new runways in relation to built-up areas (shaded). The Noise and Number Index contours are based on evidence produced at the Public Inquiry by F. Andrew Sharman, FICE, of Sir William Halcrow and Partners

Turnhouse affected 3.01 per cent of all air transport movements between 1965 and 1970 (BAA, 1971 –13), a rate considered unacceptably high. The number of terminal passengers who used Turnhouse in 1969 was 612,500, and air transport movements numbered 10,400 (BAA, 1971 –10).

The Local Communities

In 1960 people living in the village of Cramond formed an Association: 'To promote the amenity of the community of Cramond and to safeguard its heritage'. At its formation there was no thought of airport development or any threat of aircraft noise; it was, and is, a local community association, holding meetings mainly of social, literary and historical interest. There is a strong sense of community among the people. It is probable that Cramond has been continuously occupied from the time of the Roman garrison in 142 A.D. to the present day. There was a church here in the sixth century, while the village itself is essentially as it was in the eighteenth century. Cramond remained a village until after the Second World War, but house building accelerated in the 1950s and 1960s, and by 1970 the land was almost entirely built-up on the right bank of the River Almond from Cammo to the sea.

In 1966 new buildings, of a delicate design, were constructed at Cramond for the Dunfermiline College of Physical Education, the only college in Scotland for training specialist women teachers in gymnastics and dancing; the Scottish Education Department meets all its capital and running expenses. In 1971 there were 430 residential students.

Almost without exception the houses in the Cramond area are owner-occupied, with a preponderance of young married people with small children. Unquestionably it is a very well-educated and highly articulate community, and the wealth of professional skills among local people is exceptional. For the airport inquiry, expertise was immediately available in every field required: meteorology, civil engineering, economics, medicine, etc. The president of the Cramond Association was a civil engineer with special experience of airfield construction. It is difficult to imagine a community better suited to constructive public participation in planning.

Seven kilometres to the southwest, the community of Newbridge provides a sharp contrast with Cramond. Almost all its residents rent their homes from the local authority, Midlothian County Council. The houses are grouped in Newbridge Village itself, Lochend and Ratho Station. Unemployment followed the post-war decline of the oil-shale industry and local coal mining, and Newbridge was scheduled as a Special Area and a Development Area by the County Council. In 1963 an industrial estate of 120 hectares was created at Lochend (Grimson Report, 1972, p. 25), where many Newbridge residents work. Though less affluent, they value their community and their homes just as highly as people at Cramond.

Important local issues other than the airport development claimed the attention of Newbridge people in 1969 and 1970. A motorway interchange was being built on the edge of the village, thus separating it from Ratho Station. Not only was the local primary school too old and far too small, but it was sited at an accident black spot at the junction of the M8 and M9 motorways. Understandably, Newbridge people were actively concerned with the issue of a new school; they did not know that the planning officials had already planned their village into the ironically termed Public Safety Zone of the new runway. Councillors and county officials asserted that the airport reconstruction on BAA plans would not be environmentally damaging. It was only when the report of the public inquiry had been published that the residents were alerted to the truth.

The Planning

Late in 1967 there was increased public pressure and speculation concerning the improvement of Turnhouse. The Cramond Association was told privately by a civil servant in the Scottish Office that plans did exist for the new airport and that it might be advisable to declare the interest of the local people.

In February 1968 the Secretary of the Association and the Session Clerk of Cramond Church each wrote to the British Airports Authority and the Scottish Development Department (SDD) asking for 'detailed particulars' of the proposed runway at Turnhouse. The BAA replied that the matter had been passed to the Board of Trade (later the Department of Trade and Industry, DTI) and referred to the expected setting up of a local Consultative Committee for the airport. The Board of Trade did not reply at all. (Gimson Report, 1972, p. 22). The reply from the SDD stated only that the opportunity to object would be given when any planning proposals were advertised.

This refusal by government departments to divulge information to local people was of great importance in the case. At the subsequent public inquiry it was revealed (Gimson Report, 1972, p. 26) that as early as 1964 the Uniroyal Company were reassured by the SDD through Midlothian County Council that the Public Safety Zone of the new runway would not encroach on their factory site at Lochend. The plans for the runway were formed in the early 1960s and it was certainly not indecision about their nature that led to the refusal to disclose them in 1968. In May 1964 the Board of Trade made a 'Safeguarding Order' under its statutory powers restricting the height of building developments in the area of the runway approaches, but it has since emerged that this was held as 'classified information', so that local people would not know.

The Cramond Association made several attempts in 1969 to meet the Commandant at Turnhouse to ask for details of the projected runway development. These approaches were refused, and the Association learned of the proposals only in April 1971. The local people were thus denied an opportunity to comment or to participate in the planning stages; later, when the plans were rigidly cast, they could object if they wished.

On 1 April 1971 the British Airports Authority took over the airport from the DTI. On 21 April BAA officials met the Cramond Association and revealed the plans for the 2545 metre runway on a bearing of 70–250° (runway 07/25), with flight lines passing directly over Newbridge and Cramond. The BAA officials addressed a public meeting in Cramond on 12 May to explain their proposals. The meeting, attended by about 400 people, appointed a working party to study the available information and report back.

On 18 May the Cramond Association Committee decided to oppose the BAA planning application, and a recalled public meeting was held on 14 June. It resolved to object to the BAA proposal because of the noise nuisance it would cause, and those attending the meeting were asked to write to the Secretary of State as objectors. It was agreed unanimously, however, that no proposal counter to BAA's should be promoted which would impose a similar noise nuisance upon another community. The meeting accepted that improved air transport was required for Edinburgh and that the existing facilities were inadequate. The community has never wavered in these resolves.

This then was not selfish objection to development, which would subject other people to that which Cramond was seeking to avoid, nor a hypocritical blocking of the improvement in air transport services which local people used. The executive group had already established beyond doubt that the official BAA proposal was not a unique solution to the problem of how to improve the air services for Edinburgh and the east of Scotland.

Following informal discussions between the Cramond Association and other local bodies, the Runway Joint Committee was set up, and on 18 June the firm of Sir William Halcrow and Partners was engaged to prepare the technical case, in collaboration with Mr. Norman Fleming, a former director of the acoustics branch of the Department of Scientific and Industrial Research. As soon as formal objection to the BAA proposal was known, the Secretary of State for Scotland, the Rt. Hon. Mr. Gordon Campbell, M.P. (now Lord Campbell of Croy) 'called in' the planning application from the local authorities and appointed Mr. G. S. Gimson, Q.C. to act as Reporter at the public inquiry, with Mr. G. F. K. Donaldson, A.F.R.Ae.S. as his technical assessor.

In evidence, however, the DTI showed that the runway decision went to the Cabinet *before* the public inquiry (witness Mr. G. M. McIntosh of DTI, 2 December Public Inquiry proceedings p. 1970) resulting in the policy of document BAA (1971)—4a. If the matter was indeed then decided, the calling of the inquiry was illogical and dishonest, in suggesting that the issue was still open.

The Run-up to the Public Inquiry

Those responsible for the BAA proposals had prepared their plans over several years. In contrast, the Secretary of State allowed only three months notice of the public inquiry, setting it for 1 November 1971. This was a considerable disadvantage to the objectors, although not to the BAA.

It was virtually impossible to frame a proper objection when the BAA proposals themselves were not available beyond the general outline given at the public meeting. Although the objectors' solicitor asked BAA for details of their proposals on 22 June, they were not released to the objectors until September. BAA's slowness in detailing their plans was very harmful to the objectors and their consultants, and it may be presumed that this was the intention. The DTI evidence on the planning of the runway was received only on 13 October.

The Department of Trade and Industry was directly obstructive in another respect. During an early search for relevant literature on airport planning, and on Turnhouse in particular, the scrutiny of a paper by Heath and Oulton (1970) revealed the existence of Board of Trade reports on Turnhouse and the feasibility of a Central Scotland airport to serve both Glasgow and Edinburgh. On 14 July 1971 the solicitors asked DTI to provide these reports as public service documents relevant to the inquiry, but they procrastinated and stubbornly maintained their obstruction until twenty-four hours before a Reporter's hearing on 10 September which would have been asked to require the production of the documents. Their action was seen as a deliberate attempt by officialdom to 'nobble' the opposition and to weaken their case.

At about the same time, two very senior civil servants in the Scottish Office said that the BAA runway would be built at Turnhouse irrespective of the findings of the public inquiry. Although this was an unwitnessed private conversation on which no action could be taken, it certainly did not promote confidence in the public inquiry system in Scotland.

Both before and after the public inquiry, the objectors repeatedly approached their Member of Parliament about the tactics employed by BAA. A report to Edinburgh Corporation Planning Sub-Committee from the Chief Sanitary Inspector (the official responsible in matters of noise) recommended the rejection of the BAA plan on grounds of noise pollution along the flight lines, and the realignment of the runway as proposed by the objectors. Five days later, at the main Planning Committee, this report was withdrawn and replaced by another advocating acceptance of the BAA plans. The reason for the change was given as 'reassurances' provided by BAA, although the forecast figures of imposed noise were not altered. Some City councillors who voted not to object to the BAA proposals later admitted they did not know that the decibel noise scale was logarithmic – that 100 PNdB (Perceived Noise Decibels) represented double the noise of 90 PNdB, and 110 PNdB four times 90 PNdB, and thus they did not appreciate the benefits that realignment offered.

While the objectors were mounting a reasoned argument against suboptimal proposals, BAA issued a stream of counter-propaganda which ridiculed opposition (and hence ridiculed public participation in planning). Their main argument was that any change in the official plans would delay the completion of the runway. The fact that several years had been allowed to elapse while the responsible civil servants refused to discuss, and even concealed, the plans for rebuilding the airport facilities was conveniently left unmentioned. The Cramond objectors believed that serious attempts were made, especially by the officials of the Department of Trade and Industry, the Scottish Office and the British Airports Authority, to prejudice the inquiry and to thwart the objectors in the preparation of their case.

As a symptom of their confidence in the justice of the case and nature of the evidence, the Runway Joint Committee decided that the objection to the BAA proposals should be advanced by the legal process only, that — in terms of an industrial dispute — the issue should be decided by the agreed arbitration procedure, without threats of militancy.

Political Considerations

Cramond is part of the West Edinburgh parliamentary constituency which was represented in 1971 by Mr. Anthony Stodart, M.P., a Conservative and then a member of the Government. As a Minister of State in the Ministry of Agriculture, Fisheries and Food, which does not operate in Scotland, Mr. Stodart, though a Scottish M.P., was a government minister without responsibility in the Scottish Office. Newbridge is part of the Midlothian constituency which was represented in 1971 by Mr. Alex Eadie, M.P., a Labour back-bencher.

The Cramond Association is strictly non-party; the Runway Joint Committee Executive was led by Mr. Ronald MacIntosh who was also Chairman of the West Edinburgh branch of the Labour Party, and included, as Campaign Organizer, Mr. A. M. Fletcher, who subsequently became Conservative M.P. for Edinburgh North.

From the outset of the controversy, the M.P. for Midlothian, Mr. Eadie, took the line of Midlothian County Council in outright support of BAA. This support for the proposals which would impose such a vast noise burden on his Newbridge constituents was a surprising illogicality. The Reporter at the inquiry was to say later (Gimson Report, 1972, p. 101), 'The situation' (i.e. the noise imposition) 'at Newbridge would be more severe than should be imposed on any community'. He could not understand 'why the seriousness of the disturbance to be expected there (even on the basis of BAA's evidence) was not recognised by BOT, DTI or BAA and notice of it given to MCC' (i.e. to Midlothian County Council). Mr. Gimson concluded (Gimson Report, 1972, p. 103) that Newbridge might be found to be uninhabitable on account of aircraft noise, yet the political representatives at County Council and in Parliament supported the proposals.

At a public meeting (2 February 1973) Mr. Stodart was told that improved air services for Edinburgh could be provided by plans which would impose less noise on Cramond and on the rest of west Edinburgh, with no more noise for any other community than in BAA's plans. He said that although as a member of the government he could not be seen publicly to disagree with a government decision or disassociate himself from it, he was active in pressing his constituents' case by buttonholing fellow government ministers, including the Prime Minister.

The local councillors in Cramond played a minor part in the airport controversy. They may have felt that there was some conflict between their commitment as representatives of a ward which was substantially opposed to the BAA plans and their positions as business men, since the local Chambers of Commerce strongly supported BAA plans.

The Public Inquiry

Mr. G. S. Gimson, Q.C. held the inquiry in Edinburgh. It began on 1 November 1971 and ended on 3 February 1972, in all occupying thirty-eight days.

Part I of the Report, including the Findings in Fact, was circulated to those represented at the inquiry, for consideration and amendment. Mr. Gimson then wrote Part II, ending with his Recommendation to the Secretary of State. The full Report was dated 1 September 1972, although not published until 26 January 1973, fifteen months after the inquiry opened.

The BAA as applicant for planning permission was represented by Mr. J. H. McCluskey, Q.C. and Mr. D. A. O. Edwards, Advocate. The principal objectors to the planning application (nine organizations and about 350 individual objectors) were represented jointly through the Runway Joint Committee by Mr. R. A. Bennett, Q.C. and Mr. John Murray, Advocate. The Dunfermline College was represented by Mr. D. Bruce Weir, Q.C. Several people and interests were represented separately from the principals, either in support of BAA (such as DTI and Midlothian CC) or in objection.

The BAA case was strong and presented with ruthlessness. It began by forecasting the probable increase in air traffic until 1985 (BAA, 1971 −10). This indicated between 72 and 85 air transport movements on a summer day in 1985. The existing services were inadequate. The turbo-prop aircraft on the Edinburgh–London route were obsolescent and their successors would need a longer runway of 2545 metres (effectively 2347 metres in each direction with displaced thresholds). An extension of the existing runway 13/31 would not suffice; it would not solve the crosswind problem nor allow the installation of Category II Landing aids. It would also impose a considerable noise nuisance over southwest Edinburgh (Gimson Report, 1972, p. 7). These judgements were not disputed by the objectors. The operational safeguards for runways were set out in Civil Aviation Publication 168 (BAA, 1971 − 15).

An issue which assumed great importance related to the Public Safety Zones (PSZ) (BAA, 1971 −16). PSZs are created at busy airports to prevent people congregating in areas where there is a higher than usual risk of an aircraft accident, immediately beyond the end of runways. In the zones the DTI advises against all planning developments likely to increase the number of people living, working or congregating for recreation. The PSZ is a trapezium-shaped area; at the end of the runway the zone is 305 metres wide, fanning out to 698 metres at a distance of 1372 metres from the runway end. New houses may not be built in an existing PSZ. But the Edinburgh inquiry established a precedent for the PSZ of a new runway being imposed on an existing village. No one stopped the planners from putting Newbridge into the PSZ of BAA's runway. The Reporter at the inquiry said, 'That sticks in my gullet!'

The crux of the BAA proposals lay in the constraints accepted in aligning the runway. The principal physical constraints (BAA, 1971 −17) were:

1. The River Almond along the north side of the new runway.

2. The Edinburgh—Forth Bridge railway line to the east, on an embankment about 5 metres high.
3. The Lochend Industrial Estate to the south.
4. The M8 and M9 motorways to the southwest of the runway.
5. The two high railway embankments which meet to the southwest.

When these constraints were taken in conjunction with the need for 2545 metres of flat ground, the alignment limits imposed by wind direction, and the freedom from obstructions on the aircraft glide paths, the choice of runway sites was severely limited. The product was runway 07/25 (see Figure 4.1). This had the advantage of linking up with the existing runway 13/31 to provide an alternative in severe crosswinds.

The main objection raised to the plan for the BAA 07/25 runway was that its use would impose a vast noise burden on a very large number of homes, and on schools and colleges under the flight paths. The BAA forecasts of the aircraft noise (measured in PNdB — which is a logarithmic scale) were challenged as underestimates. The objectors commissioned sound measurements at Abbotsinch airport. The Reporter said, 'The alternative proposals which they put forward are the result of a more balanced study of the situation than any hitherto carried out and they provided the only comprehensive data on the very important question of noise' (Gimson Report, 1972, p. 90); 'I should add that the full extent of the noise problem at Newbridge was apparent only from the *data* produced by these (Cramond) objectors' (Gimson Report, 1972, p. 104).

The noise levels forecast are extremely high, rising to over 125 PNdB at Newbridge; at this level noise is not merely a nuisance but is in the range of possible physical damage to hearing, especially in children (Gimson Report, 1972, p. 60).

At a public inquiry into a planning application the objectors need not provide alternative plans, but in this instance the Runway Joint Committee asked the consultants to do much more than block the development. The objectors' case was that inadequate investigation had been made on the best location of the airport to serve Edinburgh, a view supported by the material so unwillingly released by DTI prior to the inquiry. Three major airports (the enlarged Turnhouse, Abbotsinch and Prestwick) within a distance of 95 kilometres were unjustified. A Central Scottish Airport (CSA) accessible to Edinburgh, Glasgow and central Scotland generally would be infinitely preferable. The concentration of air services would give greater convenience when changing flights, economy in operation, and such a concentration of passenger demand as would support direct air services to Europe, which neither Abbotsinch nor Turnhouse could do separately. The consultants identified a site for the CSA at Airth, near Falkirk, and evidence at the inquiry showed that it was technically feasible and would greatly reduce the total aircraft noise pollution for people in Scotland. It was clear at the inquiry that the Board of Trade (DTI) had not investigated the possibilities.

The objectors further proposed, but only if the CSA were ruled out, that a new runway should be at Turnhouse on a different alignment from that chosen by BAA. An alignment of approximately 06/24 would produce a northeasterly flight path

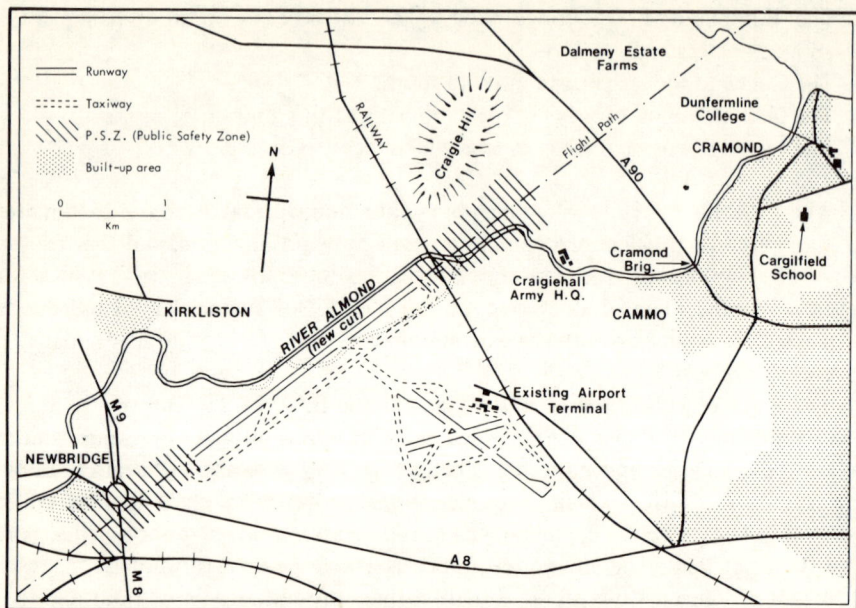

Figure 4.3 Edinburgh Airport: The Cramond Association plan which would have taken the northeast flight entirely over farmland to the sea.

over open farmland west of the River Almond all the way to the sea, thereby reducing the noise burden greatly at that end. The cost of the BAA scheme was given as £9.7 million at 1971 prices, and the Cramond Association (CA) alignment was estimated at an additional £2 million (Gimson Report, 1972, p. 98) (Figure 4.3). Against the additional construction cost, the objectors said, must be set the saving of the consequential expenses of the BAA scheme, such as the sound-proofing of the Dunfermline College and the Army Headquarters building at Craigiehall.

The Ministry of Defence (MOD) had not seen the newspaper notices about BAA's plans for Turnhouse, and therefore the Army did not appear as objectors at the public inquiry (Marre, 1974, para 78), only becoming aware of the noise threat in October 1971. Working with what proved later to be considerable underestimates of the incident noise, a DOE technical officer estimated the cost of sound-proofing Craigiehall as up to £0.8 million (1971). In the light of that figure, MOD informed SDD on 28 January 1971 that the BAA plans would cause heavy additional expenditure from public funds, and asked SDD to inform the Reporter of this. SDD did *not* do so, and there was even some attempt in the Sottish Office later to deny that the Army had made any approach.

The BAA runway created a PSZ which included part of the headquarters building. The Ministry of Defence issued a press statement that the Institute of Sound and Vibration Research at Southampton University had advised that the building would not require sound-proofing, but this had to be withdrawn hastily when Southampton University made it clear that they had not even been invited to look at the problem. As the Headquarters is sound-sensitive and will experience noise greater than 125 PNdB (DOE estimates 60 NNI (Noise and Number Index) — see Roskill Report, VII, p. 329), it is not credible that an expert would say nothing need be done. The objectors concluded that it would have been politically inconvenient to admit that the Army Headquarters would require sound-proofing or resiting since that would have eroded the apparent cheapness of the BAA alignment. The authorities crudely lied and suppressed the truth in support of the official plan. Assuredly the Army could not be allowed to leave Craigiehall (at a cost estimated in the press at £6 million) while the Newbridge residents were to be left in their PSZ.

The Cramond objectors may well have reduced their chances of success (and they certainly increased their costs) by raising the case for the CSA. It was not a casual decision. CSA was seen as a wiser development and a better investment for Scotland. Abbotsinch was running at a large financial loss annually. Turnhouse would be no better, and the European direct flights, the darling of the Edinburgh business community, would probably be an illusion. Also the objectors were influenced by the recognition that their 06/24 alignment did nothing to help Newbridge, although it did much to relieve the noise at Cramond.

In brief, the CA alignment 06/24 would have greatly reduced the noise for more than a thousand families northeast of the airport; would have made life no more impossible for Newbridge people than BAA proposed; would have cost more in direct construction, mainly by the river diversion; would have caused a few months delay in the completion of the work; but would have saved a large amount in sound-proofing at schools, colleges and the Army Headquarters, or still more in the cost of their having to be rebuilt elsewhere; would have reduced greatly the need for noise reduction procedures in flying and limitations on airport operations; and would have imposed some cost in industrial expansion in the future on sites in the PSZ at Lochend (although it is a doubtful proposition that assurances regarding freedom from PSZ imposition should ever have been given to industrialists while the people of Newbridge were not informed that they had been planned into one).

The Public Inquiry Findings

The Reporter considered the BAA application to be subject to three major objections:

1. The inclusion in the PSZ at Newbridge of an existing population of about 500 people plus road users, and the risk to the public below the flight path at the other end of the runway;
2. The effect of aircraft noise at Newbridge;
3. The effect of aircraft noise at Cramond.

He thought that the first was immediately fatal to the BAA application and that either of the others must lead to its rejection. Together they appeared un-answerable, there being inadequate separation of the runway and the neighbouring communities.

Mr. Gimson recognized that the rejection of BAA's plan would create difficulties for southeast Scotland. 'This appears to me to result from delays in the past and also from inadequate investigation of the implications of the proposals before they were made the subject of this application.'

He suggested two possible solutions; either a CSA in a central location (probably necessitating interim improvements at Turnhouse) or a runway on a different alignment at Turnhouse, which might require reconsideration of the future of Newbridge village.

Mr. Gimson then recommended formally that BAA's application for planning permission should not be granted. The objectors had won the public inquiry.

The Decision

In a decision letter to the objectors dated 26 January 1973, seventeen weeks after the date of the Report, the Secretary of State, then Mr. Gordon Campbell, M.P., said that BAA should go ahead with the construction of their runway on their plans without any alteration, in flat contradiction of the public inquiry decision.

In the waiting period between the Report and the decision, there was a succession of newspaper information 'leaks' which, with little doubt, originated in the Scottish Office. They may have been intended to test public reaction to the impending overturning of the public inquiry Report or perhaps to force the hand of the Secretary of State who, at that stage, may have been still inclined to accept to accept the Report and refuse the BAA application. Whatever their intention, they were regarded by the objectors as prejudicial, scandalous and the very negation of fair decision-taking.

The Secretary of State's decision produced intense anger in generally mild and law-abiding people at Cramond. Some immediately formed a Runway Action Group, believing more could be gained by militancy than by legal argument, although still supporting the Runway Joint Committee. It was a 'noisy' group, effectively making known to a wide audience the injustice of the overturning of the public inquiry, and dedicated to stopping the runway.

Appeal

The Runway Joint Committee carefully considered the possibility of an appeal against the Secretary of State's decision but the objectors' lawyers advised against appeal to the Court of Session, as there was no ground for asserting improper procedure in the preparation of the planning application.

It was decided, however, to take the case to the Parliamentary Commissioner for Administration, the 'Ombudsman', then Sir Alan Marre, who is charged with the investigation of cases of maladministration.

The Commissioner's subsequent report (Marre, 1974) pointed out that some of the complaints referred to him related to the actions of authorities who were outwith his jurisdiction, the principal one being BAA, which underlined immediately the extraordinary difficulty of bringing airport planning to the Commissioner's attention at all.

Sir Alan Marre examined the files of government departments and found no maladministration as such; everything had been done legally, however unwisely. The approach to the Parliamentary Commissioner achieved nothing, and the Scottish Office and BAA thought so little of the matter that construction work on the runway went on unhindered by the possibility that it might be stopped as a result of the Commissioner's report to Parliament.

His report contains some obvious inconsistencies. When dealing (para. 35) with DTI's failure to reply to the letters in February 1968 asking for information about the plans, he says that they admitted the omission but, 'there was no deliberate effort to withhold information'. In paragraphs 46 and 47, however, he repeats the arguments given to him by SDD and DTI against early release of information, which make it clear that they withheld the information intentionally.

Publicity and Expenses

During the campaign the Runway Joint Committee issued a local newsletter, *Runway News*, to inform people about the fight and to mobilize their help.

The objectors' expenses amounted in all to £26,000. In the three months ended 30 November 1971, the appeal for funds brought in £14,060 from 810 people, of whom 743 gave £25 or less. By the end of the inquiry, contributions amounted to £18,000.

Very condescendingly the Secretary of State in his decision letter said he would not award inquiry expenses against the objectors (who had won the inquiry!). This was in marked contrast to the recommendations of the Reporter (Gimson Report, 1972, p. 104); the objectors had been put to very great expense as a result entirely of mistakes and misjudgment by government agencies and had produced valuable technical material. The Reporter said that the failure of BOT (DTI) to reply to the objectors in February 1968 left them without information of the BAA plans which were then complete, and he accepted that this added to the length and complexity of the inquiry.

The Parliamentary Commissioner for Administration (Marre, 1974, p. 45), said that the Runway Joint Committee had gone to considerable expense to provide evidence 'which they believed ought to have been obtained earlier and was necessary and material to the Secretary of State's consideration of the applications. And I have invited SDD to consider whether there might not be a special case for, exceptionally, some substantial contribution towards the Committee's expenses.'

By the time he left office in February 1974, Mr. Gordon Campbell had not got around to that recommendation except to say he foresaw difficulties. His successor in office, the Rt. Hon. William Ross, M.P. was prompt in announcing that nothing whatever would be paid to the objectors.

Conclusion

Many Cramond people feel that it was an error of judgement to play the legal game; militancy and even outright violence, although they shunned it themselves, would perhaps have ensured success, which is more useful than victory. It seems that, in order to win any issue against a set of official plans, the objectors should avoid the established investigation and inquiry procedure. In this instance, success would have required the issue to become a political one, not a planning process; the planners and the civil servants had predetermined that there would be no public participation in the planning, presumably because they were aware that the plans would not stand careful scrutiny. It seems likely that none of the politicians involved really understood the technical matters of noise or grasped the idea of 'swinging' the runway alignment.

The actions of SDD, DTI and BAA in refusing to answer letters in February 1968 show that they intended to withhold information; they were not in favour of early release of planning information (Marre, 1974, paras. 46 and 47). The planners knew that they were proposing developments which would be very damaging to the environment of people in Newbridge and Cramond, and they sought to conceal the facts in order to minimize opposition to the scheme. They seem to have concealed their plans even from the Scottish Education Department who were building schools and the Dunfermline College directly under the flight path.

The propriety of a government department in giving an assurance to a commercial firm about the PSZ of a runway development which was not in their granting, which then was not even the subject of a planning application and which affected the home environment of thousands of people already resident in the area (which the commercial firm was not), is an open question – to put it mildly.

A long and scrupulously fair inquiry ended with the BAA plan being rejected. When the Secretary of State overturned the inquiry he produced no valid reason for doing so; in effect, he merely asserted that the judgement of his planners was best. If he intended all along that the runway should be built on BAA's plans, why did he commission the inquiry at all? Perhaps he never really believed that BAA might lose it. Should not a Secretary of State who overturns a public inquiry recommendation be required to say why he is doing so?

The factor which seemed to weigh heavily with Mr. Gordon Campbell was the possibility of delay if the BAA plans were altered. Considering the time spent in some of the processes of decision-taking in this case, it was the weakest of arguments. Had discussions taken place during the early stages (even in early 1971) much time and money could have been saved, and the inquiry avoided. A river diversion and an 06/24 alignment runway could have been built in less than the twenty-two months of the wasted inquiry procedure. There would also have been a vast saving of public and private funds spent in the inquiry, and the externalities of the cost–benefit analysis would have shown other plans considerably more desirable than those of BAA which were bulldozed through.

As a general principle, if the objection is upheld at an inquiry, is it not just that the Reporter (who is acting as a judge) should be able to award expenses, as a judge may do to a successful pursuer in court? The Secretary of State may grant expenses against frivolous objectors if he wishes, and it is surely inequitable that government planners should be able to act unwisely and anti-socially, yet that redress may be obtained by the private citizen only at his own expense. More particularly, would it not be reasonable that where the Secretary of State overturns a public inquiry decision which has upheld the objection he should be bound to recompense the objectors financially in order to offset the denial to them of the fruits of the inquiry?

The vital issue of this case has nothing to do with noise levels or the details of runway design. By far the most important matter arising from it is the credibility of the planning process in Scotland. Cramond had so many advantages: a case that was technically good enough to win the public inquiry, even though it lacked preparation time; local determination to mount the case and affluence enough to raise more than £20,000 locally to fight it; education and expertise in every field needed to judge the planners' work and to devise realistic alternatives. If these people could not succeed, what chance has a working-class community that is similarly threatened? Perhaps like Newbridge they would not recognize the threat, or would pin their faith on the faith on the local councillors or M.P., and not even begin to raise an effective opposition. Perhaps like the soldiers in MOD they would not even read the notice in the newspaper that something was being planned. More likely they would see the notice and would recognize the threat, but would scarcely begin to generate the enormous drive required to oppose officialdom.

If a citizen is in serious dispute with his neighbour, or with the Inland Revenue, or with a giant company, he may enter the legal process of objection, appeal and arbitration (in Scotland from the Court of Session to the Inner House on appeal and even to the House of Lords if the matter tests a point of law) with the absolute certainty that 'the other side' will not, in any way whatever, be able to 'get at' the judges, to advise them privately or influence them other than in open court. The citizen knows that if he wins his case in the Court of Session, the appeal court judges of the Inner House will not reverse the decision arbitrarily; they will do so only in response to reasoned argument in public. No amount of 'participation' would substitute for that system of redress and protection. It is the fact that the legal system is known to be non-manipulative that gives people wholehearted confidence in it.

In sharp contrast, the planning process in this country deservedly does not enjoy general acceptance and credence, precisely because those who make major plans also advise the 'court of appeal'. The planners judge both their own plans and the objections, in a system which allows the public inquiry decision to be arbitrarily overturned and in which the final appeal finds the Ombudsman washing his hands of it because he has no jurisdiction over one of the disputants. The public planning system is not non-manipulative.

Good planning identifies people's needs and takes proper care of them without the public having to take special steps. In that sense, public participation is a non-essential. But it is vital that the system of objection and appeal should be just and be seen to be just.

This case showed a serious inadequacy of the planning system, in that, quite deliberately, the planners could keep their scheme secret from the community until there was no flexibility in it and until it was too difficult for society to fling it out and tell the civil servants to try again. The real tragedy was the demonstration of absolutism among professional planners and administrators who closed ranks whenever an effective objection was raised; it made a mockery of public participation in environmental planning.

References

BAA (1971) —1 to 24. Productions by British Airports Authority at the public inquiry 1 November in support of a planning application for a new runway and terminal complex at Edinburgh.

Campbell, G., 1973. Decision letter, 26 January, Scottish Office.

Gimson Report, 1972. *Report of the Public Inquiry under the Town and Country Planning (Scotland) Acts 1947—69 into the application by the British Airports Authority for permission to construct a runway, etc. at Edinburgh Airport: 1st November 1971.* Reporter G. S. Gimson, Q.C. Edinburgh, September, p. 115.

Heath, J. B. and Oulton, W. N., 1970. *A Cost-benefit Study of alternative Runway Investments at Edinburgh (Turnhouse) Airport:* Board of Trade Paper, September, p. 29.

Marre, Sir Alan, 1974. *Report of the Parliamentary Commissioner for Administration*, London, 18 January.

Roskill Report, 1971. *Report of the Commission on the Third London Airport*, London, HMSO.

5
The London Motorway Plan

J. M. THOMSON

A kind of insurrection took place in London between 1969 and 1973. Although no one was hurt and the exchanges were invariably civil, it was nevertheless more than an ordinary political quarrel. Thousands of citizens not normally involved in politics were so incensed with the way their elected governing bodies were attempting to improve their city that they went to unusual lengths to oppose and eventually overcome the will of established authority.

This account of the battle is not intended as a history but rather as the impression of someone closely involved. As such, the author does not expect it to agree exactly with other people's impressions. As after a real battle, it is difficult to reconstruct exactly what happened, or when, and which were the decisive. moves; indeed the task is more difficult, because one is dealing with a battle of minds and hearts, and who can say when and why a man changes his mind or his values?

Whatever the exact reasons for what happened, everyone will agree that it should not have happened and action should be taken to prevent such situations occurring again. And yet what took place in London was very like, although quite independent of, the simultaneous conflicts in other big cities such as San Francisco, Toronto and Boston. Subsequent motorway resistance movements in countless cities throughout Europe and North America may have been inspired by the success of others; but in London, where the issues and the eventual success were greatest, the conflict was pursued in virtual ignorance of such events elsewhere. The emergence of these public movements in different parts of the world indicates that the underlying trouble is not a local or temporary deficiency in the government of London but some deeper failure of democratic systems in large cities to deal with major planning problems. The events in London may throw light on this important problem and on possible ways of resolving it.

The London Story

Origins of the Plan

Until the 1960s the planning of roads in London, as in other cities, was based on the unchallenged idea that if existing roads were incapable of carrying their traffic speedily and without congestion there was a need to 'improve' them or to build

60

new ones. The need was not always met, of course, because the supply of money was never sufficient and major buildings or other 'untouchable' institutions stood in the way. But the idea persisted that anyone in possession of a motor vehicle, no matter where he came from or what his business, should be able to drive it and park it without hindrance or payment on any road in the city, and the road system should be made capable of providing this facility for whatever number of people desired it. With the rapid growth in ownership of cars and commercial vehicles the

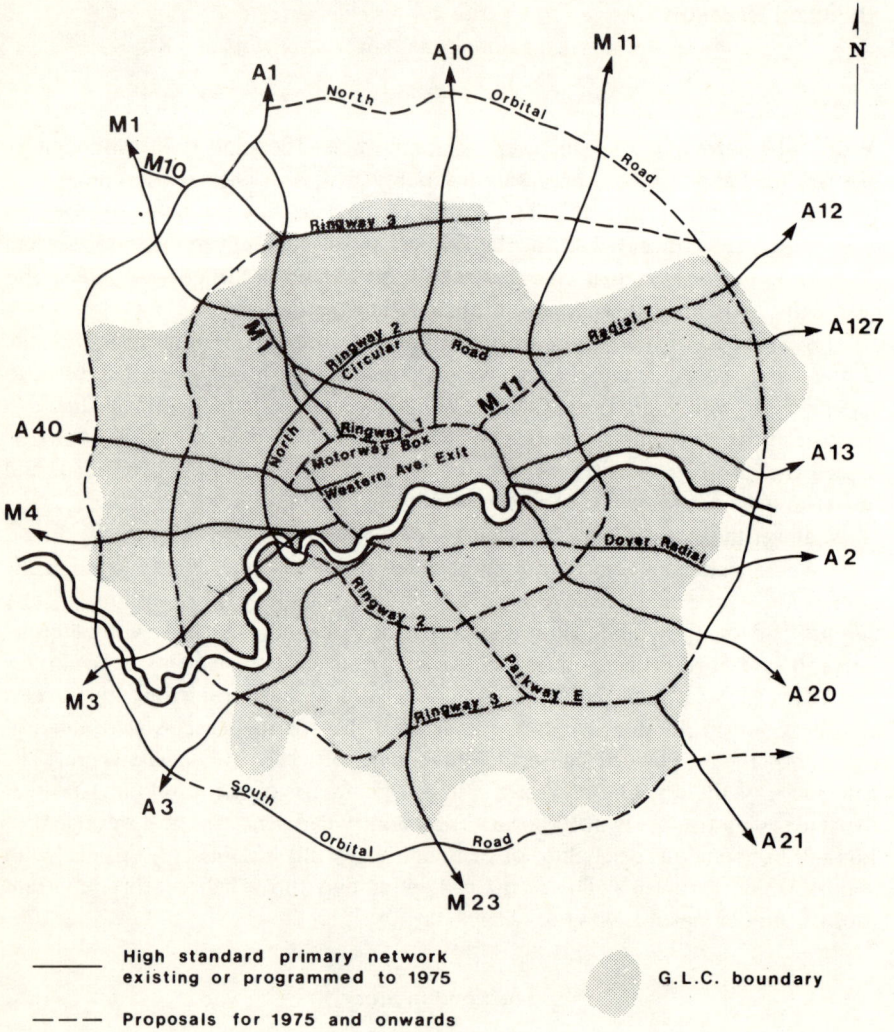

Figure 5.1   Motorway Proposals 1969

demands upon the road system increased correspondingly and the highway engineers of the old London County Council (LCC) and Ministry of Transport (MOT) raised their sights from piecemeal schemes to the creation of a whole new network of roads to be superimposed upon the old network.

The origins of this new network lay before the Second World War in the Bressey Plan but the first proposals for a completely new network were made by Abercrombie in 1944. Not for twenty years, however, was there any prospect of obtaining the enormous sums of money needed for such a major project. Meanwhile the traffic continued to grow and the highway engineers did all they could to increase the capacity of the roads by cheaper methods.

In 1962 the London Traffic Survey (later to become the London Transportation Study) was launched, with the objective of predicting future 'needs' and testing the adequacy of road plans evolved by the LCC. These plans were broadly similar to Abercrombie's and consisted of a ring-radial structure of motorways. The innermost ring, to be known as Ringway 1, was regarded by the Greater London Council (which superseded the LCC in 1966) as so obviously necessary that the Council publicly announced and committed itself to the project in 1966 long before the LTS was finished in 1969. The Council evidently expected this news to be welcomed by the public. The following year the full plan became known; four ringways, including the Outer Orbital Route lying right outside the GLC boundary, and about twelve radial motorways coming in to Ringway 1. The exact line of most of these roads was not decided, except for Ringway 1, where the plans were furthest advanced.

The GLC was bound by statute to produce a development plan for the metropolitan area by the end of 1969 for submission to the Government and (hopefully) adoption by 1971; this would replace the 1961 plans for the area. In February 1969, therefore a draft of the Greater London Development Plan (GLDP) appeared, in which the motorway proposals formed by far the most important part. No other concrete proposals were made for transport. This plan was duly presented to the Government with little modification, thus committing the Council in the strongest possible way to the construction of a comprehensive web of motorways. A map indicating the principal elements of the London motorway network, actual or proposed, is presented as Figure 5.1.

The Authorities

In the ensuing struggle, many authorities were involved together with numerous private organizations. Although by and large the authorities were ranged on one side and the 'public' on the other, this was not altogether true.

The leading role was played, of course, by the GLC but it may well be that a more influential part was played by several government departments. The Ministry of Transport was still responsible for many roads in the GLC area and had co-operated closely with the GLC in preparing the plans; and it was known (at that time) to be even more strongly in favour of urban motorways than the GLC themselves. On the other hand, the authority responsible for development plans was the Ministry of Housing and Local Government (MOHLG) which, on account of its responsibility for housing and general town planning, might be expected to be less wholehearted about road plans which demolished thousands of homes and demanded an immense share of public funds for capital investment. Thirdly, and potentially of great influence, there was the Treasury, which possessed the responsibility not only of allocating funds to the spending departments but also of ensuring that they were spent on worthwhile projects. Since approximately 80 per cent of the total cost of the motorways was expected to come from the Treasury, its influence was inescapable. The Government clearly wished, however, to stay in the background and sustain the impression that the new Council was the real planning power in its area.

If the Council had thus to look up to three powerful Whitehall departments it also had to look down to thirty-two London boroughs. While not possessing the power to veto the strategic plans of the GLC, the boroughs could cause obstruction and delay if they chose to be unco-operative. Representing on average a quarter of a million people each, the boroughs possessed quite large highway and planning departments, some of which were capable of putting forward a formidable technical case if they wished.

Finally there were the public transport authorities, namely, London Transport and British Rail, both of whom clearly had the resources to make a powerful impact in the debate. The interest of BR lay mainly in the radial lines from the outer suburbs and beyond; although these lines carry about 400,000 commuters every day to Central London, the main concern of BR was not so much to maintain this commuter traffic, which was unprofitable at the margin, as to maintain the off-peak traffic. The proposed motorways could be seen as a threat to this traffic. London Transport, on the other hand, were vitally interested to maintain the concept of a public transport system — bus and Underground — as a complete, comprehensive, inexpensive alternative to the private car as a method of moving about the metropolis. The credibility of LT as a complete urban transport service was already wearing thin in some places as bus services became less frequent and less reliable. A motorway network, although offering the doubtful possibility of some relief to congestion on bus routes, could be seen as incompatible with the level of service that LT had traditionally aimed to provide, unless big operating subsidies were forthcoming; and GLC policy was firmly against such subsidies.

A number of important changes occurred among the authorities during the period of the conflict. The GLC (like the LCC before it) was controlled by Labour during the preparation of the motorway plan but power was gained by the Conservatives from 1967 to 1973, when they were ousted by the Labour Party. At Westminster a Labour government ruled until 1970 when it was replaced by a Conservative one. Of considerable significance was the creation by the new Conservative government of the Department of the Environment (DOE) in 1970, bringing together the MOT and the MOHLG in one department under a senior Cabinet minister responsible for the environment.

Meanwhile the political composition of the boroughs was also changing. At the beginning of the story, in 1967, the inner London boroughs, apart from the City,

Westminster and Chelsea and Kensington, were solidly red and the outer suburbs almost completely blue. By the end, in 1973, many boroughs had turned from Conservative to Labour. Thus the Tory GLC which began in 1967 with boroughs that were mostly sympathetic but with a government of the opposite colour, finished in 1973 with boroughs that were largely hostile but with a government of its own party.

Another highly significant change arose with the decision of the government to hand over control of LT to the GLC. Although the GLC did not take over until January 1972 the knowledge that this was going to happen probably had a profound effect upon the behaviour of LT during the preceding period.

The Public

It is a little more difficult to identify the organizations representing 'the public'. Since, by definition, they are bodies which have a clear interest in the issue but no authority, there is no obvious dividing line between those that were really involved and those that were only marginally concerned. One might have expected certain established professional institutions to take a lively interest in the strategic planning of London. The Royal Institute of British Architects set a fine example, but it was not followed by other institutions. There existed in London two university departments specializing in transport and traffic, paid for by the public and led by two renowned professors, but one avoided any involvement in the issue while the other sold his services as a consultant to the GLC during the Inquiry.

A few voluntary organizations were drawn naturally into the conflict, for instance, the Pedestrians Association and the National Council for Inland Transport, but they possessed insufficient resources to make any great impact.

The principal representation for the public came from two organizations of contrasting character, which played completely different but essentially complementary roles. One of these was LATA, the London Amenity and Transport Association. LATA was the creation of a small group of professional people, known as the Transport in London Group, who came together in 1965 because of a common concern for the way in which London was deteriorating as a result of developments in the transport system, which itself was also deteriorating from every point of view. Although the situation was no worse in London than in most other Western cities, the Group foresaw a dreadful future when they contemplated the powerful administrative machine relentlessly pursuing a costly and destructive transport policy which they believed would prove totally counter-productive. There were in London many civic societies, residents' associations and other amenity improvement groups working on a local scale, sometimes covering a whole suburb, sometimes just one or two streets. These groups could be counted on, almost invariably, to share the general views of the Transport in London Group, but although some of them had been established a long time there was no co-operation between them to deal with London-wide problems. Each little society confined itself to its local problems; none was able to take an effective stand on the immense and difficult problems of metropolitan planning and policy.

The first vital contribution of the Transport in London Group was to conceive of and organize a federation or association of these civic and other societies throughout London. Its second crucial contribution was to ensure that the new association, LATA, was directed largely by transport and planning professionals, thus achieving a technical competence that was seldom possible in small local groups. Curiously, the creation of LATA by the civic societies in 1967 was in no way connected with the motorway plans, which at that time had scarcely touched the awareness of the public. The written aims and objectives of LATA made no mention of motorways and the Association kept an open mind on the subject until 1969. Membership was refused, on principle, to all anti-motorway groups until 1970. A principal aim of the Association was to co-operate with the GLC and the Ministry of Transport in order to promote rational policies in the interests of Londoners as a whole, not just aggrieved minorities. LATA was specifically a non-party organization.

LATA, then with the eventual backing of about 90 local groups, including practically every important amenity group in London except the Chelsea Society, could claim to represent the environmental movement and was able to do so with sufficient expertise to speak on equal terms with the authorities. The second main organization on the side of the public was the LMAG, the London Motorway Action Group, which owed its origin to local activities in Hampstead. Being the first middle-class area to be threatened by a motorway, Hampstead soon produced a strong motorway action group, closely associated with another in neighbouring Camden. In 1968 the local M.P., Ben Whittaker, together with the M.P. for Battersea North, the Rt. Hon. Douglas Jay, who lived in Hampstead and had already waged a personal battle against the motorway, which also cut through his own constituency, called a meeting of London M.P.s with representatives from the motorway action groups and set up the LMAG, with Jay as chairman and another ex-Cabinet Minister, Duncan Sandys, as vice-chairman. The LMAG was an all-party organization comprising most Inner London M.P.s, except those barred by governmental appointments, and its object was specifically to oppose Ringway 1 (at that time known as the Motorway Box) by political means. Later, Ringway 2 and the radial motorways inside Ringway 3 were also opposed. As local motorway action groups mushroomed throughout the metropolitan area, they invariably joined the LMAG.

Thus there came into existence an essentially political pressure group, strongly based in the House of Commons and capable of raising money through its enthusiastic local member groups in order to support a programme of anti-motorway publicity. Unlike LATA, its principal aim was to prevent the enormous destruction of housing to make room for motorways and the loss of amenity by householders living alongside them. Until it joined forces with LATA, the LMAG possessed little expert knowledge and was strictly an *ad hoc* pressure group representing that section of the public which stood to suffer most from the building of those motorways that it opposed.

Representatives of the public are not necessarily against the authorities but may support the authorities against other bodies of their own kind. The Chelsea Society, for instance, whose territory lay near but not actually on the line of Ringway 1, supported the road in the (probably false) expectation that it would lead to a reduction in traffic in Chelsea. More important though, was the British Road Federation, representing a large variety of industries with financial interests in road building. Its motives were obvious, of course, but it possessed large financial resources relative to its opponents and was able to carry on an effective publicity campaign using the names of carefully selected consultants in support of its arguments. In setting the interests of oil companies, concrete makers, etc., against the voluntary defenders of the social interest, the BRF may, however, have been more of an embarrassment than a help to the authorities.

Participation

The plain fact must be faced that, until 1973, there was no provision and no desire by the authorities for participation with the public. All road plans were produced in secrecy and were not made known to the public until the authorities had made up their mind what they wanted. The argument for this procedure is, of course, that it avoids causing needless alarm and anxiety. True though this may be, it nevertheless amounts to a policy of non-participation. There is no doubt that, if the public had allowed it, the GLC and the Ministry of Transport would have quietly implemented their plans without consultation, inquiry or any sort of contract with the public prior to the issue of compulsory purchase orders and other statutory obligations.

The law, of course, did provide for public inquiries into major road schemes if they attracted public objections, but individual road schemes could always be 'justified' on strategic grounds which lay beyond the competence of local inquiries. There was also provision for public inquiry into a development plan modification, which was the legal position of the GLDP, but this did not permit the discussion of strategic matters or alternatives.

At no time, so far as the writer is aware, did the authorities take an initiative in approaching the public, to ask its views and to discuss the alternatives. Certainly they were always willing to receive deputations and to give considered answers to letters. But public participation had to originate with the public. This, of course, was highly unsatisfactory since the public did not know what plans were being prepared by the authorities. Hence the public could only react – too late – to announcements by the authorities who were then willing to respond to the public reaction.

This kind of participation took place at various levels. The leaders of the public organizations would be cordially met by Cabinet ministers and GLC chairmen, while local divisional engineers would try to explain their plans to little local citizen groups. The GLC tried hard to 'sell' its plans to the public by publishing glossy leaflets, accepting invitations to speak at public meetings, agreeing to television confrontations and giving press conferences. The GLC itself organized six or eight 'public participation meetings' in large halls in different parts of London but unfortunately these came much too late, as part of a vain effort to overcome the already hardened opposition of the public.

Fundamentally, therefore, public participation occurred as a process of public reaction to an official decision which the authorities subsequently sought to defend. This process was bound to lead to conflict.

The Conflict

At first the GLC were undoubtedly convinced that their motorway plan was necessary and in the best interests of London. It seems, in fact, that they expected it to be welcomed by a public weary of traffic congestion. Had they foreseen in the early 1960s the public reaction they would doubtless have given more thought to public participation.

The reaction of the public was indeed very slow to crystallize: not, of course, that of persons directly affected but that of the majority of people who were not near the line of a motorway and who were therefore more interested in what life in London would be like if the city were criss-crossed with motorways and the volume of traffic trebled. These were the questions that LATA, in particular, was concerned to answer and for which purpose it set up an expert working party (chaired by the present writer). Not until the publication of its report, *Motorways in London* (Thomson *et al*,. 1969), did LATA come to a decision (in November 1969) to oppose a part of the plan comprising less than a quarter of the proposed motorway network, and to call for a full, wide-ranging inquiry to be set up by the Government.

From that moment, at least so far as LATA was concerned, public participation by the GLC was replaced by hostility. It is now known that a chief officer of the GLC provided the British Road Federation with a detailed attack on the LATA report, for the BRF to publish. The LATA professionals became *persona non grata* at the Ministry of Transport and the GLC.

Simultaneously the LMAG were busy campaigning for an effective public inquiry. For at least a year all demands for a proper inquiry into the long-term implications of the plan, and into alternative possibilities, met with strong resistance from the Government and, especially, the GLC. However, during the autumn of 1969 over 20,000 objections to the plan were received by the Minister, who therefore decided to set up a public inquiry which, though strictly a statutory development plan inquiry, would be expected to deal fully and freely with strategic planning objections and with alternative proposals. This was a vitally important success attributable largely to the LMAG.

The inquiry did not commence for nearly a year, largely because of administrative difficulties in assembling a suitable panel of inspectors with a team of professional advisors (assessors). The LMAG objected to one member of the panel, who was promptly replaced. In the meantime, while both sides were preparing for the great inquiry, the conflict switched temporarily to the political front, on account of the GLC elections in April 1970. The Labour party decided to oppose Ringway 1 and the Liberals were totally opposed to motorway building. A new local party, Homes Before Roads (HBR), emerged with a specific anti-motorway programme, to attract voters from the regular parties, especially the Conservatives who, of course, were stoutly defending their plan. In spite of much enthusiasm and some imaginative publicity stunts, the HBR party failed to make much impression; not only did they come nowhere near capturing a single seat but, with one possible exception, they nowhere even split the vote sufficiently to influence the choice between Conservatives and Labour. One lesson of this electoral venture was how extremely difficult it was, in a city with constituencies averaging 250,000 people, for anyone other than the two big parties to make any impact on the political scene. The Liberals failed almost as badly as did the HBR, and the Conservatives went back to County Hall to press on with their plan. Whether their victory in a local election in which most voters evidently voted as if it were a national election, i.e. according to their preference for Harold Wilson or Edward Heath, can be considered as a 'mandate' to build motorways is a debatable point.

The Public Inquiry

The GLDP inquiry lasted two years and produced enough written evidence to fill a room. Space here permits no more than a few conclusions.

The inquiry was meticulously fair and conducted at a high intellectual level, thanks to the brilliance of the chairman, Frank Layfield. Clearly, however, it could not be called public participation since the judicial inquiry process is adversarial and automatically takes the form of a conflict, as between prosecution and defence.

In spite of the high quality of the panel members and their assessors, one must recognize that not a single one of them was well equipped by experience and training to pronounce judgment on the planning of London. This was because impartiality required that they be untainted by any previous contact with the London problem and uncommitted to any views about such a problem. In the event the problem was too difficult for them. While dealing excellently with the simpler parts of their task, they ultimately failed dismally to grasp the real problem of the motorways and produced a lamentably illogical verdict which was equally unacceptable both to the authorities and to the public opposition.

Strong criticism must be made of the inquiry procedures. The nature of the legal process is to force every argument to be made half a dozen times, to lose sight of the thread of the argument, and to compel lawyers to struggle with complex matters beyond their understanding while experts are unable to intervene. The whole process is absurdly time-consuming and costly. One of the great needs is for a streamlining of inquiry procedures, to bring these affairs up to a modern standard of efficiency and productivity.

The result of the inquiry may be regarded as a disaster or a farce, according to whether one takes it seriously or not. By the end of the inquiry the GLC appeared to have abandoned the idea of building Ringway 1 but were pressing strongly for the other ringways. LATA and LMAG presented a joint case against Ringways 1 and 2 and associated radial motorways. Four London boroughs appeared for the opposition. All the principal protagonists supported Ringways 3 and 4, with top priority for Ringway 3. The panel, however, rejected Ringways 2 and 3 and accepted Ringways 1 and 4, thus producing a novel solution totally without reason and without support.

The inquiry was concerned, fortunately, with many other matters besides motorways. On other issues of transport policy the panel were very closely in agreement with the public opposition.

Political Force

Who can say why the London Labour party, which was originally responsible for the motorway proposals, gradually turned against them? Members at County Hall were placed under increasing pressure from the rank and file which first rejected Ringway 1, then Ringway 2, and finally all motorways in the urban area. It is impossible to know how far this movement of opinion was due to the public debate carried on for several years by the voluntary organizations, generously supported and encouraged by the media.

In spite of the efforts of the LMAG to keep the issue out of party politics, the Labour party decided to reject Ringways 1 and 2 and to support transport policies similar to those put forward by LATA—LMAG at the inquiry, and to fight the 1973 GLC election on this issue. They fought and won, as did Labour parties in Oxford, Nottingham, Southampton and other towns split by motorway controversy. Their first act was to publicly burn the motorway plan. Thus in April 1973 the battle was over, at least for a time.

Reflections

We live in a democratic society in which local elections are regularly held to decide who shall make decisions about things like motorways. The candidates explain their policies at great length and are duly elected or not elected. Why, then, when they try to implement their policies, should they be expected to go back to the public in some way to re-establish their mandate? Why should there be public participation in a democratic society? Is it an interference with democracy or could it be an extension of democracy? Before coming to a view on public participation one must try to establish clearly what it means, how it should work and when it is justified.

To my mind, public participation exists when those in authority take steps to discuss with certain affected members of the public (a) the nature of some problem, (b) the alternative solutions to the problem, and (c) the advantages and disadvantages of the various alternatives. In particular, the public should be approached *early enough* to have a proper chance to understand the problem and to think about it; they should be given opportunity to propose solutions or modifications to solutions *before* any options have been effectively closed; and they should be enabled to discuss fully the relative merits of rival solutions *before* the authorities commit themselves in any way to a particular course of action.

Clearly this process can be carried through more effectively with a few members of the public than with a large number. The questions then arise: who, if anyone, should be consulted like this and on what sort of problems?

It seems to me that one must distinguish between three types of problem arising:

(a) When some action is needed, in the public interest, which may have a severely adverse effect on a minority. In the case of a traffic problem the existence of the problem should be widely explained, but the possible solutions should be discussed with only those sections of the public (or their representatives) which might be greatly affected. It is clear that the simple democratic process cannot satisfy the expectations of small minorities who have to suffer in the interests of the majority;

(b) When the democratic process fails, because those in authority are not in touch or in sympathy with the majority of people affected by their decisions. This is all too likely to occur in the present state of local government where only a small percentage of voters bother to vote and few of them know anything about the candidates or what they stand for;

(c) When local government officers are incompetent. Many poor plans are produced because of the low level of competence in some highway and planning departments, and they are approved by councils and committees which have neither the time nor the qualifications to examine them properly.

The widespread demand for public participation stems from all three of these causes. In the London case there was gross neglect of the suffering imposed on minorities (witness Westway), there was practically no relation between the votes cast at GLC elections and the true desires of Londoners for the future of their city, and there was a sad, though well-intentioned, failure at the official level to identify London's real transport problems, to formulate solutions and choose between them. In all fairness to London, though, the same criticisms can be made in most large cities in Europe and North America; this indeed explains the recent epidemic of public revolt against urban transport plans.

The proper and, I believe, indispensable role of public participation lies in solving the first problem, that of minority conflicts. Full and early consultation can help minorities to feel that they have not been disregarded; it can help to produce the best possible solution to the problem and hopefully to find ways of compensating those that suffer.

But the other problems can be only alleviated, not solved, by public participation. If democracy fails, we may have to accept public revolt as a means of expressing what the public wants and does not want. If local officials are incompetent, we may expect public protest to serve as a means of correction. But the right solution, of course, is to improve the effectiveness of local democracy and raise the quality of planning and transport departments, while at the same time recognizing where a real need for public participation exists. If this can be done, there may be an end to the unruly and undesirable state of affairs prevailing at the present time.

References

Thomson, J. Michael *et al,*. 1969. *Motorways in London*, Beverly Hills, California, Sage Publications.

6

The Use of Threat in Community Decision-making: The Goldstream Case, Victoria, B.C.

COLIN J. B. WOOD

A major problem facing the managers of public goods is the integration of public opinion into the decision-making process. Some form of participation has almost always been present at the level of local government, but only recently has it become a feature of metropolitan, regional or even national governments. At the latter scales of political organization the emergence of interest and pressure groups testifies that the traditional political frameworks are viewed by many citizens as inadequate: in short, the public wants to be heard and now! The responses to this demand have varied, being the nemesis of the autocratic planner, the nightmare of efficiency experts and yet another bandwagon for the political aspirant.

There are numerous problems associated with the implementation of public participation in the decision-making process. There may be no legal requirement for a particular decision-making group to consult with the public. If an inquiry or public hearing is required, the manager may be faced with either a bewildering range of responses, or complete apathy. There may be budget or time constraints which demand quick decisions and prohibit lengthy discussion and debate. To the public, the managers may appear paternal and distant, while the agencies of government they have to deal with may seem or even are a maze of Kafkaesque proportions.

Because of these problems, and clearly only a few have been mentioned, it is essential that provision be made for input from citizens at different stages of a public decision-making situation, and that some attention be paid to it, otherwise prolonged and stressful conflict may result. This is not to assert that conflict is solely a negative and costly burden to society; on the contrary it provides a sharp reminder and signal that changes in public attitudes and preferences can and do occur. Nevertheless, any modifications to existing decision-making structures which can alleviate conflict must be examined.

This chapter examines the conflict which can occur in a community between a resource manager and the public, where no provision existed for an input of citizens' views and preferences. It took place in Victoria, British Columbia, during the late 1960s and early 1970s over the allocation of water between urban needs and the requirements of a salmon-spawning stream. The case described here illustrates how a water commissioner attempting to provide water as cheaply as possible came into conflict with conservationists trying to protect the water requirements of a salmon-spawning stream. After refusing to provide water for the fish, the water commissioner eventually changed his position under considerable indirect pressure from the public, since there were no provisions for public input into water management decision-making. It was an issue widely reported in the media, which raised both specific questions related to water supply and jurisdiction over natural resources and more fundamental ones pertaining to economic growth, environmental quality and the role of the public in community decision-making.

By examining the structure of conflict and interaction between the groups involved in the dispute, that is, the functioning system, some insight may be gained into the nature of community conflict. Hopefully, from this a clearer understanding may be obtained of the ways in which public decision-making structures may be modified to incorporate input from interested citizens.

Community Decision-making and a Framework for Analysis

A community consists of individuals and groups varying in power and organization, occupying a common location, and linked by social, economic and political interactions.[1] Individuals' rights to power are delegated via the elective process to politicians who set policy and make decisions concerning public goods and welfare, while a non-elected technical bureaucracy implements them. The structure of the system is formally defined in respect of representation, jurisdiction, time framework and amount of public participation.

Two models have been proposed to describe the *general* ways in which the community decision-making system actually functions.[2] Firstly, Maass (1962) suggests that it works as an 'upward forming consensus' where a majority of the citizens delegate power to an elected group of politicians (the proximate decision-makers) who in turn enact legislation and formulate policies implemented by the administrative bureaucracy (Figure 6.1): should inconsistencies develop between electors and elected, the latter are liable to be dismissed at the next election. If there were a free exchange of information between decision-makers and the public and active citizen participation in civic affairs we might accept this description.[3]

Secondly, the system has also been characterized as a counterflow process where decisions are made at the top by a political or economic 'elite' and flow down to confront the community 'after the fact' (Figure 6.1). Consequently, those groups which feel threatened by the decision, bargain in a gaming-type process played under uncertain conditions, until a mutually advantageous situation is arrived at.[4] Thus, groups have goals, develop strategies and resort to the use of varying tactics to achieve them.

The realities of community decision-making at the level of urban/regional government would seem to be more accurately described by the second model. The first model assumes that a free and continuous exchange of information between the decision-makers and the public occurs, is comprehended without divergent

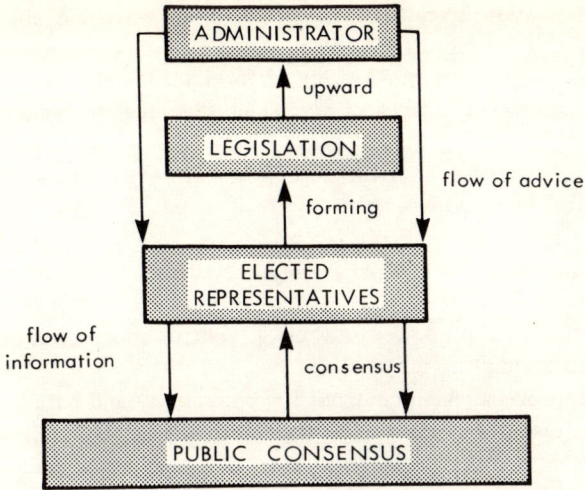

The Upward Forming Consensus (after Maass)

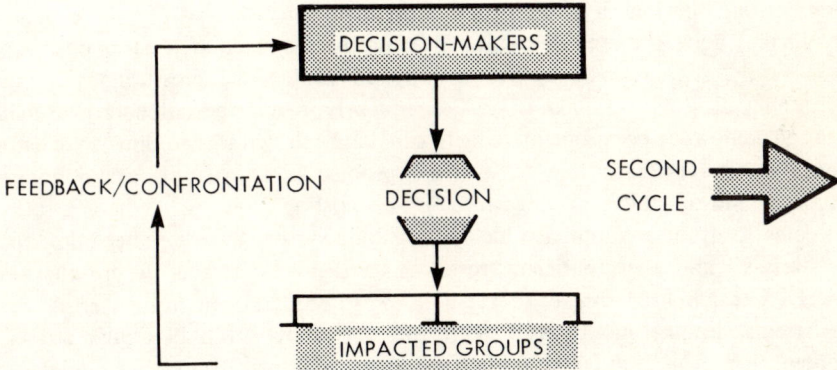

Decision-Makers as Elitists and the Gaming Confrontation

Figure 6.1 Concepts of community decision-making

perceptions and attitudes and is incorporated into the decision-making process: assumptions which are clearly unrealistic. The second model is supported by the abundant evidence concerning the power structures of communities, the behaviour of interest groups over community issues and the common occurrence of communication and attitudinal gaps between the decision-makers and the public.

In particular it would seem to be due to a situation where a majority of citizens are usually willing to delegate their interests in government, almost to the state of abdication, as long as decision-makers perform adequately and do not deviate too much from past performance. Only when they feel threatened do the public respond.

Therefore, the structure of the decision-making system may be hypothesized to function as follows (Figure 6.2):

1. The community has evolved a delegative, decision-making structure to process problems;
2. The allocation of power, authority, control and procedure is specified by Laws, Statutes, etc.;
3. Problems occur which confront the community and have to be resolved and are 'processed' according to responsibilities designated under 2;
4. The decision-makers may be ignorant of 3, may ignore them, classify them as 'routine' or treat them as a strategic problem and attempt to solve them;
5. The public responds according to the degree of perceived threat.

Many types of conflict can exist in a community; here we are concerned with the conflict which can emerge between the community and the decision-makers to whom they have delegated power. Thus, conflicts may develop if politicians are ignorant of, ignore or misread the public's wishes. For example, a city council may designate and deal with a problem as a 'routine' matter, letting the executive bureaucracy solve the problem without evaluating the reaction of affected groups. As a result, the groups may respond by contacting and pressuring aldermen, petitioning or even demonstrating. Consequently, a differentiation can be made between the 'routine problem' which can be dealt with according to existing procedures and a non-routine or 'strategic' problem which requires evaluation and decisions and a potential departure from existing policies.[5] Where strategic problems confront a community decision-making system they have been described as 'stresses', and the politicians respond to them as 'strains' where they are perceived as potential threats to the actor or system and constitute a crisis when the strains become hazardous.[6] With the occurrence of a particular strategic problem, it may generate interaction between decision-makers and impacted groups in the form of debate and controversy.

A useful approach for analysing the interaction between parties involved in a conflict is to describe it as a gaming situation where each side has goals, strategies for achieving them and tactics for effecting their strategies.[7] A deficiency of gaming models, however, is that little attention is paid to the nature of interaction between the opposed groups. Wolpert (1970) has drawn attention to the framework proposed by the psychologist Lazarus, of linking threat with stress response in understanding the interdependence between parties locked in a dispute.[8]

Consequently, the conflict which evolved over the allocation of water between an urban community and fishery conservation in the Victoria region can be portrayed as a gaming situation where the water managers and the conservationists

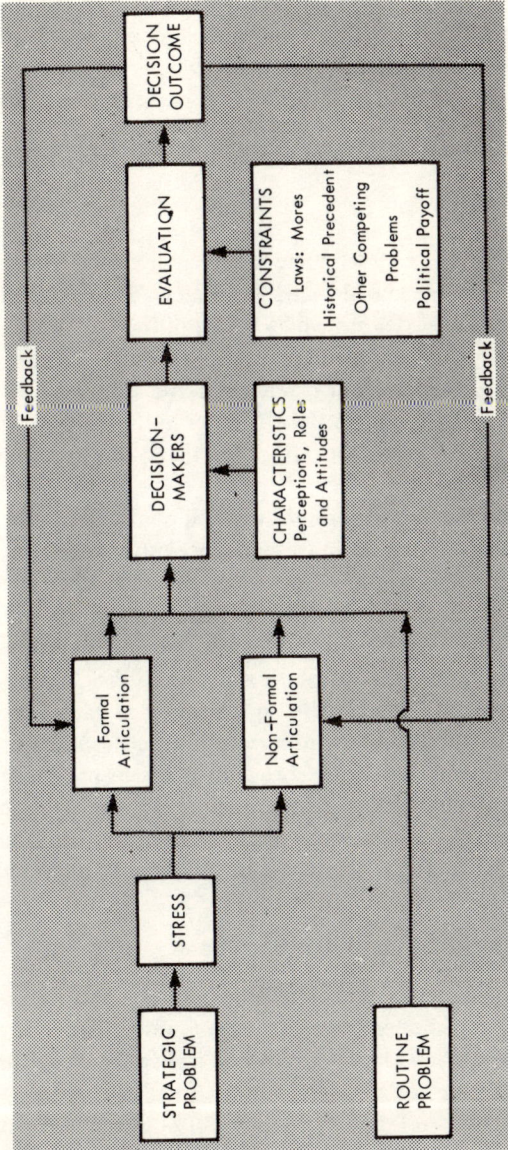

Figure 6.2 Response to environmental stress

are the chief players and threat exchange was a significant element of the interactive process. In this way it is hoped that a useful insight into the community decision-making process will be made.

The description and analysis of events is based upon interviews with many of the people who were involved in the dispute, a content analysis of newspaper articles and reports referring to the issue and a questionnaire sample survey of part of the community affected by and interested in the issue.

Conflict in Water Resource Management

The Issue

As the population of the Greater Victoria region increased from 90,000 in 1941 to 175,000 in 1968 so did the demand for water. The Greater Victoria Water Board, which manages the water system on behalf of the constituent municipalities of the metro region, responded to this demand by increasing the supply system. Until the early 1960s there was enough water left over from supplying the needs of the urban areas to keep an adequate flow of water in the Goldstream River, one of the streams in the Board's catchment area, for the salmon spawning in the Fall (Figure 6.3).[9]

However, as population and water consumption continued to increase, coupled with below average precipitation in several successive years, more water was abstracted from the Goldstream River, thus reducing the water levels and endangering spawning salmon. A major conflict appeared in the Fall of 1970 when the Water Commissioner stated that no water would be released for salmon spawning in that year. Although a major extension to the catchment system was under construction it was still incomplete, so that water supplies were very low.

As might be expected, there was intense opposition from conservation groups within the community who eventually brought sufficient pressure to bear on the decision-makers so that they altered their decision. The object of conflict was the allocation of water and the values placed on it as a resource. The conflict behaviour took the form of a gaming interaction where threats were an important tactic.

Control over the Allocation of the Water Resource

In Canada, several different levels of government with their associated executive agencies have varying jurisdiction over the use of water. The federal government concentrates on those aspects of water resource management assigned to it under the authority of the British North America Act, particularly sections 91, 92, 95 and 132. Broadly, it has sole jurisdiction over the use of water for navigation and fisheries, cojurisdiction over agricultural uses and authority to intervene in interprovincial disputes and where a water body is shared with the United States. Consequently, the provinces have jurisdiction over uses not assigned to the federal authority (for example, hydro-electric power).[10] Since some overlap would inevitably occur between the two government levels, special agencies exist to

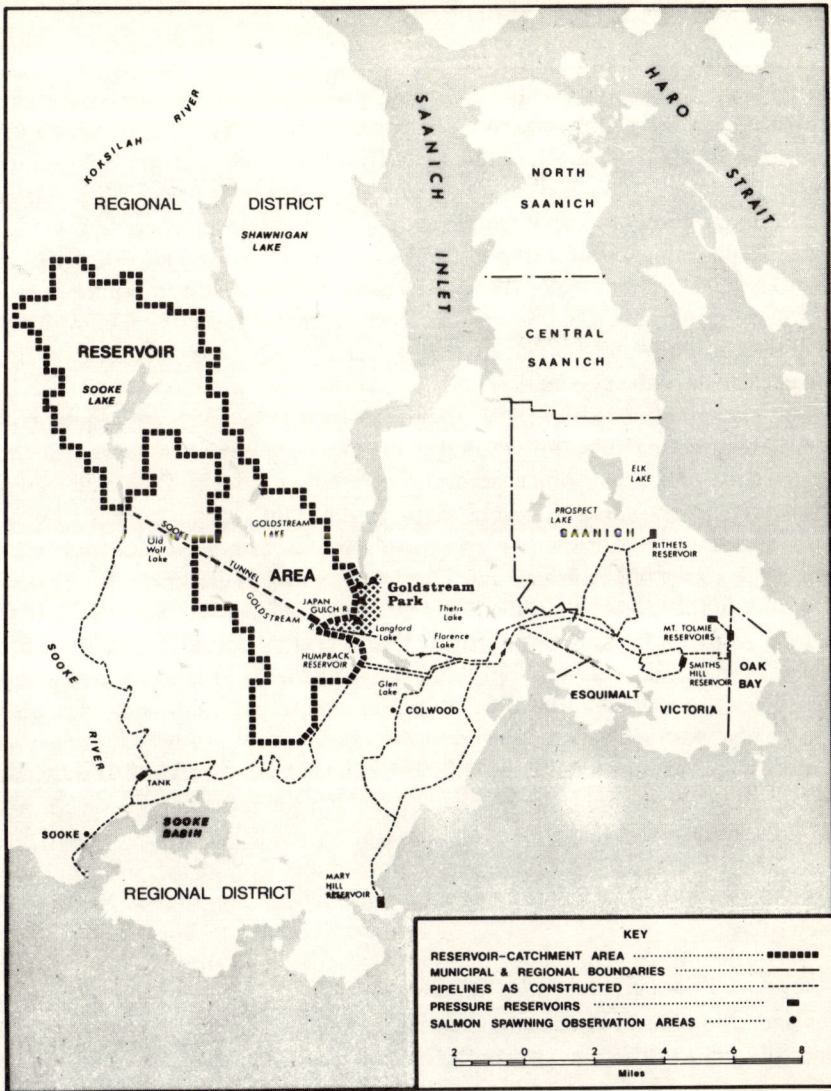

Figure 6.3 Victoria: location and water supply (reproduced by permission of Western Geographical Series)

co-ordinate and deal with the management of this resource. At the local level, water supply comes under the control of municipalities as a utility, or under that of private companies. Such local bodies and undertakings are not specifically required to consider the impact of their decisions on other types of water use unless a licence to abstract water, issued by the provincial government, was required at their inception. Furthermore, formalized channels of communication do not usually exist between this and the two other levels of government.

The Greater Victoria Water District

The growth of population in the Lower Vancouver Island area and the concomitant increase in demand for water, mainly for residential purposes, led to the successive amalgamations of local water supply systems, culminating in the formation of the Greater Victoria Water Board in 1949.[11] It was inaugurated to construct and maintain facilities for supplying water to the several municipalities which comprise the metropolitan region. The system is now managed by a full-time Water Commissioner under the control of a Water Board. The Board has seven members, and is composed of the Mayor and three aldermen from Victoria, and the mayors of Esquimalt, Oak Bay and Saanich. It makes the broad policy decisions and relies on the Water Commissioner for technical advice and running the day to day operations of the system.

Since its establishment in 1949, it seemed that the only decisions required of the Board were 'routine' in nature, related to the maintenance and gradual expansion of the system, neither of which seemed to necssitate an elaborate policy-making procedure, in view of accessible and relatively abundant supplies of water. Decisions were placed in the hands of the board, whose members were not directly responsible to the public or municipalities, financially or otherwise.

At the time of the conflict the Board also exercised a certain independence from the control of various provincial and federal agencies because, unlike most bodies which withdraw water from streams or lakes, the Water Board did not have to apply for a Water Licence from the B.C. Comptroller of Water Rights, and therefore was presumably not subject to the rules and regulations to which other water abstractors must adhere under the B.C. Water Act. The City of Victoria was granted sole rights to the waters in the Sooke and Goldstream areas under a special Act of the Legislature, enacted in 1909.[12] Because it is a publicly owned corporation, the Water District, through its Board, sets its own prices for water. It does not have to submit its rates to the Public Utilities Commission for approval as do the private water utilities.

While the Board can be held responsible for any harmful effects that the operations of the District's water supply system may have on individuals or groups, it is under no obligation to assist them in the pursuit of their own objectives, and especially where these may conflict with the District's goals and perceived responsibilities. The Board feels, for example, that it has no obligation to provide recreational facilities. Moreover, because it believes that use of its reservoirs for bathing, boating or fishing would increase costs of operation, the Board has a policy which bans the use of reservoirs for such purposes.[13] It also feels that it has no responsibility to preserve fish runs by the release of water from its reservoirs, despite suggestions to the contrary by fisheries management agencies, particularly at the federal level.

There are no formal channels of communication between the Water Board and other government agencies at the municipal, provincial and federal level. While there are sometimes informal contacts between personnel of the Commission and those in other agencies, these are usually of an *ad hoc* nature; nor are there any formal channels between the Board and the public at large. While policy-making in water management agencies often involves some form of public consultation — such as public meetings or hearings — the Water Board does not consult the public in this fashion. It relies instead on the judgement of its members and the advice of the Water Commissioner, as to what the public wants, and how it will be likely to react to policies which it puts into effect. From this brief description of the allocation of control of the water resource we can now examine the conflict which arose over its use.

The Conflict as a Game

The chronological development of events in the conflict over water use is shown in Figure 6.4.[14] The problem first appeared in the early 1960s and resulted in a

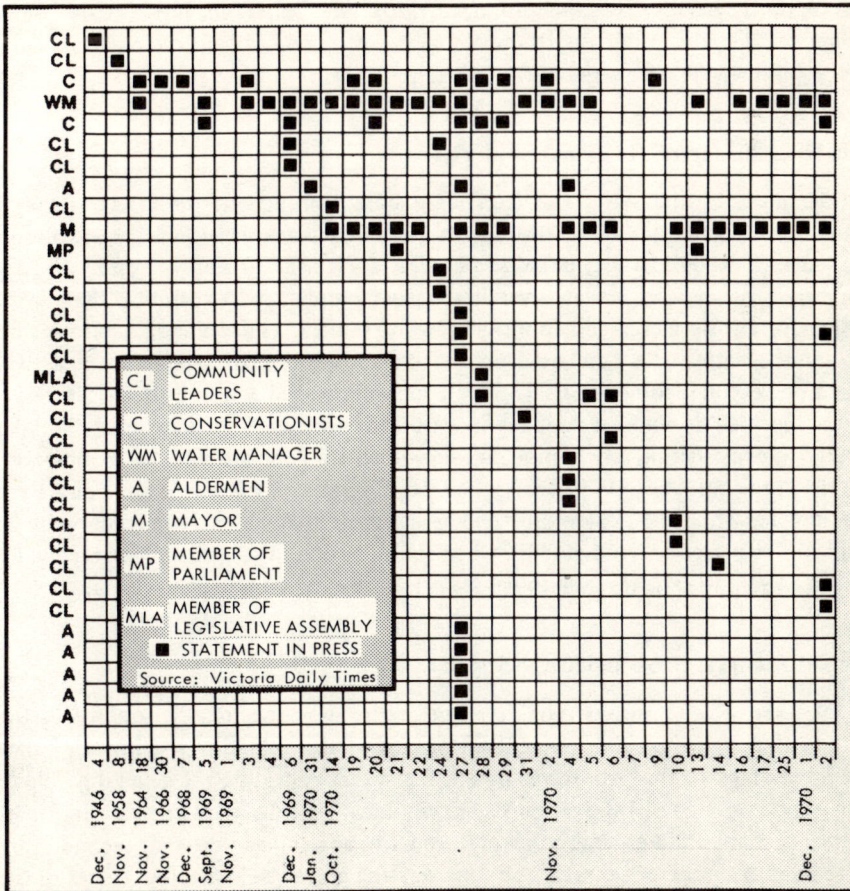

Figure 6.4 The growth of involvement in the Goldstream controversy

gradual but increasing interaction between the water managers and the conservationists, two groups with well-defined goals and a common interest in the resource. However, whereas the water managers had legitimate authority to act in terms of managing the resource, the conservationists seemingly had little power. The game had certain predictable elements such as that the demand for water would continue to grow and that the salmon would need a specific volume of water at critical periods in their life cycle.

In 1970 uncertainty was present in the variability in the amount of precipitation likely to fall, particularly prior to and during the spawning period. The conservationists were also uncertain whether water would be released, and the water managers were unsure whether water saving by the community would be possible. Neither group was confident how much water was needed for the fish. Each group had strategies for attaining their goals and reducing the uncertainty. As the issue grew in intensity, more specific tactics became necessary as each group evaluated the uncertainties and the activities of the other group. For convenience, the various groups are dichotomized into the water managers (the Water Commissioner, the Water Board members) and the conservationists (environmental groups, individuals, segments of the public).

The Water Managers: Goals and Strategies

The goals of the water managers were stated throughout the affair as selling water to the community and ensuring that an adequate reserve capacity was always available. This basic function is set out as a primary objective in the Greater Victoria District Act. As an overall strategy a policy of expanding the supply system to ensure increased supplies has been pursued. This policy concurred with the municipalities who purchased water from the Water Board and who themselves relied on revenue from water sales and hence encouraged consumption.[15] In 1964, it was decided to expand supplies to cater for projected demand until the year 2000, by constructing a new pipeline, scheduled for completion in 1970; however, at the time of the 1970 crisis, due to several delays, the extensions were incomplete. While the expansionist policy did mean that water would eventually be available, it placed a constraint on what could be done with existing water. Water had to be sold to raise revenue to help finance the expansion of the system.

Conservationists: Goals and Strategies

The goal of the various conservation groups was specifically to protect the salmon stocks of the Goldstream River as part of the natural environment.[16] The overall strategy of this group was based, firstly, on educating the general public to gain support for the conservationists' viewpoint, particularly by encouraging visits by local school children and conducted tours to spawning areas and, secondly, by increasing the stock of salmon.[17] In this way the perceived and actual values of the resource were increased. More people were encouraged to see the fish and more fish were available to be seen.

The first overall strategy was successful, since the degree of community response was a critical influence which changed the attitudes of the Mayor and Water Commissioner so that they released water for the fish. The second overall strategy was probably successful in that as stocks were increased more salmon returned to spawn, thus providing a greater spectacle for the public.

Interpretation

The decisions made by the water managers are clearly representative of the 'downward flow' community decision-making process, where a decision is made at the top and threatened groups bargain in a game-like situation to alter it to their own advantage. Yet the interaction between the two groups cannot be explained simply as one group reacting mechanically to the actions of another because of the following uncertainties.

The strategies available to each side offered a choice of actions. The water manager could control demand through rationing and pricing and thus enable water to be released for the fish. However, there was probably insufficient time to institute such measures and, as mentioned earlier, they were dependent on the revenue from sales of water.[18] The conservationists, as a group, depended on the successful co-operation of several community subgroups and public support, a condition often tenuous at best. Finally, the issue was also partly dependent on the weather — since the issue could have been resolved immediately if sufficient precipitation occurred; this had been the case in earlier incipient confrontations between the two groups prior to 1967.

Arranging the confrontation as a game situation does aid in describing the conflict behaviour of the two sides. If the options available to the community as one 'player' and the water managers as another 'player' are arranged as a simple 2 x 2 strategy payoff matrix, some insight is gained into the interaction and choices made (Figure 6.5). Thus each player has a choice of two strategies, either co-operating or defecting (not co-operating). The water managers (B) could supply water for the salmon or withhold it: the community (A) could use water or save it.

If both parties co-operate (C,C) there is a certain reward; the community saves some water and the manager releases sufficient to maintain the fish, but there are some costs. The managers will have less revenue and the consumers might have dried-out lawns! Joint action defeats the perversity of nature. There are, however, strong temptations *not* to co-operate. The community as a whole may be quite apathetic and not bother to save water, or may think that 'someone' will look after the problem at no cost to themselves while they continue to use water (D,C). The managers may keep (not release) water irrespective of some saving by the public, because of the revenue factor (C,D). Finally, if both sides do not co-operate (D,D), the community has clean cars and green lawns, and the water managers maintain revenues, but the salmon of the 1970 cycle are eliminated, a greater overall long-term loss to the community.

What actually happened? In the early phase of interaction between the two sides, the community and the water managers, the community was using water,

WATER MANAGER

strategy

		C	D
COMMUNITY	C	R, R	S, T
	D	T, S	P, P

R   reward of co-operation

T   temptation of defection

S   sucker's pay-off

P   punishment for double defection

PHASE 1.

water managers co-operate but no saving by the community

PHASE 2.

water managers apprehensive: switch to withholding water no saving by the community

PHASE 3.

conservationists encourage water saving:water managers intransigent

PHASE 4.

widespread pressure and threats result in change of attitude by water managers

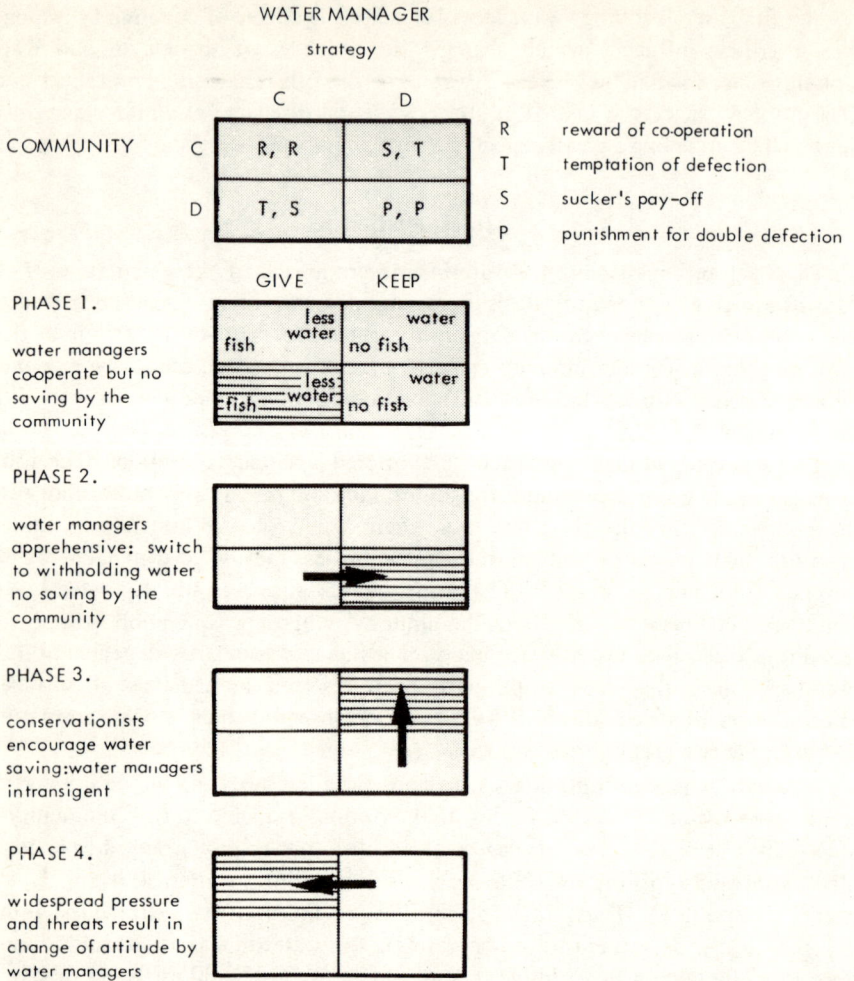

Figure 6.5 Interaction between decision-makers and the community

while the managers were persuaded by the conservationists to release water (D,C). However, as the resource diminished in quantity and the managers' perception of risk increased, they switched to withholding water, strategy D. Consequently, the two sides were locked into a double-defection situation (D,D). On the one hand, the community was apparently apathetic about the fate of the fish, while the managers were more interested in the short-run value of the game (D,D). The water managers were defecting (D), and in the absence of any other information (that the community as a whole wanted fish) were acting rationally. The penalty for giving water, if the community did not save (D,C) was too high to entertain.

The community was using water (D) because in the absence of any other information, there was no real reason to save, and was thus acting rationally. The role of the conservationists, who could see the implications of the DD trap, was only too clear. On the one hand, they had to encourage the community to adopt a 'save' tactic but avoid a 'sucker's payoff' situation (C,D) where water was saved but still not released by the water manager. The manager, in fact, used as a threat to the conservationists the likelihood of the sucker's payoff situation occurring. Therefore the conservationists had to offset the water manager's threat by using political threats and other pressures to encourage him to give water so that a co-operative situation would occur (C,C).

The Use of Threats

It is clear that during the game the strategies used by both sides changed. An important communicative act which can be linked to these changes was the use of threats by both sides, either to reinforce a strategy and thereby influence their opponents, or as a counter threat. These threats, which were exchanged almost entirely via the mass media, varied in frequency and degree (Table 6.1).[19] During the early phases of the game (in the 1960s and early 1970) they were general in content; 'people before fish' (managers), 'protect the fish against people' (conservationists) and low level.

As it became apparent to the conservationists that the managers' strategy of not releasing water was unchanged, they embarked on a specific campaign of encouraging the community to save water to protect the fish. This represented not only a direct economic threat to the water managers, but also brought into question their perception of what the public wanted: they believed that most people preferred water to fish. The managers responded with more direct counter threats, referring to the economic cost to the community, the potential damage to

Table 6.1. Frequency and type of statements made by the two principal groups to the press, which could be interpreted as threats by their opponents

Threats levelled by water managers		Total	Threats levelled by Conservationists		Total
People before fish	1964		Save water	1970 (7)	7
	1969 (2)		Fish have economic value	1964	
	1970 (2)	5		1969	
Future threat	1964			1970 (3)	5
	1967		Discredit opposition	1970 (4)	4
	1970 (2)	4	Political threat	1969 (2)	
Discredit opposition	1970 (3)	3		1970 (2)	4
Threat to property	1970 (2)	2	Protect fish v. people	1964	
Economic threat	1970 (2)	2		1969 (2)	3
			Future supplies are good	1970	1

Source: *Victoria Times* (1964–1970)

unwatered lawns, the credibility of the conservationists, and the probable failure of a water-saving campaign. Thus, the threats were now more emphatic.

The public response to the conservationists' plea was considerable (estimates vary, but probably there was a daily reduction in consumption of close to one million gallons) and meant that the game had moved to the C,D cell of the matrix.[20] The enthusiastic public response partly represented the success of the conservationists' long-term strategy of encouraging educational visits to the Goldstream River, since school children in the region became particularly keen on saving water and encouraged their parents to do likewise, and partly due to the pro-conservation coverage given by the media. The relative success of the campaign not only muted the threats levelled by the managers but showed that they were out of touch with a significant proportion of the public. The managers responded to the water-saving campaign by expanding the reasons for not releasing water, arguments which seemed rational to them, but were further threats to the conservationists (e.g. the fish were not worth saving, economic cost). Thus, the water managers, who seemingly had legitimate power over the allocation of the water, could couple the specific action of withholding water with a variety of stated threats either to the community as a whole or specifically to the conservationists — but they could not escalate action, for example, by cutting off water from those people who favoured the fish, nor could they level any kind of political threat.

As the water-saving campaign was appearing to have increasing support, the conservationists felt more confident in appealing to the other levels of government and local politicians to champion their cause. The combination of public support and encouragement from other levels of government (the Federal Minister of Fisheries referred the Water Board to the Fisheries Act, Section 120, Part 10, which compels the owners of dams and persons altering the natural flow of streams to provide sufficient water for fish), represented a political threat to the water managers aimed from above and below. In addition, the Mayor received many letters favouring the release of water. Not surprisingly, the water managers changed to a co-operative strategy (C,C) and the game had gone full cycle.

In what ways do the interactions between the parties fit in with the concepts of threat exchange and coping strategies as proposed by Lazarus? Although the conflict over allocating water was low level, in the sense that there was no personal danger to safety or health, and that violence was absent and personal abuse minimal, the conflict exhibits many of the characteristics of stressful situations such as city housing, race relations and poverty. Initially, the water managers did not appraise the conservationists as a serious threat, consequently, the coping strategy consisted of repeating earlier statements, such as 'people before fish'. The real threat to the water managers appeared to be the falling reservoir levels and the need to sell water to help finance the expanded supply system. Public attitude was viewed as supportive.

However, as the threat of the elimination of the salmon cycle of 1970/1971 loomed, the magnitude of the threat to the conservationists increased — hence the coping tactics of direct action through an appeal to the public to save water — a strategy viewed by the managers as a greater threat, particularly when some public

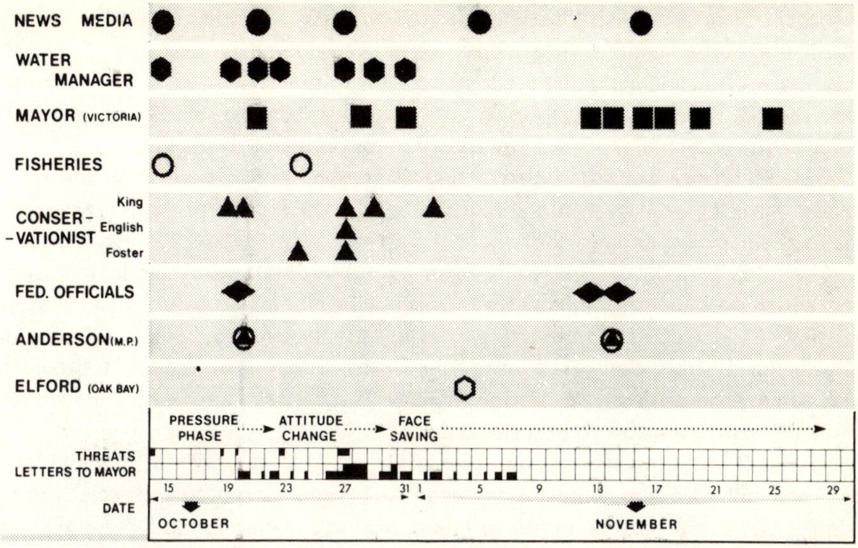

Figure 6.6 Statements in the *Victoria Times*, October–November 1970

support was forthcoming. The water managers' response was to expand the range of threats and appeal to the economic values of the community. The conservationists' response was to issue counter-threats and appeal to other levels of government, local politicians and the public. Undoubtedly, the pressure from several sources (Figure 6.6) appears to have led to the attitude change by the water managers. After the change in attitude, the water managers progressed through a 'face-saving' phase, stating that they were in favour of protecting the fish all along but that they also had to think of the community's economic interests. This in itself represents a further coping strategy, attempting to communicate their rationale for action and restore their esteem in the public's eye.

Finally, it appears that the behaviour of the water managers during the evolution of the conflict did exhibit the types of dysfunctional stress reactions posited by Lazarus. Thus, as the confrontation developed the water managers clung to the idea that people came before fish (fixation on untested hypotheses); this response was repeated many times (stereotyped response). They would only act according to the Greater Victoria Water Board Act, despite the federal legislation (problem-solving rigidity) and finally yielded when pressure came from several sources. Since there is no provision for public input, they had to rely on *ad hoc* communication channels. The use of threats as a communicative act can perhaps be related to their increasingly aggressive tone as the issue evolved.

Conclusions and Implications for Public Involvement in Water Management

It is possible to draw a number of conclusions from this examination of a resource use conflict which pertain to public decision-making in general, and water management in particular. When decisions 'flow down from the top' and sections of the community respond negatively, gaming terminology provides a realistic framework for understanding the processes of interaction between the groups involved. The concepts of threat, threat appraisal and coping strategy enable one to describe the communicative act and its influence on use of strategy.

While it is not suggested that a direct input of public views into the public decision-making process would eliminate conflict, the fact that threats are used as a major form of communication where no provisions for citizens' views are made, would seem to indicate that some form of public input would at least mitigate conflict. It would seem unlikely that stress will be eliminated from our society, but in view of the costs involved (e.g. the links between psychological stress and physiological stress cannot be overlooked) any attempt to reduce it should be welcomed. The critical question, as to *how much* stress can be tolerated and is actually needed, remains to be answered.

The case study reaffirms the general trend that the role of the public in environmental decision-making is becoming increasingly important, especially as the competition for resources increases. Public resource managers must be prepared to recognize and accommodate this phenomenon. In doing so, the present methods of gauging the public's views and incorporating them into the decision-making process are inadequate. While the 'public' is a loose and often mythical concept, a step in the right direction would appear to be at least to broaden the base of representation on bodies such as water boards. In doing this the decision-makers might be more aware of changes in public values and become conscious of the fact that water is not simply an economic commodity.

The public reaction to the Goldstream issue not only represents a keener awareness of environmental quality but also means that indirectly people are questioning the general purpose of growth, in this case of a water supply system whose pricing policy encourages people to consume more, which in turn necessitates an ever-expanding system. Thus, one of the direct implications of the issue should be a thorough examination of pricing policy and demand management.

Postscript: A New Game

The fish were saved, the mayor did not seek re-election: the water commissioner now manages an expanded system which should be adequate until the year 2000. The structure of the Water Board remains unchanged. In October 1973 recreation enthusiasts suggested that the unused Canadian National Railway track which runs through the Greater Victoria Water Board catchment area could be made into a long-distance cycle and hiking trail from Victoria to Cowichan (80 miles) (north of Koksilah River in Figure 6.3).

The provincial Department of Recreation and Conservation (Parks Branch), where the idea seems to have originated, encouraged public response and received a veritable avalanche of letters and petitions of support. Undismayed by this tactic, the water managers voiced strong opposition to the proposal, citing the previous policy of excluding public use of the catchment area and the economic cost involved in filtration if the scheme went ahead. The present situation is a stalemate with low level threat exchange between the two levels of government.

Notes

1. For recent assessments of community structure and decision-making see, T. Clark (ed.), *Community Stucture and Decision Making: Comparative Analyses*, San Francisco: Chandler, 1968. A locational emphasis is found in K. Cox, *Conflict, Power and Politics in the City: A Geographic View* New York: McGraw-Hill, 1973.
2. An excellent discussion of them can be found in T. O'Riordan, 'Towards a Strategy of Involvement', in W. R. D. Sewell & I. Burton (eds.), *Perceptions and Attitudes in Resources Management*, Resource Paper No. 2, Department of Energy, Mines and Resources, Ottawa, 1971, 99–101.
3. See R. L. Bish & R. Warren, 'Scale and Monopoly Problems in Urban Government Services', *Urban Affairs Quarterly*, 8 (1), 1972, 97–122.
4. See for example, J. Wolpert (1970).
5. This is c.f. 'programmed' (routine) and 'non-programmed' (strategic) suggested in H. A. Simon, *The Shape of Automation for Men and Management*, New York: Harper & Row, 1965, pp. 58–68.
6. R. E. Kasperson, 'Environmental Stress and the Municipal Political System', in R. E. Kasperson & J. Minghi (eds.), *The Stucture of Political Geography*, New York: J. Aldine, 1969, 481–496.
7. A. Rapoport, *Fights, Games and Debates*, Ann Arbor: University of Michigan Press, 1961.
8. R. W. Lazarus, *Psychological Stress and the Coping Process*, New York: McGraw-Hill, 1966.
9. These are returning adult salmon from fingerlings spawned four years previously.
10. In 1970 the Federal Government passed the Canada Water Resource Act, Bill C. 142, a unilateral declaration of intent to manage the waters of Canada more effectively.
11. An Act to incorporate the Greater Victoria Water District. Statutes of British Columbia (consolidated 1961), Chapter 28, Victoria, British Columbia.
12. 'Growth and Development of Greater Victoria Water Supply', Greater Victoria Water Board (no date), p. 2 (mimeo.). The city was actually given the right to negotiate with the Esquimalt Waterworks Company who held the water rights, for its expropriation. It should be noted that since 1971 the Greater Victoria Water District has been required to apply to the B.C. Water Rights Branch for a licence to abstract water from the streams in its area of operations.
13. Personal interview, Water Commissioner, Mr. R. Upward.
14. This information is based on interviews with the water commissioner and the mayor, and press statements in the *Victoria Daily Times*, 1964–1970.
15. Water pricing varies among the four large municipalities who buy water from the GVWB and then sell it to consumers. Victoria and Esquimalt have a decreasing block rate, with a seasonal price variation. Oak Bay has a decreasing block rate. Saanich has a metered flat rate. All buy from the GVWB at a flat rate.
16. This information is based on interviews with local conservationists and press statements in the *Victoria Daily Times*, 1964–1970.
17. The salmon stock which spawns, consists of 8000 Chum, 1500 Coho and some Chinook. The sports value of this population has been placed at $100,000 per year.

18. The GVWB debt is $3.25 million — requiring $400,000 in interest payments per year. Water was sold to the municipalities at 13.5c per 1000 gallons. If 5 m.g.p.d. were released it would mean a loss of $675.00 per day in revenue.
19. For a more detailed discussion of the content analysis aspects see W. R. D. Sewell & C. J. B. Wood, 'Environmental Decision-Making and Environmental Stress: the Goldstream Controversy', *Proceedings of the Canadian Association of Geographers*, Waterloo, 1971.
20. The results of a questionnaire survey of a sample of schools in the Greater Victoria area showed that there was a significant, active response by children who had visited Goldstream Park. Teachers were also instrumental in encouraging children to take an interest in the water-saving campaign.

References

Maass, A. *et al.*, 1962. *Design of Water Resources Systems*, Cambridge, Mass.: Harvard University Press.

Wolpert, J., 1970. 'Departures from the usual Environment in Locational Analysis', *Annals of the Association of American Geographers,* **60** (2), 220–229.

7

Public Involvement in the U.S. Forest Service Roadless-area Review: Lessons from a Case Study

JOHN C. HENDEE

Introduction

The U.S. Forest Service roadless-area review offers a valuable case study in public involvement.[1] It illustrates in particular how public involvement can affect land-use planning and legal classification. It affected, under the Wilderness Act of 1964 (Public Law 88–577) and the National Environmental Policy Act of 1969 (Public Law 91–190), the probable future disposition of 56 million acres (23 million hectares) of National Forest lands. It included extensive public involvement in more than 300 public meetings with a total attendance of 25,000 persons, and attracted more than 60,000 individual or group responses plus petitions bearing more than 30,000 signatures. This public input demonstrably affected both agency decisions and policies emerging from the roadless-area review.

The purpose here is to present an overview of public involvement in the roadless-area review. It is based on data and concepts developed by a task force study, led by the author to (i) determine the effectiveness of Forest Service public involvement procedures and (ii) develop new methods for analysing and evaluating large volumes of public input generated by land management issues.[2]

The study team collected data from twenty-seven National Forests and nine regional offices. A twenty-page advance questionnaire was followed by two-hour interviews with each official and his staff and a review of documents reflecting their public involvement efforts. This effort led to a comprehensive report and recommendations (Hendee et al., 1973), and development of a specially adapted content-analysis system, called CODINVOLVE, for analysing public input (Clark, Stankey & Hendee, 1974).

Background of the Roadless-area Review

The Forest Service, an agency under the U.S. Department of Agriculture, is charged with managing a nation-wide system of 155 National Forests, which includes 187 million acres (76 million hectares) of land. National Forests cover 8 per cent of the United States but include 1100 municipal watersheds, one-third of the nation's big game animals, and over 50 endangered wildlife species. They provide irrigation for 20 million acres of cropland, grazing for 7 million cattle, sheep and horses, and in recent years have experienced 200 million visitor days of recreation such as hiking, skiing, sightseeing, camping, fishing, hunting, swimming, berry-picking, etc. per annum. The National Forests accommodate more than 70,000 permits for special uses such as television-transmission sites, military installations, ski areas, private recreation facilities, reservoirs, airports and utility lines. In addition, there is an annual harvest of 11 billion board feet of timber[3] and annual extraction of 100 million dollars worth of minerals.[4] There is so much competition for the use of all the National Forest resources — timber, recreation, water, forage and minerals — that dedication of areas to any restrictive use such as wilderness preservation inevitably sparks intense controversy.

Over the years, the Forest Service, through its administrative authority, set aside in an undeveloped, roadless condition 87 wilderness-type areas including almost 15 million acres, about 8 per cent of the National Forests. Wilderness enthusiasts often voiced their fear that the agency might reverse this administrative protection and allow other uses such as logging to encroach on these wilderness-type areas. Public pressures mounted for Congress to pass a federal law to protect the areas set aside administratively by the Forest Service, as well as additional roadless tracts in National Parks and federal Wildlife Refuges. After several years of deliberation, Congress passed such a law, the Wilderness Act of 1964 (Public Law 88–577).

The Act established a National Wilderness Preservation System 'to secure for the American people of present and future generations an enduring resource of wilderness'. Areas included in the System are to remain roadless and undeveloped, and be managed for scenic, scientific, educational, historical, conservation and primitive recreation uses. No motorized access, or logging, is allowed but limited livestock grazing, mining, water resource development, hunting and fishing are permitted under strict environmental regulations. The original components of this Wilderness System are 54 National Forest areas containing 9.1 million acres which the agency had set aside, plus 5.5 million acres on 34 Primitive Areas which it was to review for potential wilderness classification within 10 years.

But this action by no means satisfied the American public's growing interest in wilderness. Environmentalists have pressed for review, study, classification and reservation of more wilderness. Recognizing the need to identify which roadless areas on the national forests have wilderness potential — and the need to appraise the aggregate impact of different amounts of wilderness classification — the Forest Service decided to examine all its roadless areas of 5000 acres or larger, plus smaller areas contiguous to designated wilderness. An inventory identified 1449 of these roadless areas on the National Forests, encompassing 55.9 million acres (23 million hectares).

The objective of the roadless-area review was to decide which of these areas should be formally *studied* for possible classification under the Wilderness Act, and which areas had resources that would probably (but not inevitably) lead to other uses.[5] The review was undertaken with extensive public involvement, to comply with requirements of the National Environmental Policy Act (Public Law 91–190) that were applicable to decisions of that magnitude and to ensure decisions that would prove acceptable to the general public.

The Roadless-area Review in Summary

The roadless-area review officially began 25 February 1971, when the Chief of the Forest Service sent a memo to the nine Regional Foresters indicating 'the need to identify those areas which still should be studied for potential wilderness classification' (U.S. Forest Service, 1973a). Each Regional Forester was instructed to inventory all roadless areas in his region. Using criteria of availability, suitability and need – and with full public involvement – each one was asked to recommend by 30 June 1972, those roadless areas in his region which should be considered for wilderness classification. After additional analysis and evaluation in the Washington Office, on 18 January 1973 the Chief of the Forest Service released a preliminary list of 235 new areas nominated for wilderness study, along with a draft environmental impact statement (EIS) as required by the National Environmental Policy Act. The draft EIS and the preliminary list were then subjected to additional public review and comment prior to preparation of a final environmental impact statement to accompany the 'final' list of 274 new wilderness-study areas released in October 1973.

Figure 7.1 shows the 1449 roadless areas identified in this initial inventory. Most lie in the extensive National Forests of the west, where rugged, mountainous terrain has limited settlement and resource development.

The roadless-area review process can best be illustrated with a diagram like Figure 7.2.[6] When the Chief of the Forest Service requested his Regional Foresters to submit a list of roadless areas, he also asked for extensive data about *each area's* environment and potential for different uses. These data were to include such things as timber volume, kinds of ecosystems, presence of rare ecological types, relative quality of the potential wilderness as calculated by a wilderness-quality index formula, opportunity costs and so forth.[7] On the basis of extensive public involvement, the inventory was also to include a variable indicating whether or not the public favoured studying the area for possible wilderness classification. All of these variables were incorporated into a systematic, computerized, program analysis called RARE (Roadless-Area Review and Evaluation) so that decision-makers could quickly and systematically review pertinent quantitative facts and qualitative judgements. Public involvement was condensed into a single, three-category, public-sentiment variable:

1. *Yes*: public sentiment favours setting this area aside as a new wilderness-study area;
2. *No*: public sentiment does not favour setting this area aside as a new wilderness-study area;

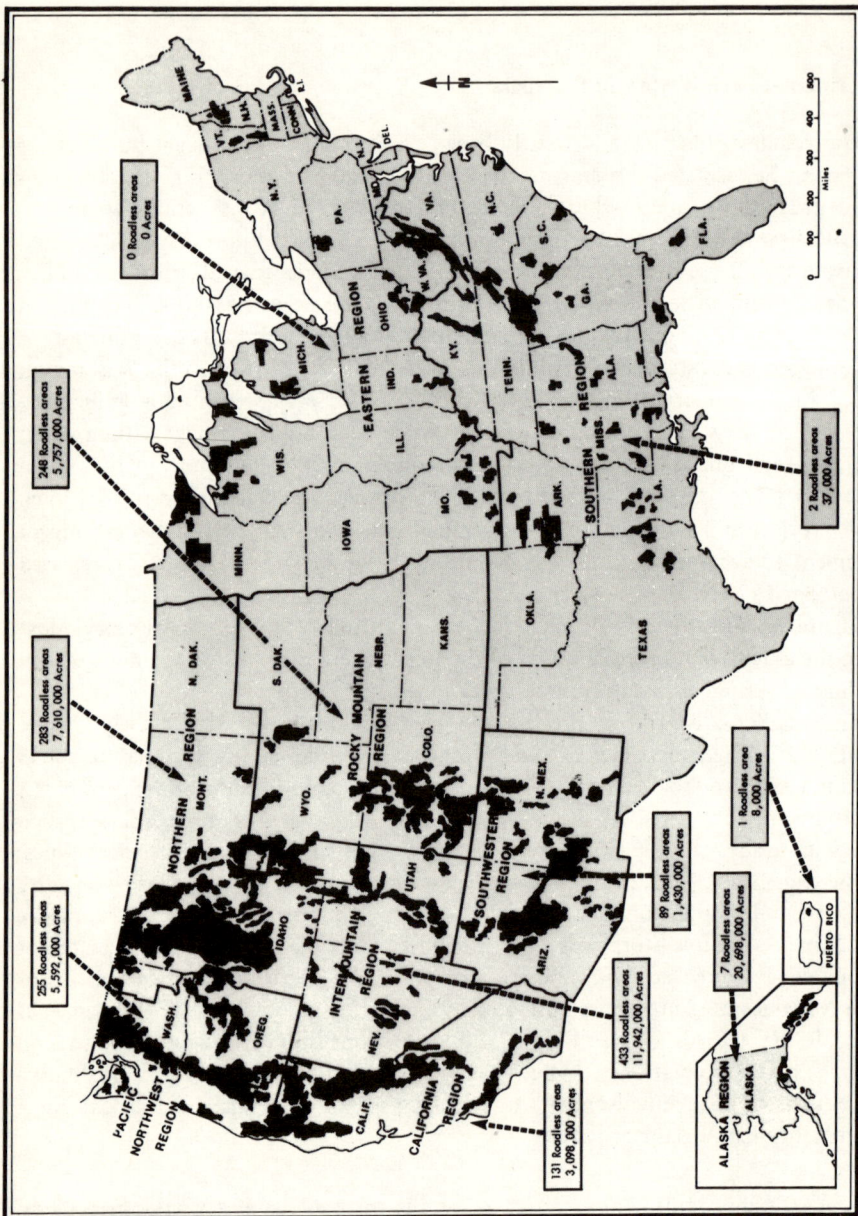

Figure 7.1 Roadless areas in U.S. National Forests

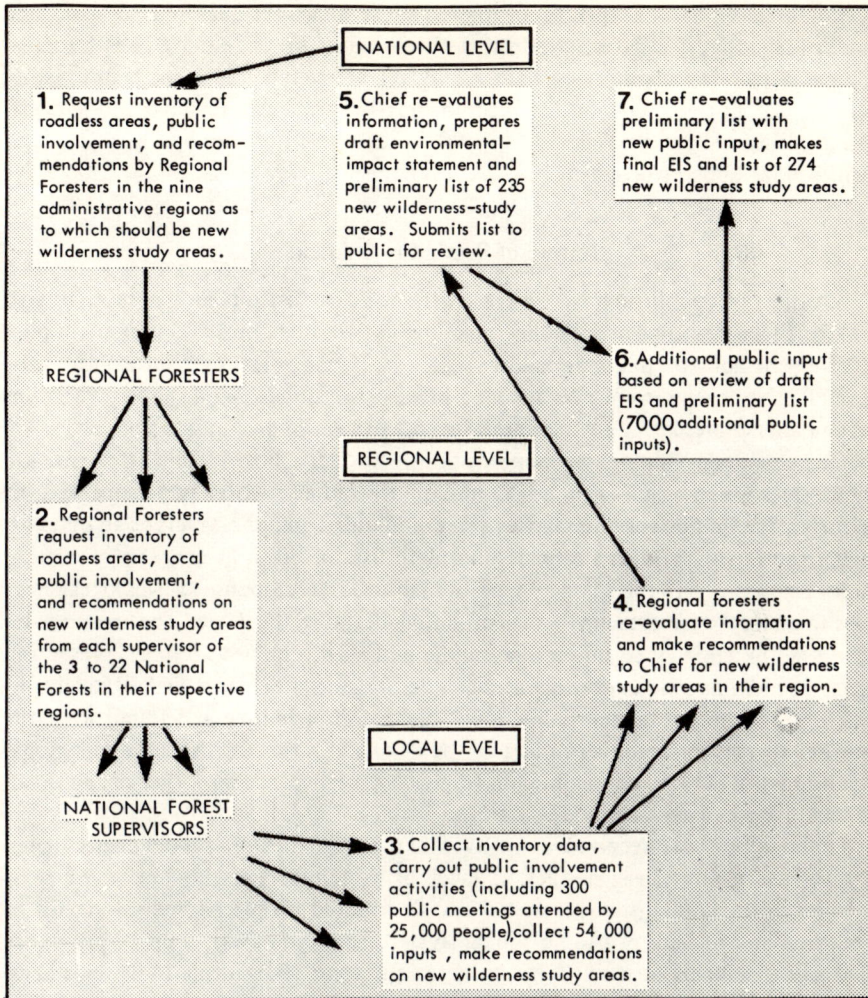

Figure 7.2 Roadless area review decision process

3. *Undecided*: no consensus by the public about whether or not the area should be set aside as a new wilderness-study area.

Therefore public involvement became one of many variables considered in the decision. But during the decision process, a few variables, including public involvement, emerged as more important than the others.

The important variables – the ones on which marginal cases were decided and which high-level officials repeatedly used in making the final decisions – were as follows: (i) public input, including the sentiments of involved citizens and organizations, and the views of elected officials and other government agencies;

(ii) potential wilderness quality of the roadless areas as measured by a quality index; (iii) cost effectiveness, reflecting the value of other resource uses foregone compared to relative wilderness values; and (iv) an overall judgement factor resting heavily, but not entirely, on the recommendations of local, regional and national agency decision-makers. This judgemental factor was influenced by the quality and quantity of public involvement (U.S. Forest Service, 1973a).

Nature of Public Involvement

A variety of public-involvement activities was carried out in conjunction with the roadless-area review. Public meetings were the most common public-involvement activity and were held by every National Forest having roadless areas, Several other means were also used to involve the public. Workshops put citizen participants representing several interests to work on impromptu teams, reviewing the issue and developing recommendations. Advisory boards and a few *ad hoc* committees were consulted for advice and input. Contacts with key persons were an important technique for tapping views of community opinion leaders as an index to public sentiment. Information was mailed to lists of previous contacts requesting their response on this issue. Questionnaires and response forms (tearsheet questionnaire) were attached to information defining the issue. The mass media were used extensively to inform the public and seek responses. Reports presenting the assessment and views of other agencies and organizations were widely sought.

The study reviewed each public input collection technique and found strengths and weaknesses for each, depending on the issue and varying with local and regional conditions. A tailormade combination of several techniques was necessary to do an adequate job in each location (U.S. Forest Service, 1973a).[8]

Public input was received in many other forms, including individually-signed citizen letters, multiple-signed letters (such as by families, neighbours or groups of friends), form letters (mimeographed and distributed by special-interest groups to be signed and mailed by people willing to endorse those views), coupons printed as paid advertisements in newspapers or as tearsheets in other media to be signed and mailed, petitions (often oversimplifying and overstating the issues to appeal for mass support) signed by tens to thousands of persons, and organization reports (often lengthy and complex with substantive resource data and interpretations) from involved citizen groups. Much of the input was general and emotional in nature, with the most extensive and most sharply focused input coming from public involvement carried out at local levels and directed at local issues and areas (Hendee *et al.*, 1973).

The numbers expressing the extent of involvement were impressive. Nationally, over 300 public meetings were held in local areas to inform the public about the roadless-area review and to solicit comments, opinions and other input. These meetings attracted about 25,000 people, and nearly 54,000 individuals or groups expressed opinions either orally or in writing. In addition, petitions bearing approximately 18,000 signatures were presented to Forest Service field officers. After release of the draft environmental-impact statement with the tentative list of new wilderness-study areas, an additional 6843 public responses were received at national headquarters with signatures reflecting the views of an additional 15,607 persons (Hendee & Clark, 1973). Thus the roadless-area review benefited from more than 90,000 expressions of opinion.

Lessons Learned About Public Involvement

Broadly speaking, five major lessons about public involvement emerged from the roadless-area review. Singling them out should not detract from the importance of some other new information also surfacing.

Five Basic Processes in Public Involvement

A major conceptual orientation emerging from the study was identification of five integral processes basic to implementing public involvement (Hendee *et al.*, 1973; Hendee, Clark & Stankey, 1974). The five processes include:

1. Issue definition: legal, environmental and fiscal constraints help to identify a range of possible land-use or management alternatives that require public input;
2. Collection: includes all the varied processes which yield input from citizens;
3. Analysis: the description of the nature, content, variation and extent of public input;
4. Evaluation: the subjective interpretation and weighing of all data that have been collected and analysed for the purposes of making a decision;
5. Decision implementation: the process of providing feedback to the public, securing a review and translating a decision into a programme of action.

Breaking down public-involvement activity into basic processes was a necessary first step in focusing the study and developing specific recommendations. However, it soon became clear that each process was so closely tied to the next that all five must be considered together in a comprehensive plan before public involvement can fulfil its potential.

The extent to which issues and alternatives are clearly defined will strongly affect the clarity of public input. The complexity of the issue at stake has important implications as to the kind of collection techniques needed to secure adequate public input. The way in which input is collected affects the way in which data can be analysed for decision-makers evaluating its importance. Any pre-conceived notions about the importance to be attached to evaluating different kinds of public input will bias the kind of input received and may hamper analysis. For example, if the public is told that petition signatures will weigh the same as individual letters, then an obvious strategy for dedicated advocates is to wage a petition war. Yet knowing the kind of input that will be regarded as most important is basic both to agency officials implementing public-involvement activity and to the public which is expected to respond.

Implementing a decision is not so much the end of public involvement as a part of it. Disappointed contestants for a decision favouring their interests must be confronted, and the public must be told how its input was handled in reaching a decision, what the decision was and how it will be implemented.

Public Input is a Major Factor in Decision-making

Some tests of the value of public involvement are (i) whether or not it helps lead to a different decision and (ii) whether or not that decision is more 'acceptable'. However, it is difficult to apply these tests because the impact of public involvement may be subtle, perhaps even invisible in the decision process. Also, it takes time for a decision to be accepted, during which underlying social factors and public sentiment can change. It is too soon to know how the public accepted those decisions which grew from the roadless-area review. But a number of direct and indirect ways in which public input affected the final decision and related issues can be identified.

There is substantial evidence underlining the importance of public input in selecting which roadless areas to designate for wilderness study. It is difficult to know exactly how much public involvement affected the development of recommendations from the field. But field officers gave abundant testimony that public involvement was valuable and even essential to the decision process (Hendee et al., 1973). At least some field officers in every region reported that public input caused them to change recommendations they had tentatively planned to make.

Further along in the decision process, headquarters officials in Washington, D.C., designated public input as one of 'four factors of primary importance in the final decision-making analysis' (U.S. Forest Service, 1973b). Also they labelled one of the other factors 'judgmental', suggesting that public input may have had a subtle influence on it as well.

The most obvious evidence of its importance to the roadless-area review is the substantial difference between the preliminary and the final lists of new wilderness-study areas. The preliminary list proposed 235 areas totalling 11 million acres. A total of 6843 public inputs reflecting the views of nearly 16,000 persons were received by the Forest Service in response to this tentative proposal. The final list proposed 274 areas totalling 12.3 million acres.

The foregoing illustrates the potential direct impact of public involvement on the decision, but some indirect effects were also apparent. The study team was repeatedly impressed with attitude changes among field officers that occurred as a result of public involvement. Many decision-makers reported initial reluctance and scepticism about the value of public involvement. Their attitudes, they said, had changed because of their experience with it, and they had come to respect it as a valuable tool in decision-making. Thus the experiences of these resource professionals in working with the public often resulted in new perspectives on the public's role in decision-making — and increased respect for what the lay public can contribute. Although indirect and subtle in its effect, such 'awakening' may be one of the most pervasive benefits of public involvement in the roadless-area review. An important observation of the study team was that commitment to public involvement by decision-makers seems to come only after experience in using it.

Systematic Analysis is Possible and Desirable

Analysis of public input (the summary of what the public said and how it varied) surfaced in the roadless-area review as one of the most complex technical problems hampering the public-involvement process. Two comments by field officers to the study team illustrate the problem (Hendee *et al.*, 1973). 'How does one begin to analyze, summarize and arrange in usable form the varied opinions of over 5000 respondents. . . .' And '. . . we didn't know how to analyze the mass of input we received, and we couldn't find anyone nearby who really knew any more than we did.' The problem of developing new methods and techniques for analysing public input was a major assignment for the study team. Three of its members and an extensive staff of graduate students and technicians worked with field officers in several National Forests to analyse public reaction to new wilderness-study areas within their local jurisdictions. It was found possible reliably to code public inputs according to the opinions expressed and the reasons, if any, supporting them. As the team worked on several local, roadless-area review cases it developed and improved a generic system called CODINVOLVE, a specially adapted content-analysis system for coding, storing, retrieving and summarizing the nature and extent of public inputs (Hendee *et al.*, 1973; Clark, Stankey & Hendee, 1974).[9]

The CODINVOLVE system summarizes all public inputs so that decision-makers can more easily review the aggregate substance of comment and thereby evaluate its decision implications. It is an open-ended approach that develops coding categories from the substance of comments received, rather than forcing all input into simple, preconceived codes. As new opinions, issues or reasons appear in the inputs being processed, new codes are developed. The system seeks to ensure that all opinions expressed are systematically recorded so that they can be related to the decision.

Most of the early applications of CODINVOLVE used edge-punch cards and needle-sort methods. But in the application to public input on the preliminary national list of roadless areas, coded data were recorded directly on a code sheet for key-punching and computer-processing. With few exceptions, open-ended coding procedures were used, i.e. if a comment differed from the logical categories that had emerged from similar comments, it was included as a new category. All comments were recorded according to the number of inputs on which they occurred and the number of total signatures these included. In the end the computer summarized the extensive data. It totalled:

| | | Form | | |
Letters	Petitions	Letters	Reports	Other
5301 (I)	155 (I)	591 (I)	502 (I)	184 (I)
6186 (S)	7549 (S)	897 (S)	655 (S)	184 (S)

(I) = Inputs; (S) = Signatures

The coding process identified all opinions and supporting reasons from all the inputs. The coding procedure included a random review of comments to identify the most prevalent opinions and their supporting reasons, systematic coding and check of each input and the creation of new categories whenever an input differed from the established categories. Those which appeared most frequently formed the basis for a report on the analysis (Hendee & Clark, 1973), also included in the final EIS (U.S. Forest Service, 1973a). These data included (but were not limited to) the following:

1. Opinions (pro or con) about the roadless-area review process and criteria for selecting new wilderness-study areas — about 1200 inputs, 1500 signatures and 30 major reasons given in support of the opinions expressed;
2. Opinions about whether the tentative list of new wilderness-study areas was acceptable as proposed or whether more or fewer areas were favoured for inclusion — about 1700 inputs with 2400 signatures and 45 major reasons;
3. Opinions directed at specific roadless areas — whether they favoured its designation as a new wilderness-study area or not, and whether they favoured enlarging or reducing the size of the area or leaving it as proposed. Most inputs included at least one comment about one of the 1448 proposed areas. These were printed out by area, showing all the supporting reasons.

Cross-tabulations were also developed to identify variations in the balance of input by the region where respondents lived, the form of the input, and who they were (citizens, organizations, etc.). This was requested by decision-makers to help them evaluate the input.

Evaluation of Public Input is Different from Analysis

An important concern affecting managers was confusion over the difference between the *analysis* and the *evaluation* of public input. *Analysis* is the description of the nature, content, variation and extent of public input, i.e. what the public said. *Evaluation* is the subjective interpretation of the importance of various kinds of public input and the integration of that with other factors in making a decision. When managers confused these two processes they were understandably reluctant to accept systematic analysis of public input because they thought the analysis would usurp their prerogative to make a decision. When applying the CODINVOLVE analysis system, the study team was always forced to explain clearly that all it could do was to describe what the public said in their input. The decision-maker would still have to decide what importance to attach to the different kinds of input and different views expressed.

The study team explored the tendency of managers to place varying degrees of importance on different input (Hendee *et al.*, 1973). More importance was usually placed on specific, written comments and less on general comments, petitions, form letters or coupons. Inputs from local people or organizations were usually accorded more weight than those from persons living far away from the area at issue. The importance placed by managers on various kinds of public input was also voiced as an issue of concern by some of the involved public bodies. They felt that information about how public input would be used was critical to their strategy for providing various kinds of it.

Professional Philosophy

The philosophy of professional resource decision-makers critically affects the extent to which they will seek and use public involvement in making decisions. The Forest Service has more foresters in its ranks than any other professional group. The philosophical perspective inculcated in them by their training, continuing professional communication and colleague contacts is a major factor in their attitude and behaviour.[10] The concept of involving the public in resource decision-making flies in the face of traditional perspectives which say that professional foresters know best how forest land should be used. The study team encountered abundant symptoms and evidence that foresters perceived threats to their professional stature and responsibilities, which in turn had an adverse effect on their public-involvement efforts. This will be a problem until resource-management professions develop a positive philosophy about public involvement as an important tool for making decisions, and institutionalize effective techniques for achieving its benefits. Some strong impressions of what this philosophy should include were developed by the study team who noted some encouraging signs of its development.

Public input is especially important to decision-makers because it is the principal source of information about what values the public holds regarding the National Forests. The 'best' use of forest resources is never evident from the resources themselves. There are wide variations in the ability of land to provide products and services, and decisions to provide any particular set of goods and services from an area should reflect public desires for those returns.

Public involvement can help to identify those desires. Meeting this public participation challenge requires considerable skill by resource managers and their professional stature will be enhanced by doing a good job of it. A constant dialogue must be maintained and feedback provided to the public because a key to continuing credibility is providing visible evidence that public inputs *are* being used in the decision-making process. Only when both resource professionals and the public can see real importance attached to public input in decision-making will either party invest the necessary constructive commitment for public involvement to realize its potential value.

Other Important Lessons

Singling out the foregoing five major lessons was difficult because some other important findings also emerged. For example, public involvement in the roadless-area review stimulated overwhelmingly local input, some input from regional levels but virtually no national input (Hendee *et al.*, 1973). Some national input is available through Congress, the White House, other executive departments and lobbyists. But the prevalence of local input which resulted from current public-involvement procedures could sacrifice legitimate national interests to more limited, local views. A classic example concerns Alaska, where strong feelings about 'Alaska for Alaskans' discredit input from U.S. citizens in the 'lower 48 states'. Yet many U.S. citizens feel Alaska is the last frontier where mistakes made in the lower 48 states can be avoided.

In building commitment to public involvement, experience seems necessary. The study team's data and impressions from interviews clearly indicate that experience with public involvement tends to develop or reinforce commitment to it. There were few negative attitudes towards public involvement from foresters immersed in the process at field levels – but suspicion and mistrust of it among those observing at a distance was occasionally encountered.

Another ingredient essential to successful public involvement is visibility of the effort. Visibility leads to credibility and trust because it shows public input affecting the decision process. Credibility is not an end in itself; it comes as a result of doing the job right and showing the effect of public input on the decision. Credibility is easier to lose than to regain, and when it is absent successful public involvement is impossible.

The representativeness of public input also arouses concern. It seems clear that views expressed through public-involvement procedures are not representative of the general public and reflect inputs from only a tiny minority of the population. The roadless-area review, which appeared to be of broad interest, stimulated input from no more than one person in a thousand: much less in some regions (Hendee *et al.*, 1973). Persons who became involved were invariably those most affected by the decision. Under these conditions, resource managers may be tempted to hide behind the silent majority – or attribute a particular view to them. This is dangerous since research indicates that no one opinion is held by the silent majority (Bultena, Rogers & Webb, 1973). Also, although many reasons may account for lack of participation, silence may be a legitimate expression of interest and concern. The study team suggested that this issue could be dealt with by differentiating between *demographic representation* which reflects the proportionate distribution of public input according to sex, age, residence, etc., and *interest representation* which reflects the extent to which groups affected by a decision are represented (Hendee *et al.*, 1973; Hendee, Clark & Stankey, 1974). The former cannot be achieved through routine public-involvement procedures; the latter must be.

The issue of quality versus quantity of public input surfaced in the study as an important concern. To resource managers, 'quality' inputs were well-reasoned, site-specific, fully informed and couched in meaningful management terminology. Such inputs are particularly useful, but they are not characteristic of the general, often superficial and emotional input received. Whether well-reasoned and detailed or not, all input expresses values, and definition of these values is the overriding objective of public involvement. Recognition of this, and the importance of both quality and quantity dimensions of public involvement, is crucial to the successful use of public input in decision-making.

Conclusions

The roadless-area review was a major public-involvement effort for the U.S. Forest Service, and a crucial shakedown for procedures, techniques and commitment to involving the public in the decision process. Not everyone was happy with either the public-involvement process or the resulting decisions. Many critical comments focused on the process, reflecting both legitimate criticism and disappointment.[11] Hopefully, all that was learned will be reflected in improved public-involvement procedures for future use – and strengthened commitment as well. Steps in this direction have already been taken with the issue of a new Forest Service 'Guide to Public-Involvement in Decision-Making' (U.S. Forest Service, 1974). For the Forest Service, the roadless-area review was a significant turning point in developing both commitment to, and techniques for, public involvement in decision-making. Only time will tell whether or not public involvement will continue to be a critical input in decision-making. But experience subsequent to the roadless-area review is encouraging. The public is continuing to participate in important decisions, although their involvement seems tied to the amount of controversy and publicity surrounding an issue. For their part, resource managers, more than before, are seeking public input and are using it with greater skill.

Notes

1. Case studies of public involvement are valuable as documentaries, or as systematic studies of processes. Several of these studies are especially instructive, notably: Citizen's Advisory Committee on Environmental Quality (1973), Barton & Warner (1971), Lyden & Thomas (1969), Milton (1973), Campion (1972). The reflections of participants in public involvement efforts also reveal valuable information about the process. See, for example, Frear (1973), Gale (1973) and Sandor (1971).
2. The preparation of this chapter benefited from the comments, suggestions and substantive contributions of a number of people, notably colleagues in the U.S. Forest Service Public-Involvement Study Team: Dr. Robert Lucas, Wilderness Management Research Project Leader, Missoula (a social geographer); Mr. Robert Tracy, then Supervisor, Targhee National Forest, Idaho, now Assistant Regional Forest, Alaska Region (a forester); Mr. Tony Staed, Washington Office Division of Information and Education (a public relations and media expert); Dr. Roger Clark, Research Social Scientist, Recreation Research, Seattle (a forester and sociologist); Dr. George Stankey, Research Social Scientist, Wilderness Management Research, Missoula (a social geographer); and Mr. Ron Yarnell, Recreation Research Technician, Seattle (a forester and planner). In addition the comments of Gene Bergoffen, at that time director of Legislative Affairs for the U.S. Forest Service, are gratefully acknowledged.
3. Local Log Scale, in 1972. See U.S. Forest Service (1973a).
4. Estimated Mines Wellhead Value, U.S. Forest Service (1973a).
5. In the final selection of wilderness-study areas as a result of the roadless-area review, the Forest Service stressed that subsequent, routine land-use planning would also consider wilderness classification as a possible alternative use for areas not selected for wilderness study during the review – non-selected areas.
6. There were some exceptions to this general procedure.
7. For detailed information on the basic data compiled for the decision, see U.S. Forest Service (1973a).

8. Guidelines for public input collection techniques were subsequently set out in the document, U.S. Forest Service (1974).
9. Reports of the use of the CODINVOLVE techniques of assessing public views include U.S. Forest Service (1974); and Hendee & Clark (1973); Clark & Stankey (1975).
10. Studies of the effect of professional socialization on natural resource managers are reported in a number of contributions to the literature, such as Bultena & Hendee (1972), Sewell (1971), Sewell & Burton (1971), Henning (1970), Kaufmann (1969), Reich (1962), Craik (1970) and Sewell & Little (1973).
11. Milton (1973) and U.S. Forest Service (1974).

References

Barton, Thomas E. & Katharine P. Warner, 1971. 'Involving Citizens in Water Resources Planning, the Communication—Participation Experiment in the Susquehanna River Basin', *Environment and Behavior,* **3** (3), 284—306.

Bultena, Gordon L. & John C. Hendee, 1972 'Foresters' Views of Interest Group Positions on Forest Policy', *Journal of Forestry,* **70** (6).

Bultena, Gordon L., David Rogers & Vince Webb, 1973. 'Public Response to Planned Environmental Change — A Study of Citizen Views and Actions on the Proposed Ames Reservoir', Ames: Iowa State University, Social Report 106.

Campion, Thomas B., 1972. 'Public Involvement in Decision-Making on the Shoshone National Forest', M.A. Thesis, University of Colorado, Boulder, Colorado.

Citizens' Advisory Committee on Environmental Quality, 1973. *Citizens Make the Difference: Case Studies of Environmental Action,* Citizens' Advisory Committee on Environmental Quality, 1700 Pennsylvania Avenue, N.W., Washington, D.C., 20006.

Clark, Roger N, George H. Stankey & John C. Hendee, 1974. 'An Introduction to CODINVOLVE: A System for Analyzing, Storing, and Retrieving Public Input to Resource Decisions', USDA Forest Service Research Note PNW—223, Pacific Northwest Forest and Range Experiment Station, PO Box 3141 Portland, Oregon.

Clark, Roger N. & George H. Stankey, 1975. 'Analyzing Public Input to Resource Decisions: Criteria, Principles and Case Examples of the CODINVOLVE System', *Natural Resources Journal,* **16** (1), 213—236.

Craik, Kenneth H., 1970. 'The Environmental Dispositions of Environmental Decision Makers', *Annals of the American Academy of Political and Social Sciences,* pp. 87—94.

Folkman, William S., 1971. 'Public Involvement in the Decision-Making Process of Natural Resource Management Agencies with Special Reference to the Pacific Northwest'. Paper presented to a meeting of the American Sociological Association.

Frear, Samuel T., 1973. 'Confrontation vs. Communication', *Journal of Forestry,* **71** (10), 15.

Gale, Richard P., 1973. 'Communicating with Environmentalists: A Look at the Receiving End', *Journal of Forestry,* **71** (10), 653—655.

Hendee, John C. & Gordon L. Bultena, 1972. 'Capture-Conformity Orientations of Foresters in the U.S. Forest Service'. Paper presented to Annual Meeting of American Sociological Association. (Mimeo available from U.S. Forest Service Recreation Research, 4507 Univ.Way N.E. Seattle, Wash., 98105.)

Hendee, John C. & Roger N. Clark, 1973. 'Summary of National Public Response to the Roadless-Area Review Draft Environmental Impact Statement'. In U.S.

Forest Service, 1973 Final Environmental Impact Statement – Roadless and Undeveloped Areas, Selection of the Final New Study Areas from Roadless and Undeveloped Areas Within the National Forests.

Hendee, John C., Roger N. Clark & George H. Stankey, 1974. 'A Framework for Agency Use of Public Input in Resource Decision-Making', *Journal of Soil and Water Conservation*, March–April, pp. 60–66.

Hendee, John C., Robert C. Lucas, Robert H. Tracy, Jr., Tony Staed, Roger N. Clark, George H. Stankey & Ronald A. Yarnell, 1973. *Public Involvement and the Forest Service: Experience, Effectiveness, and Suggested Direction*. A report from the United States Forest Service administrative study of public involvement, GPO Washington, D.C. $5.00.

Henning, David H., 1970. 'Natural Resource Administration and the Public Interest', *Public Administration Review*, **30** (2), 134–140.

Kauffman, Herbert, 1969. *The Forest Ranger*, Baltimore: Johns Hopkins Press.

Lyden, Fremont James & Jerry V. Thomas, 1969. 'Citizen Participation in Policy-Making: A Study of a Community Action Program', *Social Science Quarterly*, **50**, 631–642.

Milton, William John, Jr., 1973. 'A Critique of the Methodology of the Forest Service Roadless Area Inventory Impact Study'. M.A. Thesis, University of Montana, Missoula, Montana.

Reich, Charles, 1962. 'Bureaucracy and the Forests', The Fund for the Republic Inc., Santa Barbara, California.

Sandor, J. A., 1971. 'Public Involvement in National Forest Management', in Craig W. Rupp, Gordon D. Taylor, John A. Sandor and Harold Eidsvik, *The Problems of Park Management in Canada and U.S.A.* Weyerhaeuser Lecture Series, March 1971, Lakehead University Forestry Association and School of Forestry, pp. 21–33.

Sewell, W. R. Derrick, 1971. 'Environmental Perceptions and Attitudes of Engineers and Public Health Officials', *Environment and Behavior*, **3** (1), 23–59.

Sewell, W. R. Derrick & Ian Burton (eds.) 1971. *Perceptions and Attitudes in Resource Management*, Ottawa: Information Canada.

Sewell, W. R. Derrick & Brian Little, 1973. 'Specialists, Laymen and the Process of Environmental Appraisal', *Regional Studies*, July, 161–171.

Stankey, George H., John C. Hendee & Roger N. Clark, 1975. 'Focusing Social Science Skills on the Use of Public Input in Resource Decision-Making', *Rural Sociology*, **40** (1), 67–74.

U.S. Congress, 1964. Wilderness Act of 1964, Public Law 88–577.

U.S. Congress, 1969. National Environment Policy Act of 1969, Public Law 91–190.

U.S. Forest Service, 1973a. *Roadless and Undeveloped Areas (Final Environmental Statement), Selection of the Final New Study Areas from Roadless and Undeveloped Areas within the National Forests*, Washington, D.C.: U.S. Department of Agriculture.

U.S. Forest Service, 1973b. *New Wilderness Study areas – Roadless Area Review and Evaluation*. Current Information Report No. 11, U.S. Department of Agriculture, Washington, D.C.

U.S. Forest Service, 1973c. 'Press Clippings', U.S. Department of Agriculture, No. 15, Washington, D.C.

U.S. Forest Service, 1974. *Guide to Public Involvement in Decision-Making*, Washington, D.C.

8

The Public Hearing as a Participatory Device: Evaluation of the IJC Experience

MARGARET SINCLAIR

The Public Hearing

One of the most popular public participation techniques used by government agencies in Canada is the public hearing. During the month of June 1975, there were at least ten separate hearings taking place in the city of Toronto alone. These covered such diverse topics as transportation, immigration, the marketing of beef, lead contamination and the future of Metropolitan Toronto. A public hearing is usually understood to be a large formal gathering in which any person who wishes may present his views, usually by means of written testimony, which is read to a board, commission or agency. These groups are usually government-appointed bodies whose function is to study a problem and make recommendations to the government. It is sometimes a legislative requirement of the agency (e.g. the Ontario Municipal Board, the Environmental Hearing Board of Ontario). Communication is usually one-way; i.e. the hearing body listens to the public, but does not invite dialogue.

Public hearings may be held at various points during the course of investigation. The timing of the hearing is an important point, since it affects the degree of public influence. Generally, there is more opportunity for public influence and involvement when hearings are held at the beginning of a study rather than at its completion. There are three stages at which most hearings seem to be held. These are listed below, with Canadian examples.[1]

1. Preliminary hearings. These are held before the study begins in order to identify general information and opinions, as well as specific problem areas. An example is the set of hearings which the Royal Commission on Violence in the Communications Industry (Ontario) held in the fall of 1975 as the first stage in its investigation into the effect on society of the increasing exhibition of violence in television and movies.
2. Pre-final decision hearings. These are held for the purpose of receiving

reaction to general policies or recommendations which are only tentatively adopted. For example, hearings were held across Canada in the summer of 1975 by a Special Joint Committee of Parliament to gather reactions to the federal government's Green Paper on Immigration Policy.

3. Final hearings. These are held to provide a forum for reactions to a definite action proposal outlined in a final report or in a draft piece of legislation. Example: hearings before a House of Commons Committee considering an Environmental Contaminants Bill, which would regulate many aspects of industrial activities in Canada.

There is a subset within this third type of hearing, which is a hearing to evaluate the plans of a project proponent who wishes to start a large specific project or activity. Permission to begin the project depends on the hearing outcome, although the decision can always be overturned by a higher authority. One of the most open sets of public hearings ever undertaken in Canada is in this category. The issue is a proposed natural gas pipeline through the Mackenzie River Valley in northern Canada. Three weeks of hearings were held in Yellowknife, the capital of the Northwest Territories, and then the Commission, chaired by Mr. Justice Berger, visited more than twenty small Arctic communities. The timing, setting and length of the hearings were a reflection of the communities' wishes. The number of lawyers who could attend was limited, and the citizens of the area (mostly Eskimos) were given complete freedom to speak (Toronto *Globe and Mail*, 7 March 1975).

As a technique for public participation, the public hearing has several advantages, which explains its use by so many agencies. It was probably one of the earliest methods used (i.e. in twentieth-century society) and, because of this tradition, it has acquired a fairly high degree of legitimacy. Furthermore, it is a 'large group' meeting with potential to reach many people. From the agency point of view, it is relatively quick, inexpensive, and easy to administer (*vis-à-vis* other participation techniques).

Yet, in spite of the widespread use of the public hearing, there has been much criticism of this method, particularly as the demand for 'meaningful' public participation increases. The hearing has serious deficiencies as a participatory device and as a technique for involving the public. It tends to be a 'one-shot' exercise. A hearing is announced, individuals or groups present testimony, and that is usually the beginning and the end of their involvement.

The format of the public hearing tends to elicit negative responses. When there is a report or proposal to comment upon, those who disagree with any aspect of it are more likely to appear at the hearing than those who agree. Positive comments do not seem necessary; it is a case of silence meaning consent. The format does not encourage discussion of possible changes or alternatives. Moreover, the seating arrangement seems to enforce the confrontational nature of the hearing. The usual procedure is for the citizen to face the board members, who are in a row and on an elevated platform. This formal approach may inhibit many speakers, but for those who strongly oppose the proposal/report, the effect is minimized.

In addition, hearings usually suffer from lack of a representative audience. Without a supplementary technique (such as a systematic opinion survey), the hearing board is never sure how representative the views are that it has just heard. A sociology professor described one set of hearings as:

an exercise in futility and likely to give rise to quite misleading conclusions . . . [They] elicit the views of entirely unrepresentative sections of the population, particularly extremists representing minority positions. (Letter to the Editor, *Toronto Star*, 13 April 1974.)

In evaluating the hearings which took place as a part of the 'public inquiry into the transmission of power between Lennox and Oshawa', Dr. O. M. Solandt, a noted Canadian scientist, wrote (1975):

There is no question that every citizen in the affected area and even in the entire province has a perfect right to appear and give his views to the Commission. Unfortunately, only a narrow cross-section of those potentially concerned appeared before the Commission . . . For example, virtually no one but the Ministry of Transportation and Communications presented a submission on behalf of the travellers on Highway 401 or other major through highways in the area, and in order to get a reasonable picture of public attitude toward the Ganaraska Forest, the Commission had to plan a special seminar and invite people to come to present their views.

There is also the criticism that public hearings are more open to manipulation than other techniques of public participation. David Estrin, a Director of the Canadian Environmental Law Association, has outlined two ways in which hearings might be classified as manipulative. The purpose of hearings in the first category is to generate public support for the hearing body's recommendations or plans. (If one agrees with that body's report, this could be considered positive manipulation.) At their worst, these hearings are part of a slick public relations programme, designed to 'sell' a project or principle: the positive attributes are emphasized, the negative aspects glossed over, and alternatives ignored. Hearings under this category might also take place when a government desires to take strong action, but feels the need to elucidate the problem, and thereby gain public support, before bringing in what otherwise may appear as harsh legislation. Estrin cites the 1974–75 Cliche Commission inquiry into the province of Quebec's labour problems as hearings of this type. Out of the Cliche Commission revelations came laws putting four large construction unions under provincial government trusteeship (*Globe and Mail*, 22 July 1975).

The second category is the opposite of the first, in which public hearings may be an important part of a scheme whereby a government not anxious to take action on a controversial issue may gain reasons for inaction. Particularly in hearings involving complex issues, the public may indeed become bored with the controversy or confused by the differing expert viewpoints. The government then appears to have some justification for delaying action until 'clear evidence' emerges. It must be admitted that in conducting the hearings, there has been a time delay. This is a criticism of public participation by various managers and government personnel. For example, an Ontario Hydro executive recently said that the public voice in Hydro planning is delaying projects up to five years and will have major impact on the cost and reliability of electric power (*Globe and Mail*, 4 March 1975). It was noted earlier, however, that public hearings are one of the quickest and easiest-to-administer methods of public participation. Furthermore, there is some evidence that a public participation programme may actually be the most efficient and cost-effective way of making decisions. The public may identify some unforeseen consequences which would have delayed or prevented the proposed plan (Thayer, 1971).

Dr. Solandt sees another source of manipulation during public hearings — by vested interests within the public:

> As a result of my experience during the two series of hearings, I feel that . . . the public hearing mechanism may be evolving into an institutional structure by means of which a minority can short-circuit the established mechanisms of democracy and achieve its own ends without the opposition ever being mobilized or heard.

Dr. Solandt made this comment in response to the concept of participatory democracy as an expansion and refinement of the democratic process. The concept may not be unsound; rather, the fault may be with the public hearing as a method of democratic participation. As one government sociologist (Vindasius, 1974) has stated:

> It is not the public hearing approach that is wrong, rather it is the way it has been used. A public hearing would be more appropriate after a good information programme has been underway for some time, supplemented by a series of workshops and public meetings which enable the participants to discuss the issues and raise questions. At this stage, a hearing would be more meaningful to both the planners and the public since the latter would possess adequate information for presenting well-formulated briefs.

The end result of the public's involvement should be a decision which has taken account of public wishes. This is the true test of public participation. To clarify the different levels of participation, Arnstein (1969) has constructed a 'ladder' which consists of eight rungs, each corresponding to a progressively higher degree of citizens' power in determining the end product. Most public hearings would fall somewhere in the one-to-four range, which is low-to-middle on the participation scale. Arnstein's definition of rungs three and four seems to describe public hearings:

> When they are proffered by power-holders as the total extent of participation, citizens may indeed hear and be heard. But under these conditions they lack the power to insure that their views will be *heeded* by the powerful. When participation is restricted to these levels, there is no followthrough, no 'muscle', hence no assurance of changing the status quo.

This illustrates one of the major deficiencies of the hearing as a participatory device.

In a report on public participation in water resources planning, Glasser *et al.* (1975) evaluated twenty-three techniques which are often used in public participation programmes. As Table 8.1 illustrates, the various techniques were evaluated on the basis of their communication characteristics and their capability to deal with six resource education and public participation objectives. The categories chosen and the ratings given are subjective, based on the collective experience of the three authors The ratings are based on a simple set of numbers (1, 2 and 3) representing low, satisfactory and high degrees of achievement, respectively. For example, a rating of '2' for 'degree of user sophistication' for public hearings means that the audience requires a satisfactory level of technical knowledge in order to participate effectively at the hearing. A zero means 'none' or 'not at all'. A blank means not applicable.

The categories used by the authors are further defined (with comment) as follows: (i) 'Degree of public contact achieved' refers to the number of persons that the technique can reach; for example, a few people or a vast audience. (ii) 'The degree of impact on decision makers' assumes the ultimate decision-makers are not present. It does not evaluate whether the decision-makers are required to accept the public's input, but only the effect it may have on them: very little ('1') or significant ('3'). Thus, Arnstein's criterion for true public participation is not addressed. (iii) 'Degree of user sophistication' refers to the level of technical knowledge required by the audience. A '3' is given if the audience does not need to be literate. (iv) 'Ease of use and preparation' refers to the skill needed by agency personnel to implement the technique in a public involvement programme. Glasser *et al.* have rated 'little skill needed' as '1' and 'special training required' as '3', presumably because special training would result in an experienced leader, better able to involve the public. If the expertise were not available, however, an agency might wish to choose a technique rated as '1' which has been defined as 'low'. In this case, a technique which requires little skill would be an advantage. (v) 'Ability to respond to varied interests' refers to the degree to which the technique can deal with varying points of view. If it can respond to only a few needs, a '1' is given, if many needs, a '3'. (vi) 'Degree of two-way communication' refers to the possibility for dialogue between the planner and the public.

The objectives of resource education and public participation (the second major category) are not explained by the authors, and seem to be quite straightforward.

These ratings were made in the context of a water resource agency and would not necessarily apply to other situations; for example, a public participation programme in an urban renewal project. The authors suggest that a variety of techniques be used together for the specific information and participation needs of the people. Different techniques are more suitable at different stages in the public participation process. For example, any of the small group meetings (Group B) would be appropriate for identifying alternative solutions, whereas the community interaction techniques (Group E) would be better for evaluating the plan after it has been implemented. Thus, the decision to use any of these techniques depends

Table 8.1. Capabilities of public participation techniques for communicating and education/participation

Techniques for communicating and involving the public	Degree of public contact achieved	Degree of impact on decision-makers	Degree of user sophistication	Ease of use and preparation	Ability to respond to varied interests	Degree of two-way communication	Inform/educate	Identify problems and values	Get ideas/solve problems	Feedback	Resolve conflict/ research consensus	Implement solutions
Group A – Large group meetings												
1 – Public hearings	2	1	2	2	0	0	1	2		1		
2 – Public meetings	2	1	2	2	0	1	1	2		1		
Group B – Small group meetings												
3 – Presentations to community groups	1	3	2	2	3	3	2	2	2	2		
4 – Site visits	1	2	3	2	2	3	2	3		2		
5 – Advisory body	1	3	1	2	3	3	3	3	3	3	2	
6 – Task force	1	1	1	2	2	3		3	2	3	2	
7 – Role playing exercises	1	1	2	3	2	3	3	3	3		2	
8 – Values clarification exercises	1	1	2	3	2	3	2	3	3		2	
9 – Workshops	1	1	1	2	3	3	2	3	3	2	2	2
10 – Delphi exercises	2	3	2	3	3	3	1	2		3	3	3

Group C – Organizational approaches

Item										
11 – Regional and/or local offices	3	2	3	2	1	2	2	3	3	2
12 – Citizen representation on policy boards	2	2	3	2	2	3	2	2	1	3
13 – Ombudsman and community advocate		2	3	2	2	2	3	3	3	2
14 – Public interest centre	2		2		2	1	2	3	3	1

Group D – Media

Item										
15 – Information pamphlets, brochures, and summary reports					1	1	1	2	2	1
16 – Slide and film presentations			3		2	1	1	3	3	2
17 – Tape recorded information network			2	2	2	2	2	2	3	2
18 – Radio talk shows			1		2	3	3	1	3	3
19 – Press releases and news letters					1	1	1	2	2	3

Group E – Community interaction

Item										
20 – Response to public inquiries					1	2	2	1	1	1
21 – Attitude surveys – mailed, telephone and personal interviews	3	2	3		2	3	3	3	3	2

Group F – Legal mechanisms

Item										
22 – Citizen suits	3	3	3	3	1	2	2	3	1	3
23 – Environmental impact review statement	2	3	3	3	2	3	3	1	1	1

on the stage of the public participation process and the weight that the agency itself gives to the various categories. Therefore the agency would choose techniques which best suit its own needs and goals.

From Table 8.1, it can be seen that public hearings are not rated very highly. Two of the six communication characteristics have been given a zero, and three of the education and participation objectives are not met.

Using Glasser's framework, and keeping in mind the other comments which have been made about public hearings in this section, the public hearings of a particular agency will be examined. The International Joint Commission has been chosen as a case study for this exercise. For the most part, only those aspects of the Commission's hearings which are common to all public hearings will be discussed, so that generalized comments can be made.

The International Joint Commission

The International Joint Commission (IJC) is a joint Canadian-American institution which has a mixture of quasi-judicial, investigative, advisory and monitoring functions. Created as a result of the Boundary Waters Treaty of 1909, its purpose is, broadly, to prevent disputes regarding the use of boundary waters and to make provision for adjustment and settlement of questions that may arise along the common frontier. The border between Canada and the United States is 5525 miles long, and more than two-fifths of this is water, including the Great Lakes and St. Lawrence River system. The Commission's responsibilities include not only boundary waters but also rivers which cross the boundary. Thus, the Commission has a large area of jurisdiction and, throughout the years, it has played an important role in continuing the peaceful relations between the two countries (Bloomfield & Fitzgerald, 1958).

The Commission consists of six Commissioners, three from Canada and three from the United States. They are not appointed to serve national interests; rather, they are appointed to act as a single unit. Impartiality has been one of the Commission's strong points and, in its whole history (which dates from 1912), there have been only three instances, out of more than ninety cases, upon which the Commissioners have been divided of have failed to reach an agreement (Ross, 1974).

Under the 1909 Treaty, there are two major roles for the Commission. The first (quasi-judicial) role involves the approving or withholding approval of any use, obstruction, or diversion of boundary waters on either side of the border which would affect the natural level or flow on the other side *or* any obstructions in transboundary rivers which would raise the level in the upstream country. Approvals in this category have included diversion of water at Sault Ste. Marie for power generation, and works for the development of power in the international section of the St. Lawrence River. The second major role of the Commission, and one which is much more flexible, is that of investigation and subsequent recommendation to the two governments. Under Article IX of the Treaty, either government may refer to the Commission any question or matter of difference arising between them involving the rights, obligations or interests of either in relation to the other, or to the inhabitants of the other, along the common frontier. On receipt of such a question (called a Reference), the Commission appoints an international Board to investigate the problem. Some examples of past References are the development of the water resources of the Pembina River, preservation and enhancement of the American Falls, and air pollution in the Detroit—Windsor and Port Huron—Sarnia areas.

Article XII of the Treaty provided that 'all parties interested therein [i.e. in any inquiry or matter within IJC jurisdiction] shall be given convenient opportunity to be heard'. Thus, some sixty years ago, the IJC became one of the earliest agencies to conduct public hearings, and these provided 'a degree of public participation opportunities ... that, in a binational forum was unique for its time'.[2] Public hearings are held in the locality which is affected by the problem under study, usually at the beginning of a study, sometimes in the middle, and always at its completion. They are held in locations on both sides of the border.

In the early years of its history, the Commission's primary function was the processing of applications for projects involving private parties or, at most, very local interests (Canada—United States University Seminar, 1971—72). The early References were engineering or technical questions which did not seem to arouse widespread interest on the part of the general public. Hearings were held, but these were often poorly attended by the general public, and they did not receive wide coverage by the press.

In recent years, however, there has been an increase in the public's interest in the IJC, a cause and effect of fuller media coverage. This is partly a manifestation of the trends described elsewhere in this volume: disillusionment with traditional institutional and political structures, dissatisfaction with expanding bureaucracies, rising educational levels, the questioning of the concept of progress as measured by economic growth, and increasing concern about the environment. The demands for public participation and the growing environmental movement have affected every resource management agency. Actually, one of the major studies undertaken by the IJC may have contributed to the growth of the environmental movement. In 1969, two international boards made a final report to the IJC based on their investigation of water pollution in the lower Great Lakes. The report received a considerable amount of publicity, as did the subsequent public hearings conducted by the IJC in early 1970 to receive public reaction to the report. One of the recommendations of the report, that a programme of phosphorus control be implemented, initiated a furious debate between environmentalists and detergent manufacturers. Out of this study, and the resultant IJC report and recommendations to the governments, came the signing of the Canada—United States Great Lakes Water Quality Agreement on 15 April 1972. This brought the Commission more into the public spotlight than it had ever been before.

In addition to the water quality studies, the IJC was concurrently studying other quite controversial subjects. Two studies which received considerable publicity dealt with the environmental and ecological consequences of flooding a transboundary river valley, and the feasibility and desirability of further regulations of the water levels on the Great Lakes. With respect to this latter study, which the two governments had requested in 1964 as a response to very low lake levels, the International Great Lakes Levels Board presented both an interim and a final report in 1973, at a period of peak levels. The preliminary hearings held by the IJC in May 1965 had been poorly attended by the general public. During the four hearings, there had been fifty-nine written or oral submissions; two-thirds of these represented government departments or agencies, and only one-quarter were from individuals or local organizations (Swanson, 1971). In contrast, the hearings in May and June 1973, which discussed the Board's interim report, were well attended (e.g. approximately 400 people attended the Rochester, New York hearing), and some heated exchanges took place. This time, property owners were affected by the high water levels, and many of them held the IJC responsible for the damage occurring to their property.

In summary, the International Joint Commission is a unique agency with a long tradition of studying water-related and other problems along the Canada–United States boundary. Although it is gradually introducing new methods of communication with the public (e.g. a newsletter in the Great Lakes area, descriptive brochures and an annual report on its activities), its major (formal) communication link with the public is still the public hearing. For these reasons, it presents a useful opportunity to evaluate public hearings as a technique of participation.

A report evaluating the IJC public hearings, including recommendations, was prepared by Sinclair (1974). This report was based on perusal of the verbatim transcripts of the hearings, discussion with various persons in the field, personal observation at many of the hearings, and the results of a questionnaire sent to participants at three sets of hearings in 1973. The questionnaire, which asked about various aspects of the hearing and the respondent's satisfaction with these, was returned by 231 participants (a 55 per cent response rate).

An Evaluation of the IJC Experience with Public Hearings

The adequacy of the IJC hearings as a technique of public involvement can be considered in terms of the categories outlined in Table 8.1 by Glasser *et al*. The six 'Communication Characteristics' are discussed first.

Degree of Public Contact Achieved

The public hearing can reach a fairly large audience, by means of its publicity techniques through the mass media. Space is often supplied for several hundred people at IJC hearings. To announce the hearing, an official notice must be placed 'once each week for three successive weeks in two newspapers, published one in each country and circulated in or near the localities which, in the opinion of the Commission, are most likely to be interested in the subject matter of the reference' (IJC Rules of Procedure). In practice, the notice gets much wider circulation, being sent to other appropriate newspapers and to a variety of community groups, conservation groups, industries, government agencies, individuals, etc. A general

Table 8.2. Ranking of various aspects of the IJC public hearings by questionnaire respondents

	Very good	Good	Neutral	Poor	Very poor	Mean rank
Advance Publicity						
Amount of advance publicity	8.8% (19)	33.5% (72)	20.5% (44)	17.2% (37)	20.0% (43)	3.06 3.05
Kind (type) of notice	6.8% (14)	33.7% (69)	25.9% (53)	15.1 (31)	18.5% (38)	
Amount of time before hearing	10.1% (21)	34.1% (71)	17.8% (37)	17.3% (36)	20.7% (43)	3.04
Format (general organization)	13.5% (28)	55.5% (117)	16.1% (34)	11.4% (24)	3.3% (7)	2.35
Time (e.g. 9:30 a.m.)	19.6% (42)	44.4% (95)	16.8% (36)	13.1% (28)	6.1% (13)	2.42
Day (e.g. Thursday)	13.5% (28)	42.0% (87)	29.5% (61)	11.6% (24)	3.4% (7)	2.49
Location (e.g. school auditorium)	30.0% (65)	42.4% (92)	10.6% (23)	8.3% (18)	8.8% (19)	2.23

Note: The numbers in brackets refer to the number of respondents answering each question. Total N = 231.
Headings for Table 8.1.

press release is usually sent out to announce the set of hearings. For the first time, for the fall 1974 hearings on the final Great Lakes levels report, paid announcements on radio and television were made and interviews were held with the local press. Yet, in spite of the effort made to publicize the hearing, respondents to the questionnaire ranked the advance publicity the weakest aspect of the public hearings (see Table 8.2).

There are several reasons for this. The notice in the newspaper is an 'official' one, placed in the legal section of the newspaper. The print is small, and the wording very formal, so that it does not attract much attention. Secondly, major groups such as area planning commissions and district municipalities are often omitted in the mailing list. However, publicizing an event seems to be a perennial problem. Dr. Solandt found the same difficulty:

> . . . In spite of all this publicity [newspapers, radio, even a mass mailing] citizens continued to appear at the hearings complaining that they had not known that planning for the transmission line was going on.

The IJC faces the same problems, complicated by two national jurisdictions and, often, a wide geographical area. The onus appears to fall both on the agency to supply free and open access to information and on the public to be informed. Public participation implies a commitment and a sense of responsibility for all concerned.

Attendance at the IJC hearings varies according to the issue, the location, the time, the day, the weather, etc. Sometimes the room is filled to overflowing, while at other times, there is only a handful of attendees. Yet there is no doubt that the audience at a hearing is not representative of the general public. Sills (1975) and others (Buttel & Flinn, 1974; Kohl, 1975) have pointed out that the environmental movement is somewhat elitist; in fact, environmental concerns, which have been an important consideration in recent IJC studies, are often in the nature of class issues. Similarly, many of those involved in public participation programmes have a relatively high socio-economic status. The respondents who answered the questionnaire about the hearings were no exception: 79 per cent had a family income of over $10,000 per year, as compared to a Canadian national figure of 19.2 per cent, (Statistics Canada, 1971 Census) and more than half (56 per cent) earned over $15,000 (comparative Canadian figure: 6.0 per cent).[3] Of the 21 per cent earning less than $10,000, many were retirees and students. Similarly, educational levels were high, and 92.3 per cent of the respondents had at least high school graduation, as compared to the national figure of 30.4 per cent.[4] Also, two-thirds of the sample (67 per cent) were employed in the professional or business categories. Also, as might be expected, they were more active: almost half of the sample were members of environmental groups. Similarly, 47 per cent had, at some time, complained to a water management agency about a specific problem at least once; and many, much more often.

The implication of this socio-economic analysis of attendees at the hearing is that a representative audience is not in attendance. This remains a basic problem of all public participation techniques: how to identify the relevant public bodies and how to involve them effectively. A public hearing does not try to 'involve' the public in the way that other techniques do (e.g. workshops, citizen advisory groups), but it *is* a goal to make the event of the hearing widely known and, hence, open to everyone. This is a fundamental problem of publicizing a hearing across a broad spectrum of public interests and often a wide geographic region. Then having informed the public, a further problem is accounting for the unrepresented viewpoints; i.e. non-respondent bias. This has yet to be resolved by the IJC.

Degree of Impact on Decision-makers

It is the practice of all six Commissioners to attend the public hearings. By virtue of their personal attendance then, at least the possibility exists for some impact to be made. The Commissioners listen to every oral submission and often ask questions of the 'witness' for clarification or further information. It is possible, however, that written submissions do not receive as much attention, although they are included in the verbatim record.

The Commissioners are not the ultimate decision-makers, however, for matters referred to them by the governments for investigation. Although they do decide which recommendations they will make to the governments, they do not have the power to implement them. The ultimate decision-makers are far removed from the hearing, and it is very difficult to determine the effect on them of the briefs submitted there. Certainly, the IJC, as an institution, commands respect and its recommendations are always seriously considered by governments, if not always adopted. For a true evaluation of the impact of public input, however, there should be an examination of the briefs presented at the hearings and their relationship to the subsequent IJC report to the governments as well as to the governments' final decision. However, this is rarely done with any agency and its public hearings.

Degree of User Sophistication

Most of the IJC References are technical (e.g. water apportionments, pollution studies), and this was one reason for the relatively minor degree of public interest before the environmental movement gained momentum in the late 1960s. The IJC studies are usually broad in scope and there are a number of complex factors to be considered. For these reasons, the audience must be relatively technically oriented.

Copies of the report to be discussed are usually available (although sometimes difficult to procure), but these are often very lengthy documents (e.g. the International Great Lakes Levels Board report to the IJC was 293 pages, with seven separate appendices, one containing three volumes!). In such cases, however, the IJC often produces summary reports of the Board's main report, which are clear, concise accounts oriented to the layman. When respondents to the questionnaire were asked if there was any information they lacked when preparing their presentation, the affirmative answers (38 per cent) fell into the following three categories:

Some scientific or technical data (e.g. amount of water diverted into Lake Superior)	44% (32)
Unavailability of report or report available too late	33% (24)
Other, including format of meeting, agenda, information about the IJC	23% (17)
Total	(73) (38%)

In a formal public hearing, the audience must be more prepared and aware of the issue than for other public participation methods, which are less formal and allow for two-way communication. The purpose of the hearing is to receive opinions, views and information, so the 'burden of proof', so to speak, is on the audience. Furthermore, those who present submissions must be prepared for cross-examination. This can be a formidable experience for members of the public, particularly for those not accustomed to public speaking. One respondent to the questionnaire described it as 'a little like I was being cross-examined by lawyers who were attempting to shake my credibility'.

Ease of Use and Preparation

A public hearing requires relatively little skill to prepare and carry out, especially in the IJC's case, where public hearings have been conducted for more than sixty years. This is an advantage for the agency, since there is less time and effort expended. This is not to depreciate the time and effort which is needed to conduct a good public hearing, but it is less than that required by many other methods.

Ability to Respond to Varied Interests

Glasser *et al.* have given this characteristic a zero for public hearings, since the hearing format does not allow for response. A zero seems to be somewhat unfair, since, theoretically the purpose of the hearing is to invite as many interests as possible to appear. In the IJC case, varied interests are identified in the form of the different submissions but, as an 'impartial jury', the Commissioners do not try to resolve any conflicts, which is perhaps the intent of Glasser *et al.*'s category. A resolution may occur in the final report, but not at the hearing.

Degree of Two-way Communication

This characteristic has also received a zero, and this is one of the weakest aspects of the hearing method. Officially, there is to be no response from the Commissioners, since they are at the hearing to receive information and not to give it. The witness cannot ask questions of the Commissioners.

Yet this is also changing. The rigid practice of one-way communication is gradually loosening. The hearings now begin with an introduction by the Commission Chairman, followed by a brief summary of the study by its Chairman. The Commission Chairman may allow questions (to the study Chairman only) at the end of the hearing if there is enough time. Unfortunately, the size of the audience is an important determinant of the communication allowed. If the hearing is poorly attended, then the formality is lessened; the Chairman can accept questions, and he will ask for further comments from the audience. If there is an overflow attendance, however, there is a possibility that not everyone will be given the opportunity to speak, let alone ask questions.

There are many disadvantages to the practice of one-way communication. The audience can become very frustrated. A sincere quest for further information may be unrewarded and the value of the hearing for the public participant is negated. Similarly, a good relationship is not built up between the agency and the public.

A further disadvantage is that inaccurate statements may not be corrected in spite of the cross-examination by Commissioners referred to earlier. This can lead to incorrect reporting in the press and false impressions on the part of the audience. This is a serious deficiency from the standpoint of public information and, again, points out the inadequacy of using the formal hearing by itself as a method of public involvement.

The second major category discussed by Glasser *et al.* is the evaluation of

'Objectives of Education and Participation'. Such an evaluation should help to determine the extent to which the hearing can identify the problems, values and solutions as perceived by the public, and how far the hearings furnish a means of feedback. It should also provide an indication of the ways in which problems can be resolved.

(1) *Identify Problems and Values*. Of the six objectives listed by Glasser *et al.*, it is this first one which is closest to the official purpose of the IJC's public hearings. It particularly applies to preliminary hearings which occur before the actual study gets underway. For example, the press release which announced eight preliminary hearings in late 1972 stated that they were 'for the purpose of receiving information relevant to the subject matter of the studies'. For other hearings, the purpose is to receive reaction to a report.

But again, the problems and values identified are those of the attendees at the hearing. The Commissioners, or any hearing board, cannot evaluate how representative these are of the total public.

(2) *Inform/Educate*. The function of informing and educating is met to a minor degree. As mentioned above, there is often a summary report available for the public. This outlines the problem and the Board's findings. At the hearing, the Board Chairman will usually give a brief talk. In addition, there may be a question period, if time permits. The deficiency here, of course, is that the public is presented with a completed report and asked for comments. Public input has not been a continuous process during the course of the study, so the educational benefits are minimized.

(3) *Feedback*. Although Glasser *et al.* have given this objective a '1' (indicating a low degree of feedback), in the case of the IJC hearings and most others in Canada, there is no feedback. This is one of the weakest aspects of the public hearing process. A person presenting a brief receives no indicative response from the Commissioners and no communication about the final report to the two governments. This is quite frustrating for public hearing participants, given the interest they have shown in attending the hearing and the time and effort spent in preparing a brief.

(4) *Get Ideas/Solve Problems*; (5) *Resolve Conflict/Research Consensus*; (6) *Implement Solutions*. In the case of the IJC, neither the purpose of the hearing nor its format allow for accomplishment of the above three objectives. It is the Board's responsibility to advise the Commission on solutions to the problem, and they may, in the process, mediate conflict. (This is usually done without public input, but there are signs that this might be changing. For example, in 1973, the American Falls International Board published a brochure containing a detachable postcard questionnaire as one method of learning the public's view.) The final acceptance of the IJC's recommendations and their implementation, however, depend on the two governments.

There is another objective met, which is not indicated in Glasser *et al.*'s chart. This is the 'positive manipulation' function referred to by Estrin (1975). The incorporation of public participation techniques into a programme tends to build up public support for the agency and for the programme. This may be an important consideration for the IJC since the two governments are not bound to accept its recommendations. Thus, public pressure, which may develop as a result of the hearing and its attendant publicity, may prove most effective in getting legislation passed or governmental action taken in response to the IJC recommendations.

Conclusion: Implications for Theory and Practice

The public hearing is likely to remain as an important vehicle for public participation in Canada, at least for the next decade. It has legitimacy as a traditional mechanism; it is relatively easy for agencies to utilize; and it can reach a large audience. As more and more agencies and commissions accept the value of public participation, the hearing will continue to be used. As a technique of public involvement, it fits in more easily with the idea of 'representative democracy' (as opposed to 'participatory democracy'). It may be considered almost as a form of plebiscite – a chance to express an opinion for or against a proposal.

There is evidence that the public hearing is becoming less formal. Certainly this has been happening to IJC hearings. There is now more two-way communication, a layman's summary report, and less emphasis on requiring the thirty copies of a written submission which are asked for in the IJC official notice. Many other agencies are now holding public meetings, rather than hearings. The notices for these are often eye-catching, rather than legalistic, and they are published widely.

In the past year, there have been several innovations in public hearing procedures of Canadian government agencies. The most publicized has been the Mackenzie Valley pipeline hearings, described above. Another is the proposed set of hearings into the long-range planning of Ontario's electrical power system. An independent commission of inquiry has been established to consider a wide range of social, environmental and economic factors. The Ontario government, as an experiment in public involvement, is, for the first time, providing funding for potential participants at the hearings.

Yet the many negative aspects of public hearings must not be overlooked. Their formality, 'one-shot' approach, lack of good two-way communication, lack of a representative audience – all these factors lessen their effectiveness as a technique of public involvement. As one technique used in a broader programme of public participation, it has merit, but used by itself, it is clearly inadequate.

In order to develop a good public involvement programme, the hearing should be used in conjunction with one or more of the techniques listed in Table 8.1. For example, to define the problem initially, a public meeting could be held to identify citizen interest in a programme and to introduce the concept to the community. As the study progresses, and alternative solutions are considered, small group meetings would be useful. Perhaps the agency might form a citizens' advisory group, which would aid in designing the final plan. A public hearing might be held at this stage to receive any comments to the proposed plan. Used in this manner, as one of the techniques in the evolutionary public participation process, a public hearing can perform a useful function.

Notes

1. The following categorization is adapted from: David Estrin, 24—25 June 1975, 'Public Hearings: Some Comments on their Use and Effectiveness', presented at the IJC Public Participation Workshop, Ann Arbor, Michigan.
2. Letter to Patricia A. Bonner from Maxwell Cohen, Chairman, IJC, Canadian Section, dated 22 May 1975.
3. The results from the questionnaire and the Statistics Canada figures are not completely comparable. The former is given in 1973 dollars, the latter in 1970 dollars. Respondents to the questionnaire were asked to give total family income, and the Statistics Canada figures refer to the income of the head of the household. (Table 76, Catalogue 93—711, Volume II, Part 1, Information Canada, Ottawa, Ontario, February 1975.)
4. This figure is given for the total population, fifteen years and over. (Table 9, Catalogue 94—763, Volume III, Part 6, Information Canada, July 1975). It corresponds to the questionnaire population, since very few, if any, less than fourteen-year-olds appeared.

References

Arnstein, Sherry R., 1969. 'A Ladder of Citizen Participation', *Journal of the American Institute of Planners*, **35** (4), 216—224.

Bloomfield, L. M. & G. F. Fitzgerald, 1958. *Boundary Waters Problems: Canada and the United States*,Toronto: The Carswell Company Limited.

Buttel, Frederick H. & William L. Flinn, 1974. 'The Structure of Support for the Environmental Movement, 1968—1970', *Rural Sociology*, **39** (1), 56—69.

Canada—United States University Seminar 1971—1972. 'A Proposal for Improving the Management of the Great Lakes of the United States and Canada', January 1973.

Estrin, David, 1975. 'Public Hearings: Some Comments on their Use and Effectiveness', presented at the International Joint Commission Public Participation Workshop, Ann Arbor, Michigan, 24—25 June.

Glasser, Roslyn, Dale Manty & Gerald Nehman, 1975. 'Public Participation in Water Resources Planning', presented to the International Water Resources Association (UNESCO), Paris and Strasbourg, France, 24—29 March.

Kohl, Daniel H., 1975. 'The Environmental Movement: What Might it Be?' *Natural Resources Journal*, **15** (2), 327—351.

Ross, C. R., Commissioner, U.S. Section, 1974. 'The International Joint Commission — United States and Canada', presented at the American Society of International Law Panel, Washington, D.C., 27 April.

Sills, David L., 1975. 'The Environmental Movement and Its Critics', *Human Ecology*, **3** (1), 1—41.

Sinclair, M., 1974. 'An Evaluation of the IJC Public Hearings', presented to the International Joint Commission, September.

Solandt, O. M., 1975. *Report of the Solandt Commission: A Public Inquiry into the Transmission of Power between Lennox and Oshawa*. Toronto, Ontario.

Swanson, Diane, 1971. 'Public Perceptions and Resources Planning', in W. R. Derrick Sewell & Ian Burton (eds.), *Perceptions and Attitudes in Resources Management*, Resource Paper #2, Policy Research and Coordination Branch, Department of Energy, Mines and Resources, Ottawa: Information Canada.

Thayer, Frederick C., 1971. *Participation and Liberal Democratic Government*, Toronto: Queen's Printer.

Treaty Between the United States and Great Britain Relating to Boundary Waters, and Questions Arising Between the United States and Canada, signed 11 January 1909, Washington, D.C.

Vindasius, Dana, 1974. *Public Participation Techniques and Methodologies: A Resume*, Social Science Series No. 12, Inland Waters Directorate, Water Planning and Management Branch, Department of Environment, Ottawa, Ontario.

9

Public Participation in Environmental Decision-making: Substance or Illusion?

Helen M. Ingram and Scott J. Ullery

Introduction

The participation of new, environmentally oriented public participants in decision-making has two facets, one procedural and the other substantive. The procedural aspect of participation entails giving interested public participants an opportunity to air their views and perhaps creating for them the illusion of substantive impact. Even if their advice is rejected, participants may feel they have at least had their day in court and are more likely to accept policy decisions. Procedural participation is a precondition for substantive participation, which, of course, is more demanding because it is measured by the extent to which the public actually affects policy. It requires information channels in decision-making to be tuned so that the public can become an important contributor to the information upon which policy choices are made.

The National Environmental Policy Act of 1969 (NEPA),[1] has established procedures for collecting environmental information with the ultimate objective of actually reducing the destructiveness of decisions affecting the environment. Federal agencies proposing actions with substantial impacts upon the environment are required by Section 102 of the Act to prepare detailed environmental impact statements and make them available for interagency and public comment. The process of preparation and review, an entirely new form of federal interaction, was to link agencies making proposals which might previously have ignored information about environmental impacts with environmentally sensitive citizens and other agencies representing environmental points of view.

The purpose of this chapter is to assess the extent to which procedural rules and regulations such as those prepared under NEPA actually alter the flow of information upon which decisions are based. First, it examines NEPA procedures to identify the opportunities for developing new channels of information. Second, it identifies the factors which can be expected to structure and restrain the flow of information. Finally, it evaluates the changes which have actually occurred in the channels of information during the years of NEPA's implementation.

The National Environmental Policy Act of 1969

NEPA sets forth some bold goals in its statement of policy. The Act declares that it is the continuing policy of the federal government to create and maintain conditions under which man and nature can exist in productive harmony. Administrative agencies are directed, to the fullest extent possible, to interpret policies, regulations and public laws in accordance with NEPA's goals, and to add environmental impact to the traditional criteria by which agencies evaluate their actions.

The major techniques which Congress has chosen to assure federal agency implementation of these ambitious objectives (referred to as 'action forcing' by their designers) are essentially procedural requirements, which do not set specific performance standards nor prohibit environmentally detrimental activities. The most important of the procedures is the requirement that federal agencies prepare a detailed environmental impact statement to accompany 'proposals for legislation and other major actions significantly affecting the quality of the human environment'.[2] In preparing impact statements agencies are directed to consider environmental factors such as the environmental impact of the proposed action, any unavoidable environmental damage, alternatives to the proposed action, the relationship between local short-term uses of man's environment and the maintenance and enhancement of long-term productivity, and any irreversible commitments of resources involved in the proposed action. NEPA further provides that the impact statement should be subjected at various stages in its preparation to review by federal, state and local agencies and should be made available to the President, the Council on Environment Quality (CEQ), and the public.

The general procedural requirements of the Act have been translated into a timetable of specific steps to be taken by agencies in accordance with guidelines established by the CEQ. These steps are identified in column 1 of Figure 9.1. The guidelines provide that agencies must prepare a draft statement to be circulated to other agencies and to the public for review and comment at least ninety days before an action may begin. The Environmental Protection Agency (EPA), which has jurisdiction over most forms of environmental pollution, has a special procedural resposibility to comment on actions affecting its areas of jurisdiction.

An agency must consider the comments it receives and formulate a final statement which is responsive to these comments. Under the Act CEQ receives the final statement. Although it has no power to reject a statement or forbid a proposed action, presumably CEQ can react either to the contents of the statement or to the procedure followed. A final extraordinary procedure implied by NEPA is the option which environmental litigants may exercise for court review.

Associated with each of the procedures outlined in Figure 9.1 are possibilities for the creation of communications channels, set out in column 2. Two-way communication is intended. In gathering data necessary to prepare detailed statements, agencies are expected to call upon the skill of multi-disciplinary experts and become sensitized to environmental impacts. The availability of impact statements which spell out the costs of proposed actions in environmental terms is

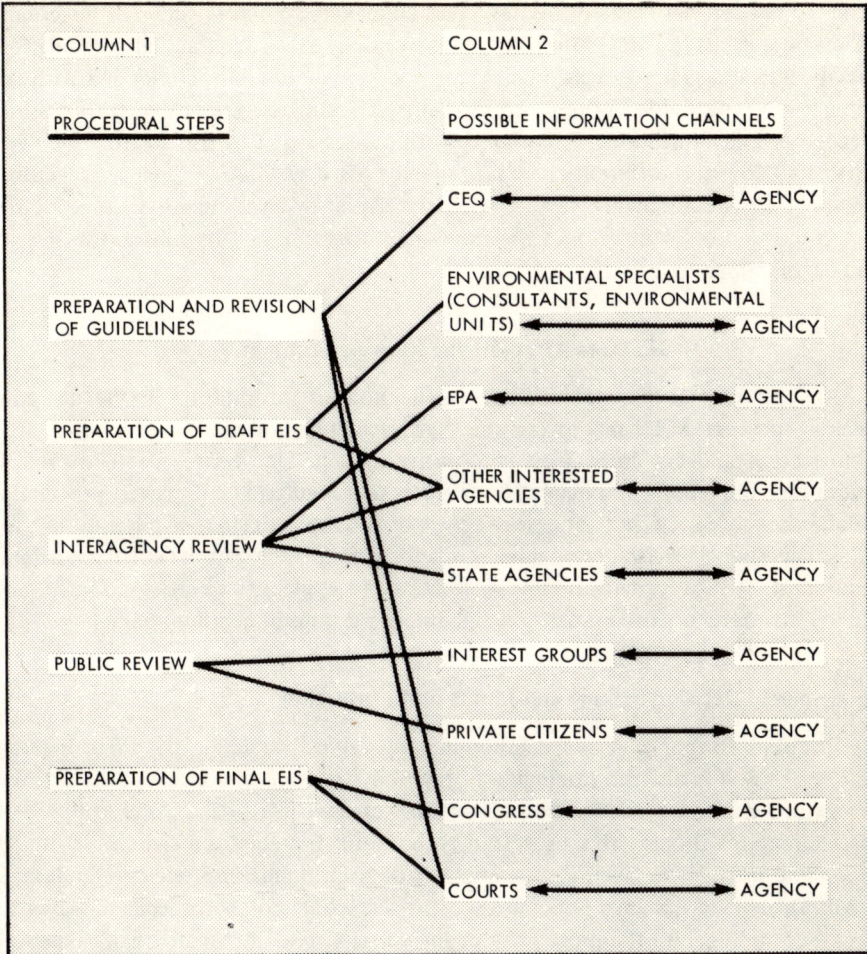

Figure 9.1 Procedural requirements of NEPA and associated possible information channels

intended to activate environmental groups and environmentally oriented agencies. The review and comments of these interests are meant to burden proposals threatening severe environmental impacts in the competition with other, less damaging, investments of federal funds and energy. The sponsoring agency is expected to modify the proposal or, in severe cases, to drop it. Agencies preparing environmental statements are to be kept honest by the interagency review process and, ultimately, by the threat of a court suit if impacts are ignored or slighted in the document (Dreyfus & Ingram, 1976).

The central question in this article is whether the basic intent of NEPA has been fulfilled: i.e. have the new procedural requirements substantively altered the communication networks of agency decision-makers so that fewer environmentally damaging decisions are made? In other words, has environmental information, newly introduced into decision-making processes successfully contended with the numerous expected structures and restraints effecting its generation, transmission, reception and utilization? To assess the effectiveness of new information we need first to know the differential impact of NEPA's procedures on agency decision-making. In the following section of this chapter we will identify some of the important factors which affect the flow of information and its substantive impact on decision-making.

Factors Affecting the Flow of Information

Any attempt to expand or improve the flow of information in the decision-making process will have to contend with a number of factors which structure information and can impede its substantive impact. One technique to overcome these impediments is to change formal rules and regulations; however, procedural change is necessary but not sufficient to produce substantive alterations. An understanding of the factors which work to maintain the gap between procedural and substantive information flow is necessary to explain the participation of new environmentally oriented citizens public interest groups in decision-making.

Incremental Decision-making and Limits on Information

Idealized formulations of decision-making typically include the identification and ranking of goals, the cataloging of methods for achieving those goals, and the investigation of possible consequences of seeking these goals. As a counsel of perfection this process this process may be both desirable and defensible, but it does not provide an accurate description of decision-making reality (Lindblom, 1968; Dror, 1968). Such a policy-making process would compel a decision-maker to seek out and analyse the great mass of information relevant to the many issues at hand. If such a decision-making strategy could be followed, the result would most probably be protracted indecision, if not complete confusion. Somehow the decision must be cut down to size.

The decision-making strategy that Braybrooke and Lindblom (1963) call 'disjointed incrementalism' is a better approximation of the real world. The information needs of this strategy are more realistically limited. Only policies which differ incrementally from the status quo are seriously considered, and, in consequence, decision-makers focus upon a quite limited number of alternatives in making choices. Further, not all the consequences of any alternative are, in fact, taken into account. There is a tendency among decision-makers to concentrate on the direct and immediate effects of decisions and to discount the remote, the imponderable, the intangible and the poorly understood. The practical decision-making strategy dictates that a decision-maker attend to the short-run consequences in the hope that the long run will take care of itself — or that some other decision-maker in another setting will take care of it.

The Agenda

The agenda, i.e. the class of decisions with which decision-makers are occupied and for which some amount of information is required, is an important factor which bears on the relative difficulty of introducing a new item, such as the environment, into the flow of information. The intent of NEPA was to place environmental quality on the agenda of every federal agency whose actions might have significant impact. While a new agenda item like the environment may not at first be fully accepted, at least it cannot be totally ignored if even a very minimal procedural compliance is mandatory. From the perspective of altering the flow of information the initial change must be to stop neglect.

Of course, any gathering of new information as a result of the addition of a new agenda item will not by itself necessarily produce a change in agency actions. Arrow (1974) has pointed out the distinction between 'experimental' decisions, which are instrumental determinations to collect information, and 'terminal' decisions, which determine the actual disposition of benefits and costs. If the decision-maker's perception of a new agenda item is one of uncertainty regarding its consistency with the established agenda, it will be dealt with experimentally. Procedures will be established to collect information, but mechanisms for integrating this information into substantive decision-making will remain undeveloped. The information may be adequate for substantive needs, but, nevertheless, will probably be kept separate from the well-established substantive agenda. However wide the gap between procedure and substance may be, experimental decisions may provide the impetus for the eventual substantive integration of a new item into the traditional agenda. The presence of obviously relevant but disregarded information will eventually come to bother the decision-makers, who may eventually be pressed to explain why they ignored the additional information.

Character of Communication Networks

Any decision-making system has a network of communication channels that services it with information. Channels of communication are the various means by which information is delivered: telephone calls, letters, public hearings, meetings, research reports. The channel which is chosen may be more or less suited to procedural or substantive communication. The need to gather information for agenda items which are regarded as experimental may be satisfied through relatively formal channels, such as research reports and public hearings. Procedural channels tend to be easily established and easily ignored. Terminal decisions require the additional kinds of information that are easily transmitted in less formal face-to-face communication. The type of channel utilized in terminal decisions must facilitate feedback. That is, an immediate response is communicated for each transfer of information. Deutsch (1966) has argued that a communication network in which feedback occurs sets in motion a learning process which in turn modifies subsequent behaviour.

With the introduction of a new item to the agenda decision-makers have a choice of which new channels of information to open. Channels vary in the time, effort and skill required for their use. The participation of new public interest groups is likely to occur initially through low-cost channels because there is a reluctance to invest scarce resources towards uncertain results. Agencies will be tentative in developing channels which may carry information difficult to digest. They are likely to rely as much as possible on existing channels to gather the required information.

Taken together, communication channels form a network of linkages among participants which traces patterns of influence. The structure of the patterns is closely related to the degree of a decision-maker's receptivity to new information. In general, when the points in the network are dispersed and decision-making is decentralized and non-hierarchical, there will be greater receptivity to new information. While the dispersion of administrative units and information channels may encourage the captivity of agencies by small clientele groups at the expense of public responsiveness, it can also enliven discussion within an agency and can link authority with knowledge. In a centralized system subordinates who possess a depth of knowledge in a particular area often find themselves overruled by superiors who lack the necessary information. Thus, centralization may aggravate the gap between information and power (Rourke, 1969).

Resources

Information is costly. The generation of information demands the investment of resources which must sometimes be diverted from other activities. Consequently, the development of new information channels in a network is partly dependent upon uncommitted or reassignable resources (Deutsch, 1966).

Differences in the substantive learning capacity of decision-makers is a function of the resources they possess. An organization can, with an adequate budget, competent staff and time, alter its utilization of information. The process of adjusting to new sources of information is typically slow. Decision-makers repeatedly encounter troublesome opposition and conflict and seek ways to deal with negative feedback. Decisions are altered marginally and tentatively as the decision-maker tests for a more positive response. New channels of communication are established through numerous incremental adjustments.

The bureaucratic system is conservative, and the use of organizational resources in a new way seems risky and threatening. The costs of procedural decisions simply to collect information are much lower than substantive responsiveness, which requires material resources, structural changes and intellectual resources. For this reason an agency may conceal a lack of new substance by elaborate procedures (Thompson, 1969).

One way of providing the necessary resources for the receipt of new information within an organization is to create a new unit which is segregated from the rest of the organization. Such a structural change itself requires resources; furthermore, to have substantive impact the new unit must create new communications channels with the decision-makers. To accomplish this it must overcome its disadvantage of isolation.

Being able to speak with one voice is an important resource. The environmental movement has suffered from fragmentation and internal division. The number of groups has been growing and they differ in their conception of environmental quality. A unified strategy, even on limited specific issues, is often impossible for them to agree upon and execute. Very often environmental groups are competing for another important resource, membership. A great deal of the energy and resources of environmental groups has been ploughed back into the organizations in membership and fund-raising drives. Consequently, environmental groups have often not had the uncommitted resources necessary to foster new communications channels with agencies.

A staff with a sufficient budget and appropriate expertise is fundamental to the generation of information. Much of the debate on issues such as nuclear reactor safety, thermal pollution, and air and water quality measurements takes place in heavily technical terms. Without specialized knowledge an organization cannot substantiate an independent position or even interpret data from the outside. Sometimes the amount of expertise in the private sector may equal or outweigh that of the government. In such cases the private sector can use its special skills as a source of influence over public policy.

Finally, it must be pointed out again that even if all of the necessary physical resources for transmitting and receiving new information are present they do not necessarily result in its utilization. Innovations cannot be effected without the resource of individual spontaneity and creativity which is so necessary for breaking old habits and established patterns.

Where the Information Comes From and Who Listens

The transmission and reception of information is very much affected by the participants' perceptions of each other. In any information network the flow of information is structured by a set of values, or relative preferences and priorities in the reception, screening and routing of information. Values facilitate the flow of a certain class of messages and block out others, thus affecting what information is generated, transmitted and received.

The background and experience of a decision-maker screens receptivity in favour of disciplines and facts with which the decision-maker feels familiar and comfortable, and the recruitment patterns of an agency affect its ability to collect and assimilate data. The dominance of engineers in federal construction agencies has affected their bias towards construction solutions and their lack of receptivity to environmental concerns. In recognition of the value positions associated with particular disciplines, NEPA has mandated an interdisciplinary approach to the preparation of impact statements. Given the past pattern of recruitment in most agencies, this approach is unlikely to be achieved without the selective hiring of ecologists and other life scientists at high ranks. Rourke (1969) observes that the tendency to bureaucratic conservatism in some cases can be mitigated by lateral recruitment from outside and by periodic training and retraining.

The source of information, evaluated in terms of the decision-maker's goals and interests, is a factor in determining its receipt and consideration. A decision-maker cannot simply make judgements, but must also build support for decisions. A decision-maker is most apt to listen to information coming from the constituency upon which he depends for continuing support. Agencies relate particularly to communications flowing from the groups served by agency programme – groups which ordinarily assist the protection or extension of the agency's authority, budget and jurisdiction.

Sources of information which are not supporters of decision-makers, but which hold a recognized veto position over actions, are also heeded. In actual fact, regulated groups often command a veto position over the governmental agencies assigned the task of regulating them. In the long run, enforcement of regulation depends upon voluntary compliance. Because of physical and political constraints, regulators cannot take punitive actions against every violator of standards if their number is large. Consequently, the setting of standards, and the choice of which violators to prosecute for non-compliance, depends upon what it is reasonable to expect the regulated industry to do, and what the adverse consequences would be if the industry were prevented, through enforcement action, from carrying on its trade.

Legislatures and courts often hold veto positions over agencies because they define legal authority and control funding. Groups and individuals who are listened to by legislators and judges are also likely to find agencies receptive even when there is no established clientele relationship.

Whether information is transmitted or not depends upon its expected impact. Organizations will transmit information to decision-makers when they believe it will get a hearing. The crucial decision points for stopping a dam or highway in the interests of environmental quality have not been on the local level, where development benefits have their strongest appeal, or within agencies whose missions involve public works. Instead, they have rested with the national political leaders, including members of Congress, who have been open to conservationist and environmentalist persuasion. As a result, opposition interests which fail to show up at agency hearings have a habit of surfacing later when projects reach a national decision-making arena. Any organisation is likely to place a higher value on the substantive, rather than the procedural, impact of information. When a group comes to believe that its testimony seldom affects decisions, it is likely to be reluctant to attend hearings, prepare reviews, or otherwise invest in the creation and transmission of information. An interest group or an agency will react first to what it perceives as imminent and direct effects upon its interests and will react later, and with less effort, to questions with an indirect and remote impact. The direct impact of a dam, highway or power plant is felt in jobs, growth and profit, while environmental implications are less immediate and more difficult to predict.

Content of Information

What information actually says affects whether or not it will be communicated. A type of information which has not been heard before by agencies is useless unless its relation to familiar types is determined. Agencies seek out information which supports specific decisions and they are particularly receptive to categories of information which justify and legitimize their decision-making process. Information amenable to quantification and cost-benefit analysis is especially favoured. The ratio of benefits to costs provides a rationale for not pursuing certain projects while at the same time this economic tool is flexible enough to supply a justification to projects which have strong support. As Marshall (1964) put it, 'one of the principal uses of benefit/cost analysis is to clothe politically desirable projects in the fig leaf of economic respectability. Environmental information must be related to and integ-¬ated with economic evaluation if this to be used comfortably by agencies.

Decision-makers also have a strong preference for kinds of information which can be applied to politically viable solutions. Schooler (1970) has pointed out that physical technologies produced by the physical, medical, biological and engineering sciences are preferred by policy-makers over behavioural technologies which emerge from the political social, economic and psychological sciences. Behavioural technologies have the disadvantage to the decision-maker of implying new life styles, shifts in values and changed patterns of behaviour which are likely to produce conflict. It is far more difficult, for instance, to focus on the behavioural requirements for reducing the demand for electric energy than to concentrate upon a technical solution, such as solar power, to generate more energy for everybody. This difficulty stems from broad economic ramifications and from the fact that some groups and industries will have to make do with less.

While NEPA is directed towards systematic environmental assessment, there would appear to be very few established participants in the communications network in natural resources policy who support such a message. The missions of many agencies established prior to the emergence of a strong environmental movement have been narrowly defined and often biased towards development. Even today there are few voices in the bureaucracy for a holistic environmental approach. Similarly, older conservation organizations have placed a central value on fairly narrow topics such as wilderness, parks, historic sites, and fish and wildlife. The more recent environmental movement is more comprehensive in its concerns but, especially in its early years, has had a more ideological than scientific message. Members have been attracted more by emotional than rational appeals. In many cases environmental information simply was not formulated in systematic terms nor supported by the factual data necessary to be assimilated into decision-making.

Timing

The time at which information channels develop affects the utilization and generation of information. Information is likely to have its greatest substantive impact early in the decision-making process. The chances are that a decision-maker will be most receptive to new information during the sorting-out phase of an emerging issue. If a decision-maker is uncertain about the values involved in the question, or about risks and options, then he or she is apt to be relatively open to all suggestions which appear helpful. If information is introduced late in the decision-making process, it is most likely to be treated procedurally rather than substantively. Questions have been structured and alternatives already forgone.

Ironically, the incentives for organizations to generate new information are greatest late in the decision-making process. The rewards for influencing early planning studies are often imponderable. Nothing happens to many plans, and even if they do come to fruition, it is often far in the future. Consequently environmental organizations with limited resources often generate information too late to receive more than cursory procedural treatment.

There are occasions where delay, even when it occurs late in the decision-making process, may foster receptivity to new information. An agency with a high stake in immediate action may initiate a search for alternatives. The passage of time may change the content of information in a number of channels and reopen issues which appeared settled.

NEPA's Procedural and Substantive Impact on Information Channels

The final verdict on how NEPA has altered communications channels in environmental decision-making is not yet in. After half-a-dozen years of implementation the Act is still in the process of evolving. There have been many more law review articles written on the interpretation and implications of NEPA than political science and public administration evaluations of the actual impact of the Act (Wandesforde-Smith *et al.*, 1975). Among those NEPA scholars who have taken a policy-oriented rather than a legal approach, there is some disagreement about just how much influence the Act has had and where that influence has been felt. Even so, there is no doubt that NEPA has affected who participates. However, what leverage these new participants exert in policy-making is more open to question.

Observers of NEPA see its implementation as having gone through distinct stages, moving towards but not yet achieving widespread substantive impact (U.S. Council on Environmental Quality, 1974). The CEQ, in its fifth annual report, defined the first stage as a period when 'most agencies adopted the position that NEPA did not apply to them at all — or at least not to most of their programs — or, if it did apply, an impact statement could be prepared by their administrative staff as a finishing touch when the project went forward for final agency approval.' A few agencies opposed to NEPA have tried to convince Congress to repeal the legislation, and attempted to avoid compliance altogether (Wichelman, 1974).

The transition from an initial period of interpretation and minimal compliance to a period of procedural compliance was brought about largely by environmentalists' use of the federal courts and by the CEQ. The courts, in a number of landmark decisions, and the CEQ, through its promulgation and revisions of guidelines for agency implementation, forced agencies to at least establish regular procedures. Resources necessary to handle environmental information in a non-substantive manner were developed and employed. Internal organizational changes were made and multi-disciplinary study teams were established to handle statement preparation. The needs of both government and industry have also spawned a number of environmental consultant firms.

Once procedural compliance had been accepted by, or forced upon, the agencies, some analysts saw a third phase marking a transitional step between procedural to substantive impact. 'At this point experimentation has ended and environmental analysis has been established as integral to agency decision-making. New personnel and old personnel with new responsibilities are now able to become internal advocates for what previously may have been illegitimate or insignificant policy considerations within agency decision-making' (Wichelman, 1974, p. 15). It is uncertain when this stage began, if indeed it has. CEQ, perhaps overoptimistically, has identified the issue of its August 1973 guidelines as the point after which the gap between substance and procedure began to narrow. Wichelman (1974) admits this stage has yet to be reached by many agencies.

Figure 9.1, column 2, displayed a set of linkages between agencies and potential participants in the gathering of environmental information for the preparation of impact statements. Although this information network developed to fulfil a procedural requirement, the intent of NEPA', sponsors was for new environmental information to affect decisions substantively. How have the factors acted to structure the flow of environmental information within the new linkages, so as to impart to them either a substantive or procedural character?

The Environment as an Experimental Agenda Item

Without doubt, the need to prepare environmental impact statements has forced many agencies, which would not otherwise have done so, to consider the question of environmental quality. As the Director of Civil Works of the Army Corps of Engineers testified:

> It wasn't until the passage of the National Environmental Policy Act that we really had in our hands the authority to spend money, time and effort in this field over and above what were the precedent-setting studies in which economic development and the benefit-cost ratio were the be-all and end-all (Andrews, 1976).

Once the issue of the environment was placed before them, many agencies faced great uncertainty regarding the consistency of environmental considerations with established agenda items. The pressures upon agencies to comply with the Act were too great to ignore. Conseqently agencies chose to regard NEPA as experimental and thus to minimize risk and conflict. Elaborate procedures were adopted to gather information without establishing mechanisms to integrate it into terminal decisions.

The incremental model of decision-making suggests that it is unrealistic to expect NEPA to alter significantly in six years the agenda of agencies long dominated by economic and development concerns. Whether the necessary pressure will continue to be exerted upon agencies to, in time, force substantive change, is uncertain. The pressure to incorporate NEPA fully into agencies' agendas has been lessened somewhat by the emergence of energy-supply problems and a weakened economy. For many, these items take priority over, and may conflict with, the environment.

New Environmental Participants and Formal Information Channels

The environmental impact statement process provides new environmental participants with relatively low-cost formal information channels. The written draft impact statement is widely circulated for review, and comments are published in the final draft along with agency responses. Freisema and Culhane have concluded that the process has particularly favoured environmental, *ad hoc* community and public interest groups which might not otherwise have close, informal access to decision-makers. To illustrate this, the researchers have compared comments on 1973 Forest Service impact statements with the contacts made face-to-face with rangers in districts. While consumptive users and their development interests account for 80 per cent of the rangers' personal contacts with the public, they provide only 17 per cent of the comments on the statements. On the other hand, environmentalists provide 25 per cent of impact statements comments though they account for only 7 per cent of the rangers' public contacts (Friesema & Culhane, 1976).

Unfortunately for the participation of the public in substantive decisions., it is easy for agencies to misconstrue or overlook formal written communications. The same NEPA scholars cited have also observed that it is not uncommon for agencies to ignore or creatively misinterpret the detailed and apparently compelling comments they receive, thus leaving the substance of the final EIS essentially unchanged from the draft.

These are some issues where the network of influences upon decision-making is so structured that new channels of communications opened by NEPA are peripheral. For instance, leadership in setting key policy directions, such as Project Independence in energy, is enshrined high in the executive branch hierarchy, and is remote from both CEQ and the agencies which must take the lead in impact statements. Andrews (1976) has noted the apparent rarity of NEPA's influence upon the truly major federal decisions at the policy, programmatic and legislative levels.

Resources and New Linkages

At the time of NEPA's enactment most federal agencies, their clientele and environmentalists were lacking in any capacity for gathering and assessing environmental impact information. The task is a costly one for which scarce resources have to be committed. Those actors who have lacked the necessary resources to develop capabilities have been least able to exploit new linkages with decision-makers.

In part due to the Act itself, the commitment of resources by agencies to activities relevant to NEPA has been uneven. No new funds were authorized for the preparation and review of environmental impact statements. Some have responded with only superficial structural changes, while others have developed massive retraining programmes and recruited environmentally oriented personnel. Agencies, such as the Army Corps of Engineers, that took the initiative in reacting to NEPA, tended to be those with large budgets and an existing staff of skilled analysts (Wichelman, 1974).

The resources and expertise which environmentalists have been able to muster have been few and consequently their ability to exploit new linkages with decision-makers has been limited. They lack the necessary personnel to conduct an in-depth review of the large volume of impact statements. Without such expertise independent detailed information is difficult to acquire. Their primary allies at the federal level, CEQ and EPA, also lack the necessary resources to carry out adequate and detailed reviews of agency proposals. The CEQ's staff is small, it has no sanctions to impose, its budget is reviewed by a hostile congressional committee, and its lack of initiative has caused it to lose substantial constituent support to the more activist EPA. But EPA also faces severe limitations in regard to its review of environmental statements. In existence only since 1970, much of its resources are taken up in establishing its own internal organization. Further, EPA has a number of difficult regulatory programmes to administer, including water and air pollution control, control of pesticides, radiation protection and solid waste management. Not unlike other agencies, they find that activities have priority over environmental impact review. In truth, impact statement review is a dull endeavour.

While many agencies have set up environmental units for receiving and assessing environmental information, most of these units lack the capacity for engaging in primary data collection. The private sector has not been reluctant to devote resources to research and development in the area of environmental impact assessment; and the dependence on these resources by the agencies has been quite great in many cases. Often the initial reports from which an impact statement is constructed are prepared in the private sector by special company environmental units or by consultants under contract to private corporations.

Bias in the Receipt and Transmission of Environmental Information

The receptivity of agencies to linkages with environmentalists and environment-ally oriented agencies is strongly determined by agency mission. Wichelman (1974) found that those agencies which had statutory authorization prior to the enactment of NEPA to protect or improve the environment acted most quickly to set up procedural channels. NEPA formalized what had previously been informal working arrangements between the Forest Service and the National Park Service and such groups as the Sierra Club and the National Wildlife Federation. Implementation of NEPA also served to clarify the individuals within agencies who were responsible for environmental analysis; it therefore became less difficult for environmental interest groups to communicate their concerns. However, the readiness of an agency to listen is not the same as its willingness to act. There is little evidence to date that agency initiative in procedural adaptation has closed the gap between process and substance.

The need to retain the support of traditional clientele and avoid conflict with actors in a potential veto position plays a strong role in determining who agency decision-makers will look to for information. Ideally, NEPA was to create a broad source of environmental information for agencies to call upon. Whether these new sources are actually considered seriously by decision-makers depends upon the evaluation of the political significance of these new sources.

So far, compliance with NEPA has not significantly altered the traditional sources of agency support. Agencies have been reluctant to utilize new sources which transmit information likely to produce conflict and make decisions more difficult to reach, unless they are in a veto position. Environmentalists have been most successful in utilizing the courts in forcing agencies to consider their input. In the *Calvert Cliffs* decision,[3] a United States Court of Appeals ruled that if a decision is reached without the consideration and balancing of environmental factors, the courts will examine the weight given to environmental information in the decision-making process. However, the courts have been reluctant to second-guess agencies on the substance of decisions and have confined themselves to considerations of procedural compliance.

Andrews concludes that lawsuits by environmentalists have been instrumental in forcing at least procedural compliance upon the Army Corps of Engineers. Because of its symbolic position as the federal government's bulldozing and construction crew the Corps was subjected to strong pressures by environmentalists. Within one year following NEPA's enactment the Corps was sued successfully at least eight times. As a result it complied much more quickly than its mission would have suggested.

Except for the courts there has been no actor, apart from traditional clients, capable of exerting a veto on agency activities. CEQ was given no statutory authority to overturn agency decisions, and it has been reluctant to become involved in public controversies with agencies. Congress, which has a potentially strong position in its control of agency funding, has shown a mixed reaction to NEPA. Those committees which do support NEPA are relatively weak ones within Congress. Consequently agencies have been most prone to look to their strongest source of support, their traditional clientele, for substantive environmental information.

Environmental Impact Statement Content and New Linkages

The content of the typical impact statement reflects its function as a procedural document and is ill-suited for use in decision-making. A concern with procedure often implies an excessive concern for detail, and the impact statement is no exception. The statements are often long and disjointed documents which run into hundreds of pages of needless detail and uncertain conclusions. Who reads them? Rarely are the comments of other agencies, public interest groups, and individuals integrated into the document; rather they are included in a separate section. Many statements are prepared for use as quasi-legal documents, with the accompanying morass of detail, or as advocacy documents selling a proposal.

The quality of the information contained in impact statements is typically uneven and, consequently, inadequate for use as a decision-making tool. Of particularly glaring insufficiency has been the consideration of impacts on the social and cultural environment as compared with the physical and non-human environment. With major energy developments taking place on or near Indian reservations these considerations have become increasingly salient. Friesema and Culhane, (1976) attribute this deficiency in part to the fact that 'It would be politically quite difficult for agencies to publicly debate the merits of providing positive values to one segment of society at the expense of other segments of society'. Further, it is difficult to predict social consequences in a precise manner which can be translated to decision-makers. The economic impact of a proposal is the only social consequence agencies have much facility to handle. Friesema and Culhane have found from their extensive examination of environmental impact statement documents and processes that 'The model EIS treats economic benefits as the primary justification for a project, to be balanced against adverse considerations. The typical EIS, in addition, makes an unelaborated assertion that economic impacts will be beneficial'.

There is some evidence that environmental groups are tailoring the contents of their review comments to increase impact. For instance, representatives of the Atomic Energy Commission admitted that, although many comments by environmentalists are more philosophic than scientific, volunteer scientific consultants to environmental groups have been imparting real expertise to the review process.

Timing of Environmental Information

Students of NEPA have observed that new public bodies providing environmental information in the formal environmental impact statement review process are usually brought in too late to affect decisions. While a telling written criticism may prompt an agency to make a design change in a project, the feedback comes too late to prompt a search for alternatives to the project itself. This has been the case especially on those projects in which planning was far advanced when NEPA was enacted.

There are some indications that during the half-a-dozen years of learning under NEPA's, mandate, agencies have come to anticipate communications and accommodate them early. Wichelman has found that two environmentally oriented agencies, the Forest Service and the National Park Service, have developed a set of expectations about what reviewing bodies will say; in order to alleviate difficulty and delay when the draft statements were released, these agencies have actively sought to involve potentially interested reviewers well before the draft is sent out. Thus, many controversial matters are resolved in advance, and draft statements serve simply to register publically non-negotiable disagreements. A dysfunctional consequence of this procedure to new public bodies may be that they expend their limited resources on early negotiations, and then are unable to prepare all the information necessary to make a persuasive case in formal writing.

The EIS process has been used by various participants to delay action on projects. It is not always certain to whose advantage a postponement accrues. In

138

some instances delay may make a project less feasible. However, at a time of declining public concern for the environment, time may strengthen the support for a project.

Conclusion

NEPA has created an environmental information explosion. In the half-a-dozen years of its implementation agency libraries have become filled to overflowing with multi-volume impact statements. A new industry of environmental analysts has come to expect a regular percentage of public investments in government projects from bird populations to minority group incomes. There is little evidence that the generation of all this data has substantively affected a large number of decisions. The impact statement has served as an advocacy document for governmental and private industrial projects, as a quasi-legal document, as a focus for political organizing, but not as a source of information for decision-making.

There is no question that the opportunity for the procedural participation of new environmentally oriented public bodies has become greater as a result of NEPA. The environmental impact statement process throws open to everyone the right to comment and have their remarks printed. These formal channels of communication may give the illusion of substantive participation, but only when new information is a basis for terminal decisions is substantive participation achieved.

NEPA's requirements may have created some new substantive channels of communication but these were not automatically reserved for the use of environmentalists, nor did they serve to overcome the strength of already existing channels. While environmentalists may employ some of these channels in their attempt to influence decision-making, the traditional economic development interests have also used these new channels for successfully pursuing their own ends.

The most important result of NEPA may be to legitimize a decision-making process it was meant to change. New environmental public bodies may be satisfied in the short run with the symbolic deference to their values given in NEPA's statement of goals and in the procedural attention given to their concerns in the environmental impact statement process. In the long run, however, when the objective reality is continued environmental degradation and policy inertia the failure to open substantive channels to environmental interests will expose the illusory nature of NEPA's procedures.

Notes

This article is reprinted, with changes, with permission from the *Natural Resources Journal* (1973), published by the University of New Mexico School of Law, Albuquerque, New Mexico. Revisions were supported by Grant NSF AEN74–21232A01 to the Institutional Subproject of the Lake Powell Research Project from the RANN (Research Applied to National Needs) Division of the National Science Foundation.

1. Pub. L. 91–190 January 1, 1970 83 Stat 8.52, 42 U.S.C. pp. 4321–4347.
2. As note 1, Sec. 102(c).
3. 449 F.2d. 1109 1 ELR 20346 (D.C. Cir. 1971).

References

Andrews, Richard N. L., 1976. 'Agency Responses to NEPA: A Comparison and Implications', *Natural Resources Journal*, **16**, 2, 301–322.

Arrow, Kenneth J., 1974. *The Limits of Organization*, New York: The Free Press.

Braybrooke, David & Charles Lindblom, 1963. *A Strategy of Decision*, New York: The Free Press.

Deutsch, Karl W., 1966. *The Nerves of Government*, New York: The Free Press.

Dror, Yehezkel, 1968. *Public Policy-Making Re-examined*, San Francisco: Chandler Publishing Co.

Friesema, H. Paul & Paul J. Culhane, 1976. 'Social Impacts, Politics, and Environmental Impact Statement Process', *Natural Resources Journal*, **16**, 2, 339–356.

Ingram, Helen & Daniel A. Dreyfus, 1976. 'The National Environmental Policy Act: A View of Intent and Practice', *Natural Resources Journal*, 16, 2, 243–262.

Lindblom, Charles, 1968. *The Policy-Making Process*, Englewood Cliffs: Prentice-Hall.

Marshall, Herbert, 1965. 'Politics and Efficiency in Water Development', in Allen V. Kneese & Stephen Smith (eds.), *Water Research*, Baltimore: Johns Hopkins Press, pp. 291–310.

Rourke, Francis E., 1969. *Bureaucracy, Politics and Public Policy*, Boston: Little, Brown & Co.

Schooler, Dean, 1970. 'Political Arenas, Life Styles, and the Impact of Technology on Policy-Making', *Policy Sciences*, 275–287.

Thompson, Victor A., 1969. *Bureaucracy and Innovation*, University of Alabama Press.

U.S. Council on Environmental Quality, 1974. *Environmental Quality: The Fifth Annual Report*, Washington, D.C.

Wandesforde-Smith, G. A., S. I. Schwartz & R. A. Johnson, 'Policy Impact Analysis and Environmental Management: Review and Comment', *Policy Studies Journal*, 3.

Wichelman, Allen F., 1974. 'Federal Agency Implementation of the National Environmental Policy Act of 1969: Toward a Framework for Explaining Differential Response'. Paper presented at the 1975 Annual Meeting of the Western Political Science Association, Seattle, Washington, 20–22 March.

10

The Influence of the Public on Federal Environmental Decision-making in Canada

STEVEN SCHATZOW

Introduction

Most of the demands for public participation, most of the experiments in creating public participation, and most of the research concerning public participation, have focused on the local or regional level. This chapter explores the public participation phenomenon within a national and federal context, and regards participation as merely one form of public influence. It explicitly considers the influence of the public in one sectoral area: federal environmental decision-making in Canada.

Brief definitions of some terms may be helpful. 'Decision-making' here is defined as the selection amongst alternative courses of action. In considering public influence upon decision-making, it is possible to divide such a process into three distinct stages: (i) the determination that a social problem exists which requires government action; (ii) the selection of policies to deal with the problem; and (iii) the selection and implementation of programmes and strategies.

The 'public' may be broadly defined as all those who are not government officials. In some contexts the public is perceived to consist of well-defined interest groups (such as business, farmers, citizens' groups, ratepayers, etc.) while in other contexts the public is perceived as an undifferentiated mass of people (embracing the public interest, general public, public opinion, public concern). Both of these contexts are relevant to this chapter. Most of the efforts to involve the public in decision-making have concentrated upon identifiable special interests, few have attempted to create or to focus a more general public interest.

Public participation is distinguished from public influence. Participation refers to the direct involvement of the public in decision-making through a series of formal and informal mechanisms. Public participation in decision-making does not necessarily mean that public influence is exerted; public views and opinions may be ignored by decision-makers. Influence refers to the effect of the public upon decision-making, and may operate even when the public does not actually participate in decision-making.

Participation and Influence

'Public participation' has become a major catchword during the past ten years. The demands for an increase in the role of the public in government planning, policy-making, and programme development has come from many quarters (Wengert, 1971). The demands arise from a number of different phenomena and challenge traditional notions of representative democracy. The traditionally accepted model of representative democracy can be simplified as follows: the public elects representatives. These representatives make many decisions which affect the welfare of their constituents. In making such decisions, the representatives utilize two major criteria: (i) what they think their constituents want them to do, and (ii) what they (the representatives) think is best.

It is traditionally assumed that the representative has adequate information about the opinions of his constituents. He runs for office on a specific platform; when his constituents elect him, they know his viewpoint. He is in close touch with his constituents, meeting with them, corresponding with them, listening to them. He reads the local newspapers; he has an informal network of informants; he sees the public opinion polls. His constituents contact him when they are concerned about specific issues.[1]

The demand for more formal public participation in government decision-making arises, in part, from a perception that this process has failed. Firstly, much of the evidence suggests that decision-makers do not know what their constituents want. As a result, not only are unpopular decisions made, but changes in public behaviour which are necessary to the success of the decisions often do not take place as expected (Sewell, 1975).[2] Secondly, in many situations, decision-makers are poorly informed about possible alternative policies, programmes and strategies. In addition, the rapid growth of bureaucracy during the past twenty years in industrialized countries has resulted in the delegation of increased amounts of decision-making to appointed officials who have no direct responsibility towards, nor communication with, the public.

Other impetus for increased public participation comes from a perceived need to decentralize the decision-making process, to increase local autonomy, and to allow for greater control by those individuals and groups in the population who have traditionally lacked the capability to influence government policy and programmes. It has long been recognized that certain non-governmental actors exert an important influence over government decision-making (Gable, 1958). Special interest groups have been formed specifically to influence government action. The 'War on Poverty' in the United States, with the creation of the Office of Economic Opportunity, the Model Cities Programme, and the development of the concept of 'maximum feasible participation' attempted to provide opportunities for participation for the poor, who had traditionally lacked access to decision-making. Provisions for public hearings and other forms of involvement in environmental decision-making are often perceived as opportunities for the 'general public' which has similarly lacked access.

A final rationale for increased public participation arises from observations that the society is suffering from anomie, apathy and alienation. Increased public participation is suggested as one technique to reduce this phenomenon.

'Public participation' may range from manipulation through tokenism to delegated power and citizen control (Arnstein, 1969). It is probably unrealistic to expect that decision-makers will provide for the higher degrees of citizen power, in environmental planning or any other areas. There are examples, however, when government has presented opportunities for 'tokenism' which have been heavily utilized by the public so that *de facto* citizen power does come to exist.[3]

Influence can be defined in the following manner: social control is what authorities do to potential partisans; while influence is what potential partisans do to authorities (Gamson, 1968). While influence can be exerted through participation, it can also be exerted in a number of other ways. These methods include elections, correspondence and the mass media. Organized groups may submit briefs, publish newsletters or otherwise pressure authorities. Through a combination of these methods, the public may influence the decision-making process.

As Gamson notes, however, it is often difficult to ascertain when influence is exerted and when it succeeds. A major difficulty arises from the 'static' in the communication process between the public and the decision-makers. In the absence of sophisticated methods for determining what the public wants, decision-makers may form somewhat idiosyncratic impressions of public desires and demands.

For instance, a decision-maker may conclude that the opinions expressed by a small, special interest group or by a newspaper are those of the general public. Or he may misinterpret the opinions expressed in a brief. These perceptions, which may be very erroneous, are the final link in the process by which the public influences decision-making.

Neither the influence nor the participation of the public in federal environmental decision-making has been substantial in Canada. Both influence and participation have been much more observable on the local and regional levels. This is also true in the United States to a lesser extent.

In making such generalizations, one must be careful to differentiate between federal processes and policies which are national and those which are regional and local. To the extent that federal legislation is administered on the local or regional level, with the co-operation of lower levels of government, opportunities for participation in planning and implementation increase. The major efforts to increase public participation in water planning in the United States have been carried out on a regional basis by the (federal) Army Corps of Engineers. In Canada, similar efforts, sponsored jointly by the federal Department of the Environment and provincial authorities, have taken place.

Opportunities for Participation on the Federal Level

The Definition of 'Environment' as a Social Problem

The necessary antecedents to the development of policy in an area are the definition of and legitimization of a social problem. The existence of a social problem is not defined by an objective condition with a definitive objective make-up, but rather by a collective societal decision that a problem exists (Blumer, 1971). After gaining initial recognition, a social problem must acquire social endorsement (legitimization) if it is to become the subject of major government action. Or as Downs notes, a problem must go through the stage of 'alarmed discovery and euphoric enthusiasm' (Downs, 1972).

In most instances, the public participates in the definition of a social problem and in its legitimization. Certainly, such participation occurred in the definition of the environmental crisis in the early 1970s (Sewell & Foster, 1971). There were not, however, formal mechanisms whereby the public could have directly expressed such concerns to decision-makers.

The Development of a National Environmental Policy

Decision-making on all levels of government ranges from broad policy decisions through decisions about specific programmes, to narrow, technical decisions about regulation and enforcement. It is seldom, however, that government explicitly utilizes a policy-making process; for the most part, environmental policy in Canada has developed implicitly through a series of incremental decisions about institutional structures and programmes. Since decision-makers have rarely explicitly developed policy – and even more rarely in public forums – it is not surprising that the public has had only minor direct inputs into policy development.

Public participation was encouraged, however, in two major national attempts to develop an environmental policy. In preparation for the 1972 United Nations Conference on the Environment in Stockholm, an effort was made by the Department of the Environment and the Department of External Affairs to utilize public participation in developing a Canadian position for the conference. With the assistance of the provinces, public hearings were held throughout Canada. Evaluation of the process, however, suggests less than complete success: (i) it was a last-minute effort which was poorly organized by the sponsoring departments; (ii) the inputs received from the public were not substantially utilized in the development of the Canadian position; and (iii) it appears that only a small, elite portion of the Canadian population participated.

The second major effort was the Man and Resources Conference sponsored by the Canadian Council of Resource and Environment Ministers (CCREM) in 1973. The Council, composed of ministers from the ten provinces and the federal government, had developed a fourteen-month programme to elicit public views about resource and environmental problems. After a national steering group suggested a series of major topics, the process grew from the grass-roots level. City and local groups coalesced and elected delegates to regional and provincial conferences. The provincial delegates in turn elected delegates to the national conference held in December 1973, in Toronto. While many of the participants expressed enthusiasm about the proceedings, there were complaints that the 'experts' from academia, industry and government had taken over the conference (*Globe and Mail*, 13 December 1973). Complaints were raised similar to those relating to the preparation of a Canadian position for the Stockholm Conference: public participation was irrelevant. With regard to Stockholm, not only was public input to the Canadian position minimal, but the importance of the conference itself to Canadian environmental planning was also considered by many to be minimal. 'A series of platitudes for international consumption', said one participant. Such criticisms were even more strongly voiced in regard to the Man and Resources Conference. The CCREM was not itself a decision-making body, but rather a network for informal consultation and information exchange. In addition, its existence was coming to an end. It was possible, as a number of ministers suggested, that the recommendations of the conference would be considered by the individual ministers and their governments, but far from certain.

More general public participation in federal environmental decision-making was suggested by the designation of a Canadian Environmental Advisory Council which reports directly to the Minister of the Environment. The fifteen members are appointed by the Minister for three-year terms. They include a cross-section of prominent Canadians from industry, the universities, anti-pollution groups and the scientific community. The Council has a permanent secretary and a very small support staff. Most of the work therefore must be performed by the part-time Council members themselves. The Council receives explicit requests from the Minister for advice, and also investigates issues on its own initiative. The Council has considered environmental ethics, the impacts of the McKenzie Highway, commercial and recreational fisheries, and the environmental assessment of Northern development. Much of the Council's responsibility is viewed as providing confidential advice to the Minister and therefore most of its reports have not been published.

There is little information by which to evaluate the effectiveness of the Council as an advisory body to the Minister. There are a number of problems inherent in such a body, however, when viewed from the perspective of public participation. First, the Council is a body of specialists; its members are not drawn from the general public, it is not representative of the general public, and it has no responsibility to them. Its function is an advisory one, and it is unclear if it has the right to publish information or opinions which the Minister does not regard as being in the public interest. In addition, its members serve on a part-time basis and it has no staff to investigate environmental issues.

The Development of Federal Legislation

Canadian federal environmental legislation has been developed almost exclusively by the federal agencies responsible for the different aspects of the environment. No attempts have been made so far to allow explicitly for public participation in such legislative development, although in some cases agencies have informally solicited the opinions of special interest groups.

Some formal opportunities exist for public participation in the legislative process. Committees of the House Commons review legislation after it has been discussed and generally approved by Parliament. Although the committees deal primarily with technical drafting and marginal amendments, interested members of the public are often invited to testify. For the most part, however, such hearings attract well-organized special interest groups. Most of the testimony in regard to the Canada Water Act, for instance, came from industrial spokesmen (Woodrow, 1973). Because of the technical nature of the hearings, and their location in Ottawa, it is not reasonable to expect widespread public participation.

Implementation of Federal Legislation, and Development of Regulations

The major vehicle which has been utilized by the federal government in Canada for water pollution control is the Fisheries Act. This Act, amended in 1970, creates two major pollution control opportunities for the Department of the Environment: (i) it can pass regulations limiting the amount of effluents which can enter the watercourse (Sec. 33[12]); and (ii) it can require that plans for major undertakings be submitted to the Minister, and can further require that such plans be amended or discarded because of possible environmental consequences (Sec. 33A). The Department of the Environment has utilized both of these powers. It has regulated such industries as pulp and paper and chloro-alkalies. It has demanded and considered plans for major undertakings. The legislation does not provide for public participation in either the development of regulations (standards) or the consideration of plans. Although the Department has both formally and informally solicited outside advice from experts, it has made no effort to involve the general public.[4]

The possibility of public participation in specific planning activities is included in two federal water planning and management programmes. The Northern Inland Waters Act mandates two Boards with the power to grant licences and charge fees for effluent discharge. The Act provides that public hearings must be held on all applications for licences, except where the applicant waives his right to a public hearing, and, after published notice, no other person expresses his written intention to appear (Chapter 66, Sec. (5[2]). Since the regulations under the Act went into effect in September 1972, approximately fifteen public hearings have been held. In only three cases was there no public participation. The Indian and Northern Affairs Department, which administers the programme, is evidently quite satisfied with the experience. A spokesman states that public participation has not only been valuable to the Boards in making specific decisions, but has also suggested possible changes in the legislation and regulations.

The Canada Water Act permits, but does not require, the joint federal–provincial water quality management agencies to hold public hearings. The agency 'may take into account views expressed at public hearings or otherwise by persons likely to be affected by implementation of the plans' (Chapter 52, Sec. 4(d), 1970). Although no Management Agencies have been developed under the Act, in related federal–provincial water basin planning efforts in the St. John, the Okanagan and the Qu'Appelle River Basins, public participation was included in the planning process. Sewell (1975) discusses these experiments, finds attractive characteristics in each, but expresses concern about the scope and continuity of the participation. (These Canadian water basins or regional planning experiments have their counterparts in the numerous experiments of the Army Corps of Engineers in the United States. The United States experiments have been quite seriously analysed and evaluated.[5]) Such experiments, however, are not federal in nature, although certainly they have involved federal funds and some federal control. To some extent, federal interests are also at stake. The Qu'Appelle and the St. John, for instance, are shared by two provinces, and may require a mediating federal role. Basically, however, these are exercises in regional, rather than national, planning and decision-making. While there has been substantial involvement of federal funds and in some cases, federal expertise, the major interests and controls have rested with the provinces.

The final major federally related exercise in public participation is through the Canada—United States International Joint Commission. The Commission holds public hearings in both countries when it is considering water management and water pollution problems. The bulk of the testimony, however, comes from government agencies and organized interest groups (Gould, 1972).

Influence on the Federal Level

Although public participation in federal decision-making, with the exception of regional water planning, has been negligible, public influence on federal decision-making has been much more substantial. Such influence, however, has been constrained within somewhat narrow boundaries. As noted previously, decision-making involves three main phases: (i) the decision that a social problem exists which demands government action; (ii) the selection of policies to deal with the problem; and (iii) the selection and implementation of programmes and strategies. The influence of the public has been primarily in the first category.

A high level of public concern was the primary catalyst in making the environment a priority societal issue in 1969 and 1970. It was also the major catalyst leading the federal government into large-scale involvement in a field which was traditionally believed to be predominantly of provincial concern. The acknowledgement by the federal government that the environment was an issue of major public concern led it not only to become involved in the environmental field, but also to select strategies, policies and programmes at least partially to alleviate public concern.

It is very difficult to measure the influence of the public upon decision-making. It does seem, however, that a host of federal decisions were influenced by what federal decision-makers perceived to be of concern to the public. Environmental questions which had previously been the subject of *ad hoc* discussion among some Members of Parliament, became Cabinet questions in 1969 and 1970. A national interest in water quality management problems provided justification for federal involvement in regional planning through the Canada Water Act and its preamble, which noted that the quality of the environment had become 'a matter of urgent national concern' (Chapter 52). The formation of the Federal Department of the Environment was felt to be necessary for a number of reasons: one of these was to show to the public a federal commitment to improve the environment.

A desire to satisfy the public played some part in the development of certain strategies. The utilization of the Fisheries Act as the major federal instrument for water pollution control rather than the Canada Water Act was partially based upon the speed and drama with which the Act could be utilized. The 'polluter must pay' principle, a questionable economic strategy, was promulgated to some degree as an attractive dogma for public consumption. Nutrient control regulations were quickly inserted into the Canada Water Act after expressions of public alarm about the phosphate issue, despite their lack of relevance and congruity to the other provisions of the legislation.

On what basis did decision-makers decide that the public was concerned about environmental issues? There is no evidence that environmental issues were important in the 1968 federal election. The official platforms of the major parties were quite similar (and non-specific) with regard to environmental problems (Holmes, 1973). In a survey of election issues, pollution was not even mentioned often enough to be coded (Winham, 1972). Informal communications with the public, through letters or conversations, were not suggested by the decision-makers who were interviewed as an important source of information. The citizens' environmental groups which developed in late 1969 and 1970 concentrated their efforts at the local and provincial levels and made few representations to federal decision-makers.

The two major sources for decision-makers' perceptions of public concern were the mass media and public opinion polls. Media coverage of environmental issues rose markedly in late 1969 and peaked in 1970. The phosphate issue was covered intensively, as were mercury, oil spills and 'spot' industrial pollution (Schatzow, 1973). In many newspapers, editorials were calling for federal government action (Green, 1973). While decision-makers do not view the mass media as the representative of the public or of public concern, they do regard (and correctly, the results of this study suggest), mass media as a reflection or indication of public concern.

The Gallup Organization released results of its surveys showing substantial public concern about pollution in 1970. In a Gallup Poll of 25 March 1970, 91 per cent of the respondents said that they were aware of pollution problems, a figure noted by the Institute as 'one of the highest levels of awareness in Gallup Poll history'. Seventy per cent of the respondents thought the dangers of pollution were 'very serious' (Canadian Institute of Public Opinion, 1970). In a Gallup Poll released on 2 December, 1970, (Canadian Institute of Public Opinion) respondents were asked to choose three problems to which they would like to see the government devote most of its attention in the next year or two. Pollution was at the top of the list with 65 per cent. Other surveys of environmental concern and opinion have been sponsored by federal decision-makers: the Market Facts national studies of 1970 and 1971 (Department of the Environment), the Centre pour Recherche de l'Opinion publique study in 1969 (Department of Energy, Mines and Resources), the local studies sponsored by the Opportunities for Youth programme (Edmonton Anti-pollution Group, Ecos-Calgary, both 1971), and the studies of public concern and phosphates (O'Riordan, 1971b; Sinclair, 1971); all of these studies showed high levels of public concern about pollution problems.

Such evidence of public concern was probably important in encouraging decision-makers to take action. There is no indication, however, that the public directly influenced the development of specific programmes and strategies. All the surveys suggested a very low level of public knowledge about the specifics of pollution problems and about potential strategies which might be utilized.

Obstacles to a Greater Public Participation

Would Greater Participation make any Difference?

Research does not suggest that the decisions taken by the federal government with regard to environmental issues were in any major way contradictory to public desires. The public appeared to want a governmental recognition of environmental problems, an institutionalization of environmental concern within government, and the development of programmes of environmental protection. The governmental response, a measured and cautious one,[6] appears to have been a realistic one in terms of the decline in public environmental concern since 1970.

It does seem, however, that increased opportunities for participation might have resulted in four major societal benefits: (i) a more explicit policy process with a greater and more detailed consideration of alternatives; (ii) a more educated, involved and aware Canadian public, including the development of a national environmental lobby; (iii) an explicit consideration of major issues, particularly the relationship between environmental quality and economic growth and development, which have for the most part been ignored; and (iv) a sense of public involvement to counter some of the apathy and alienation which exists in society.

While there appear to be a number of benefits for increased public participation in federal environmental decision-making, there are a host of difficulties which must be surmounted.

Is There Large-scale Public Demand for Greater Participation?

Research suggests that neither the general public nor the citizens' groups were particularly concerned with developing a greater role in federal environmental decision-making. Despite the major federal efforts in the environmental field beginning in 1969, environment was perceived by the public as primarily a provincial, regional or local issue (Stewart, 1973; Market Facts, 1970, 1971, 1973).

There are a number of reasons for this perception:

(1) In general terms, the federal government in Canada is generally less powerful than the central governments in such countries as Great Britain or the United States;

(2) Most aspects of the package that is called the environment had traditionally been under provincial control: health, control of local works and undertakings (including sewage treatment facilities), water management and natural resources;

(3) While 'the environment' might be broadly and intellectually defined as a national issue, environmental experiences are predominantly specific and local in nature. While one may be generally concerned about the issue of environmental quality, one is more apt to be specifically concerned with a particular oil spill, or fish kill, or smog, or a local body of polluted water.

One commentator has suggested that 'the concern people feel about pollution is an intellectualized concern, and is not deeply woven into the fabric of their everyday lives — the groups most concerned about pollution are not the groups who experience the most pollution' (Winham, 1972, p. 400). Winham cites his interviews which show that those residents of Hamilton who live in the areas of the city which have the highest rate of air pollution are the least concerned about such pollution and believe it to be more serious in other areas of the city. Similar results have been recorded in other surveys (Rankin, 1969; Murch, 1971).

Most aspects of environmental degradation are very gradual ones and the majority of Canadians accommodate to such environmental change. Most people become involved only in situations of environmental stress (Sewell & Wood, 1971). Such environmental stress situations, in which serious environmental degradation occurs or threatens, arise primarily on the local level (Sewell & Wood, 1971; Kasperson, 1969; O'Riordan, 1971a). When surveyed as to which level of government is primarily responsible for water pollution, Canadians evenly placed responsibility with the federal and provincial governments, with the municipalities somewhat behind, but placed the major responsibility upon sewage and garbage systems, which are predominantly a municipal responsibility (Market Facts, 1970, 1971).

The principal involvement of the public in environmental matters has been on the provincial and municipal levels. The major environmental citizens' groups which formed in Canada in 1969 and 1970 developed primarily in response to local concerns: The Society to Oppose Pollution in Montreal [STOP] (phosphates in the St. Lawrence); Pollution Probe in Toronto (phosphates in the Great Lakes), and the Canadian Scientific Pollution and Environmental Control Society [SPEC] in Vancouver (strip-mining in British Columbia). Additional groups tended to follow these early examples. Pollution Probe Toronto was followed by a host of local groups throughout Ontario and elsewhere bearing the Pollution Probe prefix. Over forty loosely affiliated local groups form the British Columbia federation. In Montreal, a French group, Societé Vaincre Pollution (SVP.) was organized to complement the work of the English group STOP (Stewart, 1973).

While national environmental groups such as the Sierra Club, the National Wildlife Federation and the Friends of the Earth moved into the forefront of the environmental movement in the United States, no such national groups developed in Canada. Chapters of the Sierra Club do exist in Canada, but are concentrated on the West Coast; there is no Canadian Sierra Club organization. The Canadian Audobon Society has attempted to change both its name and its image. In September 1971, this group of provincial naturalist federations, local societies and individuals became the Canadian Nature Federation (CNF). In its activities and in the publication of its magazine, *Nature Canada*, the organization has attempted to address itself to distinctly Canadian wildlife and environmental problems. Most of the local environmental interest groups, however, have not become members, and the CNF maintains its traditional focus on conservation and ex-urban environmental planning (Stewart, 1973).

An attempt was made in the summer of 1970 by SPEC, PROBE and STOP (amongst others), to organize a national umbrella group, the Canadian Association for the Human Environment. As a result of financial difficulties, this national group has become inactive. The local groups keep in touch sporadically, exchanging reports and newsletters, but place their major emphasis on local environmental issues. They have seldom attempted to influence federal decision-making or to press for greater public participation.

Is There Interest Within the Federal Government in Encouraging Public Participation in Environmental Decision-making?

Interviews with government officials, particularly on the federal level, which were undertaken for this study, suggest their general suspicion and dislike for greater public participation. This attitude can be divided into a number of component parts:

(1) A belief that the government through the political process represents the public and that more direct public participation is a challenge to that political process;
(2) A belief that politicians know what the public wants and do not require input on each decision;
(3) A belief that public participation is cumbersome and time-consuming;
(4) A desire not to expose the decision-making process to public scrutiny;
(5) A belief that much of governmental decision-making requires merely technical advice and that the public is not qualified to provide such advice;
(6) A fear that forums for public participation will become platforms for radical 'unrepresentative' groups to spout their concerns, and will lead to conflict and noise.

Within the past few years, the federal Department of the Environment has made numerous decisions which tend to limit seriously the role of public participation and influence on environmental decision-making. It disbanded the 'public participation section' of its water planning and management branch; it has also dissolved its section for liaison with citizen groups. It has stopped its support for research investigating public attitudes and values related to the environment. It has suggested that it regards itself as a technical arm of government, responsible for making technical decisions and evaluations and for providing technical advice, rather than acting as a spokesman for the 'environmental perspective' or the 'environmental conscience'.

As suggested earlier, two types of pressure can be put upon decision-makers to encourage them to create more opportunities for public participation. The first, direct pressure from the public, has never existed. The second is evidence that failure to involve the public has resulted in unsuccessful policies. While such evidence exists on the local level in Canada (Sewell, 1975), there is no evidence with regard to federal environmental decision-making that policies or programmes have failed because of lack of public support. In the absence of either of these pressures, it is unlikely that increased opportunities for public participation will be created by decision-makers.

Is the Public Well Enough Informed to Participate?

In order to participate in a meaningful way in decision-making, the public must be well-informed about the issues, problems and strategies. The results of research suggest that the general public has never been well-informed about environmental issues. They also suggest that government has made relatively meagre attempts to inform the public more fully.

Almost all Canadian studies of the public and environmental issues have focused on the lack of knowledge possessed by the public. An Edmonton study notes that 'knowledge of general environmental issues was poor to mediocre, except for the subject of DDT', and 'there was a shallow perception of Edmonton's local pollution problems, with poor to mediocre recognition of the relative importance of various sources of air and water pollution'. (Edmonton Anti-Pollution Group, 1972: 7). In his survey results on water pollution in rural Ontario, Dwivedi reports that 'the public is inadequately informed about such issues as environmental quality' (1973: 14). A survey of Winnipeg residents found that respondents were poorly informed about pollution problems; 65 per cent were not even aware that some portion of pollution control is funded through water and sewer charges (Rempel, 1971). The Gallup Poll reported that 37 per cent of Canadians did not know enough to evaluate Canada's position in pollution abatement relative to other countries (Canadian Institute of Public Opinion, March, 1973).

In a national environmental survey conducted in 1973, respondents were asked whether the Great Lakes were undergoing environmental degradation, and if so, what was the main cause of such degradation. While more than 75 per cent stated that the Great Lakes were polluted, few were able to identify the major contributing factor to the deterioration. Over 35 per cent did not know enough to choose any of the five options. About 10 per cent chose each of the following incorrect answers: oil spills, sewage from boats, mercury, and pulp and paper wastes. Only 15 per cent chose the correct answer: phosphates (Market Facts of Canada Ltd., 1973). This lack of public knowledge about phosphates, a subject which received extensive mass media coverage and governmental attention in Canada, is substantiated in two other surveys. In Hamilton, a group of housewives were asked about the phosphate problem; only 12 per cent gave a relatively informed answer (Sinclair, 1971). In a similar study of Vancouver housewives, over 50 per cent had no knowledge of phosphate problems (O'Riordan, 1971b). In the national pollution survey, approximately 40 per cent of the respondents did not answer questions requiring knowledge as opposed to attitudes about pollution problems (Market Facts, 1973). This phenomenon of high levels of public concern, coupled with very low levels of public knowledge, has also been reported in studies in the United States. (Rankin, 1969; Kasperson, 1969; Murch, 1971).

All evidence suggests that the mass media are regarded by the public as its main source of information on pollution and most other issues. (Sinclair, 1971; Edmonton Anti-Pollution Group, 1972; Murch, 1971). Direct information from government is a very minor source (Market Facts, 1973). The failure of the federal government to inform the public generally has been noted by the Task Force on Government Information (1971). 'Governments must acquire the power to speak persuasively and continuously . . . (or) administration will be swamped by rising tides of incomprehension and discontent' (Vol. 1, p. 1). When the Department of the Environment was created in 1971, one of the six goals set for the organization was 'to develop an environmental information and education program'. (DOE, 1971, p. 3). While the federal information output with regard to environmental problems has increased since 1971, there has been no serious commitment to improving the quality of information, and no concerted effort to develop major information programmes. Information Canada, the official government information agency, has played virtually no purposive role with respect to the dissemination of pollution information (Taylor, 1973). Despite the urgings of the Task Force on Government Information and the Science Council (1972), there are no indications that federal information output concerning environmental problems is improving.

A related problem is the tendency of the government to shroud its decision-making processes in great secrecy. Documents are routinely stamped 'secret' or 'confidential'. Thus government not only has no affirmative programme designed to inform the public, but actually limits public access to much of the information which forms a basis for decision-making. As the Science Council has noted,

There is an increasing tendency, particularly in government departments, to refuse publication on grounds such as 'the public will take the wrong meaning out of the information; the public is too ill-informed to know what the data mean;' and so on. Custodians of data should know that we have and need a nation of well-educated people; that these people have the right to make up their own minds; and that other scientists must have access to data if maximum progress at minimum cost is a goal (Science Council 1972, pp. 34–35).

Such a need was recognized by the DOE Task Force on Environmental Contaminants Legislation which recommended that the public have access to the data collected on environmental contaminants, and be encouraged to participate (Calamai, *Ottawa Citizen*, 19 May 1973). (Of course, the report of the Task Force was confidential!) The recommendations were not included in the legislation which was introduced in the House of Commons.

A public which is poorly informed about issues cannot sustain a high level of concern about such issues, is unlikely to ask for more information, to demand to be included in decision-making, or to scrutinize government action closely. It also seems clear that merely increasing the flow of paper from government to the public is not sufficient to inform the public properly. The failure of government information campaigns has often been documented. The media gave extensive coverage to pollution problems during the period 1969 to 1971 without substantially increasing the level of public knowledge.

A totally new approach to information may be necessary. a closer relationship with the educational system is one avenue (Saskatchewan, 1973). Public participation is another.

What Mechanisms could be Developed for Public Participation?

Even assuming that the impediments to public participation in federal environmental decision-making which have been discussed could be overcome, it is difficult to conceive of the proper forum for such participation. The best strategy would probably not rely upon any one method, but utilize a variety of mechanisms.

One further caution should be mentioned. All of the opportunities for public participation have resulted mainly in the participation of 'the influentials'. (Wengert, 1971). The influentials include special interest groups, academics, business and industry, and citizens' environmental groups. The 'average' member of the public generally does not participate because of his lack of knowledge and/or interest in the subject (Curtis, 1971).

None of the mechanisms discussed in the remainder of this paper are likely substantially to increase the involvement of the 'average' member of the public. It is possible, however, that such mechanisms will increase the numbers of those who regard themselves as influentials and believe that their interests are affected by environmental decision-making. In other words, the quality of the inputs from participation is likely to increase as well as the quantity:

The green paper or white paper: The circulation of proposed governmental policy as either a green paper (quite tentative) or a white paper (less tentative) has been utilized in a number of countries including the United Kingdom. In Canada, such papers are circulated both by provincial governments and by the federal government. On the federal level, however, the use of the white paper has been primarily restricted to the Departments of Defence and Finance and the green paper to the Department of National Health and Welfare. The government has not distributed any major policy papers on environmental issues since 1969.[7]

Such policy papers may encourage public reaction. Feedback can come through written responses from different segments of the public. In addition, important policy papers may become the subject of Parliamentary Committee consideration. Such committees may hold public hearings, both in Ottawa and other sections of the country, to receive public input to their deliberations. It would seem that the policy paper really provides for widespread public participation only when formal feedback mechanisms are provided through public hearings.

Public hearings: As noted previously, public hearings are utilized as part of the legislative process. They could also be used as part of the policy or programme development process on the administrative/executive level. The major difficulties with public hearings are those of time and access. Public hearings may not only delay decisions, but to be effective require that senior decision-makers devote substantial time to them.

Advisory councils: Advisory councils may provide for the prodding of decision-makers. For them to be effective, however, they require a great deal of independence from the agency to which they report; independence to set their own agenda and to publish all findings and recommendations; funds to hire independent staff; a substantial degree of public representativeness and of access to and feedback from the public. Task Forces and Royal Commissions can perform similar functions.

Environmental impact statements: Legislation in the United States (The National Environmental Protection Act) requires that proposals for all major governmental undertakings be evaluated in terms of their environmental effects. Provision is made for public hearings on such environmental impact statements. Some Provinces in Canada are considering similar legislation (Ontario, 1973).

The Department of the Environment has been given the power by the Cabinet to institute environmental assessment procedures for significant federal undertakings throughout Canada. The Department was not, however, given the power to veto or amend proposals without the concurrence of the proponent agency. The assessment procedure includes a discretionary provision for public participation.

Advocacy planning, a national environmental forum: The federal government in Canada, as Audain has noted, has become a champion of citizen participation. 'But the present government has been encouraging participation in local, not national, matters. Such a strategy may win friends . . . but a cynic might suggest that it also keeps citizens' noses out of national affairs' (Audain, 1972). The Department of the Environment has curtailed even such local support, by dissolving its sections on Public Participation and Liaison with Citizen Groups. Even if such support were to be resurrected, it is unclear if various local groups could coalesce into a national lobby. Many of the difficulties which Audain discusses with regard to citizen participation in the development of national urban policy would find their parallel in national environmental policy.

It would seem, however, that the development of a national environmental movement through the combination and co-ordination of local and regional interests offers the best prospects for public participation and influence in federal environmental decision-making. Such a process is, however, necessarily a long and arduous one, and the unwillingness of the federal government to support such a process increases the difficulties.

Conclusions

The actual participation of the public in the development of Canadian national environmental policy and programmes has been minimal. It is unrealistic to expect that such participation will increase in the future, particularly since public concern about environmental issues clearly appears to be declining, and since public pressure appears to be the only leverage which will open decision-making to increased public participation.

With 'environment' institutionalized within the federal government, one can expect that organized special interest groups, particularly industry, will continue to exert the major influence upon federal environmental decision-making. Public participation and influence are likely to remain marginal.

Notes

1. Even this simplified model ignores many of the features of the contemporary Canadian federal process. The 'representative' is not a free spirit, but is generally bound by the positions taken by his political party. Parliament itself is not the locus of decision-making power in contemporary Canadian politics, rather the locus is within the Cabinet, a subset of the Parliament. Still, individual parliamentarians do influence government policy and programmes, and the Cabinet itself is composed of elected representatives.
2. Sewell gives a number of examples where failure to assess public preferences accurately on a local and regional level has resulted in important economic and social losses: the Spadina Expressway in Toronto, the South Indian Lake, the Churchill—Nelson Diversion Scheme, etc. See Sewell (1975).
3. See Warriner (1961) and Kasperson (1969) and Sargeant (1973).
4. The pulp and paper industry, for instance, was well-represented on the Task Force which developed the Pulp & Paper Regulations promulgated under the Fisheries Act in 1971. Although initial plans provided for comments on the regulations from environmental citizens' groups, such plans were later discarded.
5. See Chevalier & Cartwright (1970) and Borton *et al.* (1970). Also see generally the *Proceedings of the Symposium on Social and Economic Aspects of Water Resources Development*, Ithaca, N.Y., 1971, for numerous reviews of the Delaware and Susquehanna experiments as well as the fishbowl approach.
6. As noted previously, the government response to the environmental issue was two-pronged. On the one hand, the government appeared to be making major changes – the creation of a new department, passing new environmental legislation such as the Canada Water Act, the Clean Air Act, the Northern and Inland Waters Act, etc. On the other hand, the government was rather slow in developing regulations and in implementing the new legislation.
7. In August 1969, the Department of Energy, Mines and Resources did produce a white paper on the Canada Water Act, primarily as a basis for discussions with the provinces. Public involvement in proposed government policy, however, seemed to re-emerge strongly in 1975 with widespread consideration of immigration policy.

References

American Water Resources Association, 1971. *Proceedings of The Symposium on Social and Economic Aspects of Water Resources Development*, Ithaca, N.Y.

Arnstein, S. R., 1969. 'A Ladder of Citizen Participation', *Journal of the American Institute of Planners*, 35 (4), 216–224.

Audain, Michael, 1972. 'Citizen Participation on National Urban Policy', *Plan*, 12 (1), 74–87.

Blumer, Herbert, 1971. 'Social Problems as Collective Behaviour', *Social Problems*, 18 (3), 298–305.

Borton, T. E. *et al.*, 1970. *The Susquehanna Communication-Participation Study*, Alexandria, Va., U.S. Army Engineers Institute for Water Resources.

Calamai, P., 1973. 'Task Force Recommends Public Access', *The Ottawa Citizen*, 19 May p. 24.

Canada Department of Environment, 1971. *Department of Environment, Its Organization and Objectives*, Ottawa: Information Canada (Cat. No. EN 21–171).

Canadian Institute of Public Opinion, 1970. 'Dangers of Pollution Very Serious', Gallup Poll Report, Toronto: CIPO, 25 March.

Canadian Institute of Public Opinion, 1972. 'Little Hope for Cleaning Great Lakes of Pollution', Gallup Poll Report, Toronto: CIPO, 12 August.

Canadian Institute of Public Opinion, 1972. 'Why 39% Doubt Possibility of Cleaning up Great Lakes', Gallup Poll Report, Toronto: CIPO, 24 June.

Canadian Institute of Public Opinion, 1972. 'Economy, Unemployment, Labour Named as Our Main Problems', Gallup Poll Report, Toronto: CIPO, 4 November.

Canadian Institute of Public Opinion, 1973. '37% of Canadians Don't Know What the Government is Doing about Pollution', Gallup Poll Report, Toronto: CIPO, 3 March.

Centre de Recherches sur l'Opinion Publique, 1969. *Sondage sur la Pollution de l'Eau*, Montreal: C.R.O.P. Inc.

Chevalier, M. & T. J. Cartwright, 1970 'Public Involvement in Planning: The Delaware River Case', in W. R. D. Sewell & I. Burton (eds.), *Perceptions and Attitudes in Resources Management*, Ottawa: Information Canada, pp. 111–120.

Curtis, James, 1971. 'Canada as a Nation of Joiners', in J. E. Gallagher & R. D. Lambert (eds.), *Social Process and Institution,* Toronto: Holt, Rinehart & Winston, pp. 146–164.

Downs, Anthony, 1972. 'Up and Down with Ecology – The Issue-Attention Cycle', *Public Interest*, Summer, pp. 38–50.

Dwivedi, O. P., 1973. 'Public Attitudes toward Pollution in the Big Otter Creek Drainage Basin', Paper prepared for presentation at the 16th Conference on Great Lakes Research, 17 April (mimeo).

Ecos-Calgary, 1971. *Pollution in Calgary*, 2 vols, Calgary: University of Calgary.

Edmonton Anti-Pollution Group, 1972. *Sources and Resources: Resource Inventory and Guide to Environmental Studies*, Edmonton: Edmonton Anti-Pollution Group.

Gable, R. W., 1958. 'Interest Groups as Policy Shapers', *Annals of the American Academy of Political and Social Science*, 319, September.

Gamson, W. A., 1968. *Power and Discontent*, Homewood, Ill.: Dorsey Press.

Gould, Jack, 1972. 'The International Joint Commission', Urban Pollution Task Report Arbiters, section 11, Ottawa: Ministry of State for Urban Affairs (mimeo).

Green, Henry, 1973. 'Survey of Newspapers', Urban Pollution Task Report Media, section 1, Ottawa: Ministry of State for Urban Affairs (mimeo).

Holmes, James, 1973. 'Party Policies', Urban Pollution Task Report Arbiters, section 6, Ottawa: Ministry of State for Urban Affairs, (mimeo).

Kasperson, R. E., 1969. 'Political Behaviour and the Decision-Making Process in the Allocation of Water Resources between Recreational and Municipal Use', *Natural Resources Journal*, 9 (2), 176–211.

Market Facts of Canada Ltd., 1970. *Public Attitude Study Concerning Pollution*, Toronto/Montreal: Market Facts of Canada Ltd.

Market Facts of Canada Ltd., 1971. *Second National Public Attitude Study Concerning Pollution*, Toronto/Montreal: Market Facts of Canada Ltd.

Market Facts of Canada Ltd., 1973. *National Public Attitude Survey Concerning Pollution*, Toronto/Montreal: Market Facts of Canada Ltd.

Murch, S. W., 1971. 'Public Concern for Environmental Pollution', *Public Opinion Quarterly,* **35**, 100–106.

158

Ontario Ministry of the Environment, 1973. *Green Paper on Environmental Assessment*, Toronto: Ontario Ministry of the Environment, September.

O'Riordan, T., 1971a. 'Public Opinion and Environmental Quality: A Reappraisal', Environment and Behaviour, 3 (2), 191–214.

O'Riordan, T., 1971b. 'Some Reflections on Environmental Concern and Environmental Action', Burnaby, B.C.: Department of Geography, Simon Fraser University (mimeo).

Rankin, R. E., 1969. 'Air Pollution Control and Public Apathy', *Journal of the Air Pollution Control Association*, August, pp. 565–569.

Rempel, G., 1971. *A Consumer Attitude Survey on Water Quality and River Pollution Control*, Winnipeg: Metropolitan Corporation of Greater Winnipeg.

Sargeant, H. K., 1973. 'Fishbowl Planning Immerses Pacific Northwest Citizens in Corps Project', *Civil Engineering*, March 186–188.

Saskatchewan, 1973. *Education for Environmental Quality*, Regina: Saskatchewan Department of Education and Department of the Environment, October.

Schatzow, Steven, 1973. 'Media Synthesis', Urban Pollution Task Report Media, section 5, Ottawa: Ministry of State for Urban Affairs, February (mimeo).

Schatzow, Steven, 1974. 'Urban Pollution Working Paper', section 26, Ottawa: Ministry of State for Urban Affairs, February (mimeo).

Science Council of Canada, 1972. *It's Not Too Late – Yet*, Report, section 6, Ottawa: Information Canada.

Sewell, W. R. D., 1975. 'Public Involvement', in *Comprehensive River Basin Planning*, Ottawa: Department of the Environment, pp. 73–109.

Sewell, W. R. D. & C. J. B. Wood, 1971. 'Environmental Decision-Making and Environmental Stress: The Goldstream Controversy', *Papers of the Annual Meeting of the Canadian Association of Geographers*, Waterloo, Ontario.

Sewell, W. R. D. & Ian Burton (eds.) 1971. *Perceptions and Attitudes in Resources Management*, Ottawa: Information Canada.

Sewell, W. R. D. & H. D. Foster, 1971. 'Environmental Revival: Promise and Performance', *Environment and Behaviour*, 3 (2), 123–134.

Sinclair, M., 1971. 'A Survey of Housewives' Attitudes', in *Proceedings of the 14th Conference Great Lakes Research, 1971*, Burlington, Ontario: Lakes Management Research Section, Canada Centre for Inland Waters.

Statutes of Canada, 1970. Fisheries Act 1932. (C.42, s.1), Amended 26 June, Queen's Printer.

Stewart, A., 1973. 'Environmental Interest Groups', Urban Pollution Task Report Public, section 3, Ottawa: Ministry of State for Urban Affairs (mimeo).

Task Force on Government Information, 1969. *Report: To Know or Be Known*, Ottawa: Queen's Printer.

Taylor, J., 1973. 'Federal Information Output', Urban Systems Task Report Arbiters, section 13, Ottawa: Ministry of State for Urban Affairs (mimeo).

Warriner, C. K., 1961. 'Public Opinion and Collective Action: Formation of a Watershed District', *Administrative Science Quarterly*, 6 (3), 333–359.

Wengert, N., 1971. 'Public Participation in Water Planning: A Critique of Theory, Doctrine and Practice', *Water Resources Bulletin*, 7 (1), 26–32.

Winham, G., 1972. 'Attitudes on Pollution and Growth in Hamilton or "There's an awful lot of talk these days about ecology"', *Canadian Journal of Political Science*, 5 (3), 389–401.

Woodrow, R. B., 1973. 'The Canada Water Act: A Case Study in Decision-Making', Urban Pollution Task Report Arbiters, section 15A, Ottawa: Ministry of State for Urban Affairs (mimeo).

11
Citizen Participation in Practice: Some Dilemmas and Possible Solutions

TIMOTHY O'RIORDAN

Participation takes many forms. It is a slippery concept easy neither to define nor to execute and, like 'democracy', it conjures up socially desirable connotations which can all too easily be countermanded in practice. The purpose of this chapter is to look carefully at three participatory experiments in British Columbia, each of which began in good faith but changed in function during execution. The cases cited all invited participation at an extra-local level, that is they incorporated urban or regional issues and not neighbourhood concerns. The very nature of such issues and the techniques employed all but precluded the vast majority of the citizenry from taking part or even from knowing about these experiments. Thus the case studies analyse a particular kind of participation, and the difficulties that each faced are illustrative essentially of the non-local form of participation where certain highly motivated individuals became involved. The case studies speak for themselves, and the dilemmas that emerge from the analysis appear to be common to all such programmes; but the search for solutions may cause us to redirect our attention to more intimate and meaningful scales of operation.

The GVRD Livable Region Programme

On 20 March 1974, the Board of the Greater Vancouver Regional District (GVRD) voted to reduce its citizen participation budget by half, to curtail its programme of activating local interest groups, to cut the number of planned regional policy seminars with citizens' groups from fifty to about twenty and not to renew the contract of the participation co-ordinator. These decisions substantially reduced the momentum of the GVRD's 'Livable Region' programme, a goals-oriented participatory experiment designed to elicit opinions from a broad cross-section of citizens as to the kinds of urban community in which they would like to live.

There is no doubt that the GVRD intended to take this programme seriously. In 1971 they hired a consultant planner to sketch out a number of 'instrumental goals' — desirable means to attain the notion of livability — and to devise a sort of 'environmental matrix' outlining the implications for the regional plan if any or all of such goals were pursued. While this matrix provided a suitable basis for discussion, the GVRD was concerned that it might excessively inhibit citizens' views by providing too narrow a framework. So in August 1972 it hired a full-time participation co-ordinator whose wide-ranging terms of reference set him off along two pathways. One was to identify and work with any citizen groups in the region, to assist them in conceptualizing their frustrations and their aspirations, to help them prepare alternative proposals to existing plans to which they were opposed, and above all to activate their interest in the regional implications of municipal planning schemes – zoning codes, shopping centres, open space provisions and the like.

The co-ordinator's second responsibility was to identify a number of topics, each of central importance to the region's future, and to establish a number of citizens' task forces which would meet regularly and would prepare a guideline report for the GVRD to consider and possibly incorporate into its future regional policy. During the summer of 1973 nine task forces (called policy committees) met and eight finally reported in February 1974. The eight policy committees dealt with transportation, government and social services, recreation, health and public protection, education, environmental management and pollution control, residential living, and government and society. (The ninth policy committee, which failed to report, discussed a rather technical matter – production and distribution – which apparently became too complicated for lay citizens to handle.) Although some members of these policy committees were invited to attend, the participation co-ordinator encouraged as many citizens as possible to participate and largely left the committees to handle their own affairs. The committees worked diligently if slowly but suffered considerable attrition of membership. In fact the final reports were composed by fewer than a dozen individuals, and in most instances by fewer than five.

On the surface the GVRD experiment was sincere and far-reaching. No other regional district in the province and indeed, to my knowledge, no other regional district in Canada had attempted anything on this scale before. The co-ordinator enjoyed considerable freedom of movement. He was instrumental in assisting a number of citizens' groups to renegotiate municipal planning schemes in favour of much more comprehensive proposals, and many people were encouraged to work with municipal planning staffs to improve original designs. The prescriptions of the policy committees were accepted in principle by the GVRD, particularly the concept of limiting population growth and urban sprawl. Subsequently the GVRD organized a series of 'in house' seminars on critical questions of optimal population, regional decentralization, open space and cluster zoning. The first of these seminars involved members of the policy committees, but subsequent ones did not. Moreover, as a consequence of the decisions outlined at the beginning of this account, there is little likelihood that any substantive citizen consultation will take place in the future. The GVRD Livable Region participation experiment has left its legacy but also its epitaph.

The Vancouver False Creek Study

The GVRD Livable Region programme was not the first participatory experiment in metropolitan Vancouver. In 1968 Vancouver City Council initiated what they claimed was an innovative participatory exercise following widespread public discontent over a proposed alignment for a downtown freeway. (Further public protest eventually led to the scrapping of the alignment and the freeway) (Pendakur, 1972). It is interesting and important to note that three of the strongest anti-freeway advocates were so angered at the political decision-making process which all but forced the freeway onto the Vancouver public without any formal debate, that they formed a countervailing political party called The Electors' Action Movement (TEAM). In 1972 TEAM won the civic elections with all three founding members elected as alderman.

The City Council proposal for 'new look' participatory planning consisted of selecting key areas within the city for which professional planners were to prepare a number of questions known as 'issues'. These would be open to public discussion by interested citizens and citizens' groups. Following the tabling of briefs, the planning department would then produce a number of highly conceptual schemes (known as 'alternatives') for the areas under consideration, and Council would again invite public response. With further clarification and specification the five or so most popular alternatives would be the genesis of a number of specific designs (known as 'proposals') prepared either by the planning staff or by consultants. These proposals, essentially variations of a theme, would then form the basis for final public discussion and, where necessary, public hearings.

This mechanism looks fine on paper. Unlike the GVRD scheme which looked mainly at goals, the Vancouver experiment was issue specific, inviting increasingly defined analysis by citizens and citizens' groups. For those concerned enough to stay with the process to its completion, the experiment appeared to offer a rare opportunity for direct consultation with planning officials.

But in practice the experiment failed. The City never pursued the three stages with any vigour, there was no discussion or dialogue amongst citizens or between citizens and planners so no one knew how alterantives and proposals were formulated. The problems encountered in this experiment can be outlined more clearly with reference to another case study, the False Creek plan.

False Creek is a shallow slough, close to downtown Vancouver, that was cluttered by industrial slums. With its excellent location and water setting the area had enormous potential for middle-income housing and amenity open space. The City owned lands to the south of the area while a large private developer owned all lands to the north. Although the latter quietly prepared a scheme for dense, high-income residential development, public attention was focused on the city-owned lands. The Council bypassed the 'issues' stage by preparing six conceptual schemes for the area. It is not clear why the crucial first step was ignored but certainly it proved to be a dangerous omission. Meanwhile, as a consequence of public discussion of the alternatives, a set of design criteria was outlined, based on a combination of moderate density, middle-income housing, civic buildings and waterfront open space. To assist in the preparation of these criteria, Council appointed a False Creek Review Panel composed of interested citizens and professionals, most of whom had worked closely with the False Creek proposal from its inception. Unfortunately the panel had no clear terms of reference, nor was it in active consultation with City Council. Because no discussion had ever taken place as to what regional and urban role False Creek should really play (the issues) the panel was divided as to whether the area should be planned to meet local needs or to serve regional demands. The major point of contention was whether there should be any housing at all. Low-income and social welfare groups advocated well-designed, low- to middle-income housing to help alleviate the severe housing shortage in Vancouver, while a number of planners and wealthy civic groups preferred a major public park and 'imageable' civic buildings. This conflict was finally resolved by compromise, with civic buildings in the western portion of the area and middle- to upper-income housing plus some public open space in the eastern portion. But in the process one city planner resigned and another was quoted publicly as noting that the area was environmentally unsuitable for housing (*Vancouver Sun*, 3 April 1974).

As with the GVRD experiment, the False Creek case was by no means a failure in citizen participation. Citizens had a substantial say in the planning process and a City Council subcommittee was struck, with the specific responsibility of incorporating citizens' views into the final design. It is doubtful whether the final mix of housing, open space and civic buildings would have been considered had not the participatory process created a significant impact on policy-making. Remember too that the very Council which initiated the False Creek Study was elected on a platform of greater responsiveness to the public.

Nevertheless critical questions remain unanswered. Whose views were heard? To what extent were conflicting opinions properly reconciled within the final plan? Was the Council really responsive to the participatory process, or was it merely paying lip service to principles and not to practice? These questions will be reviewed below.

The Okanagan Basin Agreement Experiment

As the GVRD programme dealt primarily with goals, and the False Creek study was concerned mainly with design concepts, it is useful to look at another participatory experiment that was intended to link goals to specific management issues. This is the Okanagan Basin participation programme, which formed part of the Okanagan Basin water management study. In October 1969 the Government of Canada and the Province of British Columbia agreed to finance jointly a major water management study of the Okanagan Basin in south central British Columbia. The original purpose of the study was to identify the water needs for the region to the year 2020 and to prepare a comprehensive plan to ensure that those needs were met both in quality and quantity. The planners were faced with quite a complicated task. The basin is composed of a series of lakes fed by tributary streams, many of which are diverted to irrigate the economically important orchards of the region. Some of these tributaries were highly productive fishing streams, but diversions for irrigation have seriously reduced the spawning potentials. The local tourist industry is also dependent on high-quality lake water which itself is threatened by discharges from inadequately treated municipal sewage, seepage from improperly sited septic tanks, and run-off from the surrounding orchard lands and cattle-grazing areas. It became evident that to satisfy all these conflicting demands sacrifices would have to be made by all water users at some time or other so that optimum community benefits were obtained, and that water management could not be separated from comprehensive regional economic planning, a notion that had not been fully developed in the original terms of reference for the study.

Another notion that was incorporated, albeit hesitatingly, was public participation. Senior government officials permitted its inclusion in the original terms of reference although unsure of what it might mean. Therefore they initially assigned it a low budget, intended to be used for public presentation of technical data and final recommendations. The original concept of public participation appeared to be a well-meaning form of public relations. With the recognition of the importance of water use in the future planning of the valley it became clear that public participation *had* to mean much more. By mid-1971 the budget had increased tenfold, sufficient to hire a full-time co-ordinator.

The co-ordinator was given fairly wide-ranging terms of reference though he was not as free as his counterpart in the GVRD. He quickly set to work identifying and mobilizing local groups, familiarizing them with the technical issues and assisting them to conceptualize regional goals. After nine months or so it became clear that he was no longer facilitating the process but was manipulating local opinion. This view was shared by many citizens and local press as well as the Okanagan Basin personnel. Consequently his contract was not renewed. This gave local politicians and government officials an ideal chance to scrap the programme. But they did not: in fact they pressed for stronger public involvement and a new co-ordinator.

On the face of it this was a remarkable decision. But again this emphasizes the positive aspects of all the participatory programmes analysed here. The government officials wanted participation to work. They were satisfied with the programme as it had been developed despite the difficulties experienced with the co-ordinator. They were genuinely persuaded that participation was a useful exercise which could fruitfully be integrated with the ongoing planning and technical studies. However, the delay was costly, as the new co-ordinator was faced with a half-completed management study and less than two years to remobilize the community.

The rejuvenated programme centred around six citizen task forces. Four of these were composed of individuals selected by the co-ordinator to represent various interests (agriculture, industry, environmental groups, recreation groups, etc.) in four regions of the valley. The other two consisted of specialists — one of technical experts and the other of local politicians. The *tour de force* of the whole scheme was a seventh task force, consisting of members of the other six working groups, whose job was to pull the views of the entire valley together. Its final report was intended as a synopsis of the region's views on the future of the Basin. Its major recommendations were to place environmental quality above economic growth, to ensure adequate recreational facilities for local residents, to limit projected population and tourism and, most important, to establish a basin-wide planning authority responsible not only for comprehensive planning but also for tax sharing and an ongoing participation programme.

During its four years of operation the Okanagan Study evolved from a public information programme to one of specific citizen participation. Its scope shifted focus from water management targets to regional goals involving questions of growth, immigration, regional distribution and land use controls. It protected its mandate to involve citizens' views, and there is no question that the final report of the Joint Canada—British Columbia Consultative Board took the views of Task Force Seven very much into consideration.

But today the full-time co-ordinator is no longer retained. The task forces have been disbanded, the central clearing office is no longer a hive of activity, though informal citizen consultation continues. Why has the participatory effort not been sustained? The dilemmas found in the Okanagan experiment are also found in the two other case examples cited and are now examined in more detail.

Dilemma 1: From Principles to Practice

All of these case study experiments floundered at the critical point of converting concepts into practice. In every case the political will to pursue the *logical extension* of the participatory planning process faltered, though many of the recommendations reached by the various citizens' groups were subject to subsequent political debate. In part this is because participation must be seen as an evolutionary procedure, not as a static programme. To establish terms of reference implies a cut-off both in terms of time and input. It seems that planning is all too easily dominated by preparation for decision and is not sufficiently prepared to handle participation for subsequent implementation. Possibly policy-makers are still too concerned with conceptualization and decision rather than subsequent enactment. Hence the failure to pursue hindsight analyses or to monitor the on-going effects of planning in action. To ask citizens to conceptualize notions, to provide broad policy statements and to dream up future designs is of course useful and in some senses necessary. But it is also fairly harmless. No commitments need be made, no specific proposals need to be discussed, there is no substantive threat to the political process. Power is still retained by politicians, their advisers and the relevant influential few in the community. But it would be facile to criticize participation limited to the conceptualization phase as a manipulative device, a harmless mechanism through which to promote the rhetoric of citizens' dreams. The real dilemma here is to generate sufficient will and momentum to permit this very valid form of participation to shift gear so as to be useful at the enactment stage. This requires dramatic rethinking both on the part of politicians and participatory advocates. At present the ground rules do not readily permit such a shift and this introduces the second dilemma.

Dilemma 2: Participatory or Representative Democracy

In western democracies politicians are elected to assume responsibility for government. Government means executing as well as discussing, and it also means promoting and protecting the public interest. Generally it is assumed that politicians regard themselves as representatives of constituent interests which shift from issue to issue and time to time. At the local level, however, and this is the area with which we are particularly concerned, many politicians see themselves as altruistic citizens — paternalistic trustees of community affairs — whose actions are rarely scrutinized on a continuing basis. Because their salaries are often very low they must continue in their occupations and therefore have little time to devote to community affairs unless they are willing to make considerable sacrifices in their personal lives. Hence many feel they are delegated to do a job on behalf of the community. In his investigation of such 'citizen politicians' Prewitt (1970) found that they are not generally perceptive of public opinion, especially on social issues (such as zoning, pollution control, open space) where most individuals who are not directly affected hold only weak views in any case. Citizen politicians feel indignant of vituperative public criticism and are especially distraught when that criticism stems from a hard core of 'professional participatory citizens' who, while carrying none of the responsibilities of public office, still get much publicity over their allegations of political non-responsiveness.

The dilemma here is how far to move from an imperfect but familiar arrangement of representative democracy to the uncharted waters of participatory democracy. While the democratic process is predicated upon principles of responsiveness and accountability, in practice few elected officials know much about the broad spectrum of public opinion on most issues, and few citizens have any notion as to how their elected representatives are protecting their interests. Nevertheless the representative system appears to work, for as Almond and Verba (1963) conclude, the potential for public sanction always exists. The people know it and the politicians know it, so for all its inadequacies, representative democracy is still cherished by most of the body politic.

In the present changing times, however, representative democracy may not turn out to be such an enduring concept. The demand for participation is ultimately a demand for some sharing of power. Even at the conceptualizing stage the actively committed citizenry are not entirely altruistic in their motivations. They wish to shape the destiny of their community to conform to a pattern which they would like to see. At the critical point where policies are converted to practice this struggle emerges in raw form.

Politicians are loth to let participation go too far because they never know where it might lead. They see the threat of 'non-representative' citizens undermining their authority in a similar manner to that in which professionals view the opinions of 'uninformed' lay citizens. The Okanagan Task Force Seven recommended a basin-wide authority with reform of local taxation, a notion disturbing to some municipal politicians in the valley. The GVRD policy committees were also talking about tax sharing and the possibility of metro-government, ideas equally distressing to some city politicians in the District. The new chairman of the GVRD was publicly criticized by one of his own colleagues for not being keen to push the programme any further. The fact that it got as far as it did was largely due to the milder and more sympathetic views of the previous chairman. But to blame one individual entirely is clearly unfair: for the programme to be so emasculated a majority of his colleagues must have felt the same way.

It seems that the 'participation' was confined largely to the citizenry and the professionals. In both the False Creek and Okanagan studies the local politicians, while invited to participate, in fact failed to do so. Consequently, events moved in a manner over which they had little control, but in their own minds they must have worked out what degree of participation was maximally acceptable to them. Some compromise plan between housing and open space had to be found for False Creek, so it was found irrespective of citizen protest and the publicly expressed disenchantmant of planning officials. In the Okanagan a special task force was struck expressly to involve the local politicians. But it began too late and most meetings were attended by only a fraction of its members. So the views of the Task Force Seven were never worked out in co-operation with local political opinion.

Dilemma 3: Public Participation and Citizen Representation

In all of the case studies described above essentially the same types of people participated. They are members of a relatively small corps of public-spirited citizens who hold visions of an ideal community and of a responsive political process. While certainly not selfish — for they sacrifice large amounts of time and effort, often for little demonstrable reward — they neverthelsss feel that the benefits of participation outweigh these costs. These benefits may be related to personal ideology, professional advancement, political aspirations or simply genuine public spirited-ness, but they do serve to distinguish such a group from the general body politic. This is particularly the case in goal-oriented participatory programmes where civic or ideological actors are involved. Generally they wish to see change, both in policy and in process, which they believe will benefit everybody, though naturally the goals for which they strive are personally valued. Consequently they tend to be deeply frustrated when they feel that their efforts are being manipulated for others' political ends.

The problem here is that they are not *representative* in the formal sense of the word. They are not elected nor do they actively seek constituency support. They are citizen politicians even at a more general level. They present no platforms and face no challenges should they alter their opinions. Most of the time they prefer to deal with *notions* (not *details* as planners and politicians must), and frequently when details are discussed they become bogged down in dissent. The standard forms of participation — hearings, discussion groups, task forces, review panels and the like — are pabulum for them, while those less familiar with such procedures become suspicious, disenchanted and even hostile.

Only this devoted core survives the process of attrition usually experienced in most participatory experiments. In the GVRD example it has already been noted that most policy committees were decimated and that the final reports were written and reviewed by a very actively committed few. Even in the Okanagan, where a special attempt was made to overcome this problem by carefully selecting the membership and maintaining a regional focus, a similar process of attrition occurred and again only the hard-core 'professional participants' remained. In the False Creek case only the more motivated civic actors appeared to begin with, for the process was not structured to include a widely based citizen input.

The persistence of a 'hard core' will probably remain a feature of participatory programmes. In the absence of incentives to encourage participation only a few people will be mobilized to play their part. One might well ask whether our present political and educational institutions are doing an adequate job to provide these incentives, but the fact remains that, practically speaking, only a very small percentage of population can ever participate in extra-local issues with any degree of effectiveness. An 'open door' policy plus extensive use of the media can help to widen community interest, but the vast majority of citizens will still prefer to play no direct part.

There is a touch of irony about all this. For some actors participation is a convenient path to political success. The temptation to run for local political office is particularly strong. As mentioned earlier, three members of Vancouver City Council began their political lives fighting the very City Hall in which they subsequently determined policy. Their case is by no means unique: probably as many as one-quarter of all candidates for local office now rise from the participatory ranks. The chief spokesman for the GVRD policy committees who publicly castigated the insincerity of the GVRD politicians himself ran for a federal parliamentary seat (which he failed to win). This provided a convenient excuse for GVRD politicians to ignore his demands and dismiss his allegations, which were rather exaggerated. A former mayor in the Okanagan was elected to office partly as a result of publicity gained when he castigated his local council for failing to improve its sewage treatment processes.

The irony of course is that once in power the temptation is to deny the process that put one there and which now threatens to dilute hard-won political power. Even if he is positively inclined towards participation the politician knows that the process as it is currently arranged does not produce representative citizen interest, so he can deny its validity at any time it appears convenient to do so. This was certainly the case in the False Creek and GVRD examples.

Dilemma 4: The Provision of Amenity

In the case studies described here one major point over which the politicians and the citizens parted company was that thorny question of providing environmental amenity. 'Amenity' is a vague term which is used here to cover those niceties which make collective living enjoyable. Open space, waterfront access, views and landscaping, preservation of historic buildings, creative play space, malls, balconies, gardens, pollution control, all fit into the notion of 'amenity'. These are all collective services available and free for all to use or not, as desired. Because everybody can benefit from provision of such amenities it is difficult to find a powerful lobby willing to fight for them and even more difficult to generate a consensus as to how much and of what kind they should be. To provide amenity means some sort of coercive payment – usually in the form of taxes – which is never politically popular.

If participation is not simply to be bush fire fighting – the protection of individual self-interest – much of the debate over putting policy into programmes must centre around how to provide amenity. The GVRD policy committees were unanimous in prescriptions for limiting growth, encouraging open space and higher residential densities and protecting natural and cultural amenities. While much of the False Creek controversy was created by differing views as to the area's role locally or regionally, a subsidiary battle took place over the respective roles of amenity versus functionalism in the compromise plan. The Okanagan Task Force Seven placed 'environmental quality' above economic growth. It advocated a reduction in the planned growth of tourist facilities, stiffer land use controls to protect rural amenity and regional waste treatment facilities.

Both the Okanagan and the GVRD proposals are laudable in principle but only possible to implement if some sort of regional co-ordination is guaranteed. Some areas will have to grow while others remain rural: some areas will receive lucrative tax-generating facilities while others will face an increased tax burden. This is the great political test. To what extent will local municipalities share growth and taxation for the greater community good? In both case studies local politicians showed that they were still not ready to grasp this nettle.

So while the notion of amenity is widely acepted, its formal incorporation within the planning system is not. Private developers tend to pay only lip service to it unless property values are enhanced by exciting environmental design. To provide public amenity is a chore rather than a central notion in the planning of all public and private space. But even public proposals pay lip service to amenity partly because no political lobby exists and partly because taxes are involved. So here we return to the intractable issue of representation. On the one hand politicians claim that they have many legitimate demands upon the tax dollar which is provided by all citizens, while on the other civic and ideological actors who emerge through the participatory process and who press for the provision of amenity services are not regarded as representative.

Dilemma 5: Personality and Preparedness

In both the Okanagan and GVRD case studies, the services of the participation co-ordinator were not available at the most ciritcal stages in the proceedings. The job of co-ordinator requires a particular combination of talents which is almost impossible to find in any one individual. An abiding interest in people, a knowledge of social processes and political theory, a deep understanding of planning principles, a familiarity with all kinds of technical information, a facility to explain and clarify without distortion and manipulation, a sharp wit and a keen sense of occasion and of critical events are but some of the many attributes such a person must have.

Above all, he must be flexible, ready to tackle new approaches as the occasion demands or as the programme dictates. These are not readymade qualities but must be nurtured by experience, frustration and achievement. The danger is of becoming so committed to the job as to lose perspective of its objectives. The temptation is to wield power and to manipulate wants in certain directions. Susceptibility to egomania is almost overwhelming.

In no sense can the co-ordinator be held wholly culpable for the events described in the case studies. The programmes were experimental and innovative, their terms of reference were unique, and political responsiveness was variable. The transition from policy to practice was never built-in; indeed the programmes seemed almost designed to be self-destructive at a certain critical point. The co-ordinator is faced throughout with the four dilemmas outlined above. If he activates local groups he may subvert established notions of political power and authority. If he plays the political game he may be accused of compliance by his citizen sponsors. If he heeds one set of wishes over others he is culpable of manipulation, and so on. The job of co-ordinator is probably the most difficult to be trained for and the most difficult to hold, yet it is possibly the most crucial element in the participatory process. The enormous potential of the position yet the paucity of suitable applicants must surely attest to the inadequacy of present policies in higher education. This is a challenge that must be squarely faced.

Some Possible Solutions

There are no clear-cut solutions to these dilemmas: indeed there may be no solutions at all. Participation, like common law, is moulded by case experience. There is no set pattern. What may be suitable for one area and one issue may not be appropriate for another. Even during the evolution of a programme, the participation procedures may have to be changed. Careful monitoring and hindsight analysis of a variety of ongoing programmes is a first requirement, wherever possible by some sort of independent investigation.

Probably the single most pressing difficulty facing participation is the involvement of the citizenry at large. At present most of the standard techniques such as hearings, task forces, etc., do not appear to be suitable for people concerned with local issues and day-to-day living. Many do not see the need to worry themselves with city-wide or regional problems despite the fact that most issues have both regional as well as local significance. For example, in the Kitsilano area of Vancouver, (a middle-income residential section of the city undergoing a transition from single-family to multiple-family dwellings), many residents are opposing further development of high-rise buildings. To control all growth there now would simply shift housing pressures elsewhere. Yet few of the protestors appear to care about housing densities in other parts of the city.

Somehow then the link must be forged between local area interest and a concern for the wider and longer term community welfare. It is probably fair to say that many people are vitally interested in local issues which may look insignificant to regional politicians or ideological actors. Day-care centres, playgrounds, cycle paths, traffic separation and other public amenities do mean a lot to people at the community level.

In the United States there is a current resurgence in the *practice* of community co-operation via active citizen involvement and communal concern. Many experimental neighbourhood organizations, complete with professional assistance and modest budgets, have sprung up. Their aim is to stabilize community demographic structure, put fresh vitality into neighbourhood organizations and instil a sense of pride at the very local level. Block organizations — groups of neighbours acting in concert — are also flourishing. Neighbours are beginning to help each other repair their homes, look after each other's children, form car pools, and raise money through 'block parties' to plant trees and fight developers. Many of these budding participatory endeavours are growing in stature as incipient success breeds a vital sense of community spirit in areas that once seemed to have no hope.

In Vancouver the new Director of Planning is actively promoting the formation of local area planning committees. These proposals are still at a formative stage but the aim is to put a full-time professional planner at the disposal of each committee, members of which are either appointed or elected by community groups. The committee membership will reflect a cross-section of community interests and will be responsible for transmitting community concerns to City Hall. The planner is placed in a difficult position, for though paid by City Council he is supposed to be independent both of the Director of Planning and of any particular citizens' group. His job is to translate the objectives of the community into a workable planning programme. Being employed by City Hall technically makes it easier for him to gain access to city planners and politicians, but it remains to be seen how effective he can be if his proposals conflict with established city or regional policies.

Here is the bridge between policy and operation, between local area and region, between citizen and politician. But the structure only provides the avenues and the success of the whole programme will depend upon careful resolution of the various dilemmas (still inherent even at this level) mentioned above. Many people feel that City Council did not authorize sufficient funds either to hire the necessary planning personnel or to provide an adequate budget. There remains little guarantee that the membership of the citizens' committees will be guarantee that the membership of the citizen's committees will be accountable and representative, for, even with the best will in the world, volunteer citizens will find it difficult to identify all views and to attend all meetings. Somehow these individuals must be encouraged to accept responsibility for their position: this is a throny problem which might be overcome either if they were paid and/or were granted sufficient power to make the job attractive, stimulating and above all competitive. Council are probably willing to experiment but are uncertain as to where all this will lead — ward representation? community power? The difficulty with controlled experiments is that they may be emasculated before they begin.

But it is a beginning and it is in the right direction. If participation can be directed to local area involvement then there is hope that the broader civic issues and regional questions will become of more relevance and interest to all citizens. Participation, when it is most effective, is educational, therapeutic and consciousness-raising. To be successful it must surely activate its proponents into a wider community understanding and more sober political scrutiny. The GVRD was right in intent but wrong in execution. Goals-orientation must be combined with local area political articulation, but there should also be a commitment to an ongoing process and some sharing of responsibilities. If participation is designed in part to develop a community of interest, then all participants must be prepared to make certain sacrifices in the search for a better existence. In such a scheme of things personal self-interest, suspicion and indifference are constant threats. The continuing challenge is to create a participatory arrangement where such threats are sterilized.[1,2]

Notes

1. Since this chapter was written (June, 1975) Vancouver City Council voted to reduce the budget for the local area planning programme and to deny extra planning personnel requested by the city's director of planning. The scheme is now confined to a small number of local areas, but fortunately these are parts of the city where participatory assistance is most desired and readily forthcoming from among active local groups. As a final comment, it is worth mentioning that in Britain local area participation programmes that focus on implementation as well as preparatory discussion are proving to have some success.
2. Readers might find the following references useful in following up the case studies described in this chapter:
   Guttstein, D., 1975. *Vancouver Ltd.*, Toronto: James Lorimer.
   O'Riordan, J., 1976. 'The public involvement programme in the Okanagan Basin Study, *Natural Resources Journal,* **16**, 177–196.

References

Almond, G. M. & S. Verba 1963. *The Civic Culture*, Boston: Little, Brown.
Pendakur, V. S., 1972. *Citizens and Freeways*, Vancouver: School of Community and Regional Planning, University of British Columbia.
Prewitt, K., 1970. *The Recruitment of Political Leaders: A Study of Citizen Politicians*, New York: Bobbs Merrill.

12

Participation through Centrally Planned Social Change: Lessons from the American Experience on the Urban Scene

ROGER E. KASPERSON

For America the 1960s were a testing time, a turbulent decade when the fabric of the social order seemingly began to unravel. The first half of the decade witnessed a protracted struggle over racial equality, produced widespread sit-ins at segregated service facilities and Martin Luther King's memorable march through the white violence of Chicago Streets. On the heels of this non-violent struggle for equal rights, a conflagration of 'ghetto riots' illuminated the desperation of blacks and poor whites in the decaying slums of American cities. The second half of the decade was, of course, primarily the tragedy of Vietnam, an unpopular war which bitterly divided the American nation and cast doubt on the moral rectitude of American foreign policy. In New York the repeated stabbing of a woman before a skyscraper gallery of passive witnesses seemed to symbolize an erosion of humanity in urban life, a growing indifference to the fate of one's friends and neighbours.

It was also a decade, however, which saw an evolving national recognition that these events, surrealistic as they appeared, arose from basic flaws in social structure and institutions. Critics agreed that existing governmental services directed at these problems were failing to reach the victims. The conviction grew that any new programmes must break through the inertia of existing bureaucracy and the passivity of those who lived in poverty, in the city's slums, that those who suffered from social problems must themselves participate actively in their solution. Yet the capability for effective action clearly lay beyond the limits of the city or even the metropolis. Given the magnitude of the problems, only centrally planned social change seemed then, and now, to have any prospect for widespread success.

Happily the need coincided with the 'New Frontier' and 'Great Society' administrations, national leadership committed to liberal reform. In 1964 President Johnson, in his 'Message on Poverty' to the Congress, pointed to the 'one-fifth of our people' who constitute the poor, who do not share in the benefits of American society. Shortly thereafter the Economic Opportunity Act kicked off the 'War on Poverty'. A scant two years later over 1000 'community action agencies' scattered throughout urban America were sponsoring a variety of anti-poverty programmes in which greater participation by the poor themselves in the design and implementation of these programmes was a central goal. In that same year Congress also passed the Demonstration Cities and Metropolitan Development Act, intended to rebuild decaying neighbourhoods by co-ordinating the activities of a wide array of federal, state, local and private agencies in a number of target cities, and authorized some $1.2 billion in support. This effort, which came to be known as Model Cities, also sought to create 'widespread citizen participation'. Yet by the end of the decade most proponents and opponents were in agreement — whatever else had been accomplished, the effort for effective citizen participation had failed (Rose, 1972; Aleshire, 1972; Alinsky, 1965). The most massive federal effort ever undertaken to increase grass-roots participation had not delivered. What happened? What lessons are there for other societies or future efforts?

Centrally planned social change, as represented by the Community Action and Model Cities programmes, involves a number of steps or elements: (i) an identification of the problem (definition); (ii) a social theory to explain the incidence and causes of the problem (understanding); (iii) a conceptualization of the means for intervention and social change (strategy); (iv) an institutional and organization effort to accomplish the strategy (mobilization), and (v) a sustained allocation of human and financial resources (commitment). Breakdowns in any of these components could conceivably explain any deficiencies or shortcomings in the actual social change resulting. The framework provides a useful means for evaluating the question of what went wrong.

Problem Definition and Understanding

Following the Second World War and until the 1960s, American federal and local policy virtually ignored the poor. America had long assumed that the cause of poverty lay in the basic defects of the individual. Comforted by the Horatio Alger myth of opportunity, political leaders saw little need to tamper with institutions or social structure; rather therapy for or resocialization of those who were poor seemed the more appropriate response.

Several events in the early 1960s contributed to the 'discovery' of the poor once again in American society. John F. Kennedy was shocked by the poverty which he encountered during his primary campaign in West Virginia in 1960. In 1962, Michael Harrington's *The Other America* dramatized the plight of the poor in America. The civil rights movement was also revealing the extent of discriminations against both urban and rural blacks. Robert Kennedy's preliminary work on a National Service Corps had convinced him and close colleagues of the magnitude of the poverty problem and the unresponsiveness of the existing social welfare bureaucracies.

The founders of the anti-poverty programme began with a different conception of the roots of poverty. Particularly important in this alternative view was Richard Cloward and Lloyd Ohlin's (1960) *Delinquency and Opportunity* which advocated 'opportunity theory' to explain juvenile delinquency. According to this theory, cultural goals, particularly the achievement of success and wealth, are diffused to all

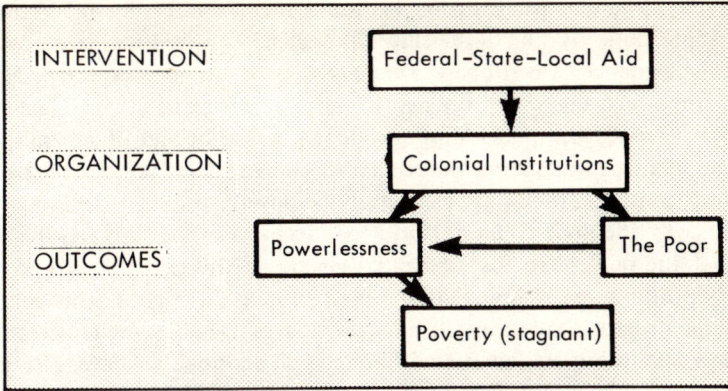

Figure 12.1 Model 1: the existing system

members of society while the social structure permits only certain members the opportunity for attaining these goals. The divergence between accepted cultural values and opportunities to realize these values breeds frustration, eventually manifesting itself as delinquency and other forms of deviant behaviour.

This conception of poverty and its effects suggested some avenues for analysis. Since a defective system and environment were now the culprits, they, rather than the individual, became the targets for change. This entailed a significant break with convential wisdom. The emphasis switched to community and institutional change. The long-run objective was to create new opportunities via institutional and structural change: what was needed was a more detailed formulation of the poverty problem to guide an ambitious effort of central intervention for change.

Figure 12.1 presents more detailed portrayal of the problem which emerged. This conceptualization of poverty centred upon an interlocking set of courses perhaps best described as the 'culture' of poverty. An array of sources provided aid through an institutional structure which was largely 'colonial', in that services were provided *for* the poor with little say or involvement by the people themselves in the institutions or programmes. The poor remained subjects, not participants, acted upon by those who purported to know their needs better than they themselves. The result was a pervasive sense of powerlessness which militated against any mobilization for change among those in need. Yet until such mobilization materialized, any major breakthrough in institutional and community structure would not be forthcoming. Thus, the problem was how to break into this closed circle to induce change — which was needed to expand opportunities and provide resources (in the Cloward and Ohlin sense). But the conceptualization of the problem did suggest that far-reaching intervention would be required.

A Strategy for Change

The strategy adopted in community action emerged from several important experiences in the Kennedy Administration. One was the civil rights movement, sustained by the direct participation of blacks in the South, by the activism of young people, and by the leadership of Martin Luther King, Jr. The other important experience was Robert Kennedy's work on a prospective National Service Corps which uncovered the massive service bureaucracy which had evolved over time to service the poor. More and more, Kennedy and other anti-poverty programme founders became convinced that this bureaucracy, remote, unresponsive and insensitive, was an important element in the poverty problem. Repeatedly they were asked why the poor could not plan for themselves. They apparently came to believe that the only hope for substantial change in this situation was to bypass existing institutions and to stimulate the poor to help themselves. This conviction that only direct participation by the poor themselves would succeed in creating the needed new institution and additional resources to continue whatever efforts were initiated by the federal government became the central plank in the anti-poverty programme. In fact, in its early stages community action was to be the entire programme.

The previous work of the Ford Foundation Grey Areas programme and the President's Committee on Juvenile Delinquency and Youth Crime was also an important influence. In the late 1950s the Ford Foundation, viewing the stagnation of social reform in the Eisenhower Administration, embarked on a new approach to the problems of American cities. In contrast with the urban renewal programme, the Grey Areas Project attempted to provide a broad, coherent attack on the slums by concentration on the school system. The programme assumed that any effective social intervention required the participation of the people involved and the development of indigenous leadership. Eventually the Foundation expended some $20 million in support of the programme.

Early in his administration, President Kennedy established a committee for community development and action programmes to combat juvenile delinquency. Emphasizing community development and self-help, the Committee awarded grants to sixteen cities over a three-year period. In each case the programme attempted to gain the active participation of affected residents and the support of local leadership.

Both programmes failed to achieve any dramatic breakthrough of participation by poor people and slum residents. But, since they emphasized both the application of Cloward and Ohlin's 'opportunity theory' to the social problems of cities and the mobilization of chronic non-participants in new 'self-help' efforts, they did create a pool of theory, people and experience upon which the Community Action Programme was to draw.

The strategy for intervention which eventually emerged may be presented in model form, as shown in Figure 12.2. Federal aid would be applied directly to the poor themselves, bypassing both the labyrinth of social service agencies ministering to the poor and the direct political authority of City Hall. The latter part of this strategy was apparently aimed particularly at southern cities. Kennedy officials believed that such direct aid would revitalize institutions because the poor would have a personal substantial stake and involvement.

The notions of 'self-help' and 'countervailing power' guided much of the

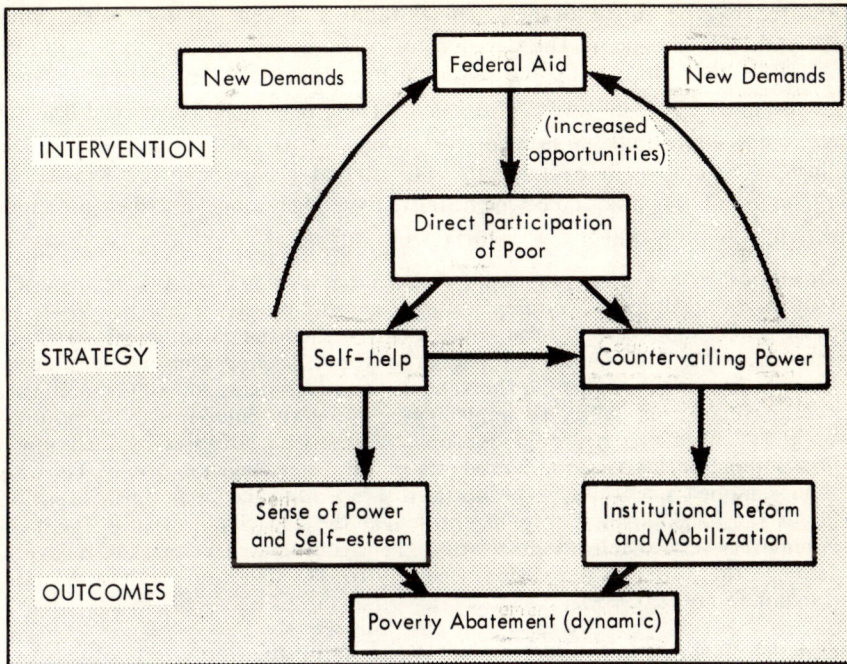

Figure 12.2 Model 2: community action programme

formulation of the Community Action Programme. The services of the welfare bureaucracy would never reach the poor, in this view, if they continued to be dominated by the welfare professional and traditional political authorities. Only when the poor could act on their own behalf to challenge those who presently determined their fate would the situation change substantively. This process of self-help would also effectively combat the sense of 'powerlessness' that passivity before colonial institutions had induced. A new sense of power and self-esteem would emerge in its place. So direct participation by the poor outside of normal community and bureaucratic authority changes was a key ingredient to community action. It was also to create the 'countervailing power' which was to encourage reform in the existing bureaucracy. It was, further, to be the lever which, through a mushrooming of new demands, would capture additional resources to combat poverty. The Kennedy people were well aware that no new administration was about to win sufficient funds from Congress to eradicate poverty. It would be necessary to initiate in one fell swoop a process which somehow would be self-sustaining and capable of capturing other significant resources.

The model depended upon common goals and rationality. Programme planners assumed that when the new community anti-poverty agency demonstrated the ineffectivenss of present institutions and programmes, there would be a common recognition of the problem and a concerted effort among the various agencies and organizations to reformulate and redirect their effort. This process would be stimulated by the carrot of new federal funds and kept honest by the direct participation of the poor. The deployment of funds was to constitute a form of 'ju-jitsu', application of limited resources at key points to capture larger resources for a sustained effort in poverty abatement. These new incentives would lead to a new co-operation and co-ordination among service institutions and a new willingness to engage in experiments and internal change. Sanford Kravitz, the co-ordinator of the task force which drafted the legislation, described the model underlying the programme:

> Our model of how the community action program would work went something like this: A community would carefully study its poverty problems, locate the most severe pockets of need, and identify them as target areas slated for intensive effort. It would plan a program for these areas that would affect all relevant institutions, that is, the schools, social services, job opportunities. It would enhance its ability to implement its program objectives by inclusion of political leadership. It would 'remain honest' to its purposes by inclusion of voices representing the poor, residents of the target neighborhoods. Thus, the model implied a central local authority to exert influence on and make decisions about the local poverty program, presumed the capacity to engage the major community-service-delivery institutions in a coordinated effort, and above all assumed the power of persuasion necessary to allocate resources to carry on the program (Kravitz, 1969).

The model, in short, was one of mobilization, of enlisting the variety of necessary institutions through challenge to the existing order in an enlightened attack upon shared goals.

The Community Action Programme

Section 202 of the Economic Opportunity Act of 1964 outlines the objectives of the programme:

> The term 'Comminity action program' means a program (1) which mobilizes and utilizes resources, public or private, of any urban or rural, or combined urban and rural geographic area (referred to in this part as a "community") . . . (2) which provides services, assistance, and other activities of sufficient scope and size to give promise of progress toward elimination of poverty or a cause or causes of poverty through developing employment opportunities, improving human performance, motivation, and productivity, or bettering the conditions under which people live, learn or work: (3) which is developed, conducted, and administered with the maximum feasible participation of residents of the areas and members of the groups served; and (4) which is conducted, administered, or coordinated by a public or private non-profit agency . . .

It is clear that the framers of the legislation gave little thought at the time or in the legislative hearings to the precise meaning or possible implementation of the now famous term 'maximum feasible participation'. Boone (1972), one of the founders of the Community Action Programme, points out that there was little interest or support for the concept. Congressional debate largely overlooked the clause, no organized constituency emerged from local areas or citizen groups to support its passage, and even President Johnson was largely oblivious of its existence. It was put there by several Kennedy men and just went through with the rest of the Act.

In the initial effort to establish a Community Action Agency in the various cities, it quickly became apparent that the poor were in no position to compete effectively with established authority and organizations for equity in the agency. As a result, Office of Economic Opportunity (OEO) officials within a year emerged as advocates of the poor. By mid–1965, some OEO regional directors, especially in the South, were insisting that non-white representation be at least one-third of the Agency numbers. Eventually in 1966, OEO formally recognized a tripartite division of representation by requiring a 'three-legged stool' for Community Action Programme boards — one-third public officials, one-third representatives of private agencies, and one-third representatives of the poor. In the effort to upgrade or safeguard the role of the poor, 'maximum feasible participation' stumbled at the first of the hurdles posed by the magnitude of the problem. 'Maximum feasible' was to be no more than one-third; the non-poor would continue to rule the poor. Community action was on its way to becoming a 'safe' programme.

The *OEO Workbook* outlines the two methods for stimulating participation by the poor in the Community Action Programme. First, the poor may be included in positions within the community action agency 'that permit the poor to influence the objectives, policies, actions, and services of the organization' (Clarke & Hopkins, 1968). Second, the poor may be assisted to develop 'autonomous and self-managed organizations which are competent to exert political influence on behalf of their own self-interest'. Both of these measures, and particularly the latter, sparked conflicts over control of the Community Action Programme. As it turned out, 95 per cent took the more autonomous course of existence outside City Hall control (Strange, 1972). It quickly became apparent that countervailing power to traditional authority could be created in American cities. The response came quickly. Only months after the inception of the Programme, the United States Conference of Mayors adopted a resolution proposed by Mayors Shelley of San Francisco and Yorty of Los Angeles:

> Whereas no responsible Mayor can accept the implications in the OEO Workbook that the goals of this program can only be achieved by creating tensions between the poor and the existing agencies and by fostering class struggle: NOW THEREFORE BE IT RESOLVED that the administration be urged to insure that any policy ... assure the continuing control of any expenditures relative to this program by the fiscally responsible local officials (Rose, 1972).

A number of mayors, such as Mayor Richard Daley of Chicago, successfully subverted the intent of the programme by appointing city department heads to the positions supposedly reserved for the poor. Other mayors and their colleagues complained bitterly to the President, the Vice-President and Congress, demanding that OEO fund only those projects approved by City Hall. The battle was over almost before it started. Compared to big city mayors, the constituency of the poor could muster little political clout with a Democratic President already beset by the Vietnam War. The Administration instructed OEO administrators to emphasize jobs rather than participation, the conservative director of the General Service Administration became Sargent Shriver's, deputy, more conservative administrators replaced reform-minded OEO personnel, and OEO began to emphasize more traditional and conventional programmes. It was through this diluting process that the programme survived in subsequent years.

Despite these problems, ther were some significant tangible accomplishments. Over 1000 programmes operated during the second half of the decade. Community action made a significant contribution to providing employment for minority groups and the urban poor. It was also a training ground for thousands of talented people denied other routes of social mobility and thereby broke the stranglehold of old-line, white politicians over young black neighbourhood leaders. There was also much learning in the numerous encounters with political elites which would stand the poor in good stead in subsequent experiences with Model Cities. Finally, the network of nascent organizations which emerged provided some lasting spillover in other areas of public policy competition.

The debt sheet, alas, is no less impressive. Levels of participation in the target neighbourhoods remained disappointingly low. Programmes rarely succeeded in attracting more than 5 to 15 per cent of the prospective participants. This, of course, is scarcely surprising given the low levels of involvement which prevail in American cities to begin with, and the long years of unsuccessful encounters with traditional political authority were scarcely conducive to an outpouring of enthusiasm. In fact, the poor were probably justified in their scepticism that commitments would be fulfilled.

Moreover, representation posed another problem. The Programme never developed any standards or detailed guidelines for selecting the representatives of the poor. Inevitably, there was a 'creaming' process which skimmed off for involvement those who were most 'reasonable' or 'acceptable' – in effect, the elites or better-off residents of the neighbourhoods. Once involved in city-wide agencies, these representatives of the poor tended to be drawn away from their own constituents and thrust into lower- and middle-rung administrative positions. One deleterious impact, then, was to siphon off the aggressive leadership into 'safe' positions, thereby decapitating indigenous leadership.

Despite the watering down of the Community Action Programme and the success of traditional political authorities in eliminating the threat of countervailing power and institutional reform, it was clear that a different model would prevail for any new federal programmes aimed at the city. Thus, Model Cities was to proceed with an alternative conception of citizen participation.

The Model Cities Programme

The architects of the Model Cities Programme resolved early on to avoid any repetition of the 'Brave New World' of community action. If the Community Action Programme aimed at new institutions, self-help and countervailing power,

Model Cities recognized established political authority. Model Cities was intended, like community action, to be a broad programme of centrally planned social change, but it was one of planning and co-ordination rather than overt politics. In fact, perhaps more emphasis was placed on improving the 'delivery systems' than on the content of what was being delivered.

The motivations for the programme were several. At the time Democrats in Congress and the executive branch were dissatisfied with the piecemeal programmes, particularly those in the housing area, aimed at the cities. The Democratic leadership had become convinced that an ambitious programme of federal spending for the cities was required. Many conservative Republicans and some Democrats were unhappy with what they saw as gross inefficiency and a lack of organization in current programmes. The urban renewal programme in particular drew criticism from liberal and conservative alike. The riots in ghetto areas during 1964 and 1965 galvanized the administration to take action on the range of problems confronting urban areas. In late 1965, President Johnson appointed a special Task Force on Urban Problems. Rejecting the Community Action model of direct funding to neighbourhood groups, the Task Force emphasized instead the need to co-ordinate the variety of piecemeal efforts into a concerted programme. The model for conceptualizating the problem reflected a throwback to the early stages of the Ford Foundation's Grey Areas Project. Instead of a systematic attack on the sources of the 'culture of poverty', Model Cities centred upon blighted neighbourhoods and the need to co-ordinate physical and social planning. The objective was to concentrate available resources and activities at all levels of government and private enterprise with liberal federal subsidies in an attack upon the physical and social blight of a particular area of the city. It was, in short, a programme directed to the manifestations of basic social processes and not to the causes themselves. To avoid controversies plaguing community action agencies, administration planners decided to nominate state and local agencies as the instruments of social change. Indeed, the programme came to recognize the victory of the mayors over the OEO 'government guerrillas'.

Despite these precautions, however, the programme required selling. While there was support for subsidization programmes, there was powerful opposition in Congress to social innovation in institutions and to participation for the poor. Republicans, in the House especially, but also in the Senate, were vocal in their opposition. Eventually, after several language changes, the bill gained the support needed for passage. It was necessary to add assurances that Model Cities would not weaken the control of local government over federal grant-in-aid programmes; to delete provisions requiring racial integration in the plans; to expand the programme to include small cities; and to eliminate the requirement for a special agency to administer Model Cities. Despite this watering-down of the bill, only a determined lobbying effort by the administration and the United States Conference of Mayors allowed the bill to squeak through the House on a 178-to-141 vote.

The programme eventually enacted consisted of two stages: planning and implementation. The planning stage was to last for two years and was to involve the development of a comprehensive city demonstration programme. The federal government supported four-fifths of the costs of this planning. Implementation of the plans would span a five-year period. Congress authorized $24 million for planning and $900 million for implementation in some 60 to 70 cities. Since all funds were to be channelled to the local City Demonstration Agency through the city council, the latter exercised *de facto* control over the programme.

With respect to participation, the language of the act, while more cautious than that of the Community Action Programme, was no less ambiguous:

(A) A comprehensive city demonstration program is eligible for assistance under ... this title if (1) physical and social problems ... are such that a comprehensive city demonstration program is necessary ...; (and) (2) the program is of sufficient magnitude ... to provide ... widespread citizen participation in the program, maximum opportunity for employing residents of the area in all phases of the program, and enlarged opportunity for work and training.

(B) In implementing this subchapter the Secretary shall (1) emphasize local initiative in the planning, development, and implementation of comprehensive city demonstration programs (and) (2) insure ... prompt response to local initiative, and maximum flexibility in programming consistent with the requirements of law and sound administrative practice ...

The phrase 'widespread citizen participation' certainly meant something less ambitious than 'maximum feasibility participation', but what? It was unclear who (minorities, residents, poor people) was to participate or how. The role of established city agencies, the emphasis on planning, the lack of guidelines or performance standards delineating 'widespread citizen participation', and the limited time available rendered citizen participation virtually impossible during the planning stage. An initial evaluation, not surprisingly, found 'inadequate participation by neighboring residents in the preparation of applications and inadequate provisions for meaningful participation in implementation phases' (Urban Data Service, 1970),

In late 1967, the Department of Housing and Urban Development (HUD) established six standards to guide citizen participation efforts: (i) an *organizational structure* to involve neighbourhood residents in programme planning and implementation; (ii) *leadership* which is acceptable to neighbourhood residents as representative of their interests; (iii) *sufficient information* with adequate lead time; (iv) *technical assistance*; (v) *financial assistance*; and (vi) *employment of neighbourhood residents* in programme planning and execution. The technical and financial assistance was particularly well-planned to citizen groups and improved substantially on the services available in the Community Action Programme. A 1968 speech by H. Ralph Taylor of HUD made explicit the evolving Model Cities position on citizen participation:

The pattern of citizen participation must be set locally. HUD will not make the Solomon's choice between competing neighborhood groups, each trumpeting its importance, virtue and priority claim as the representative of the neighborhood. ... The objective is to encourage a working relationship between neighborhood and city government that can endure long after the conclusion of the Model Cities Program. ... In this context, citizen participation is an essential and crucial element of the Model Cities Program. *It is not the objective of the program* [Italics added.] (Ripley, 1972).

There can be little doubt that for Model Cities the role of participation was peripheral rather than central. It was not, as in community action, conceived as a causal factor in the strategy of change. The Programme was not aimed at 'self-help' or 'countervailing power': quite the reverse. Resident participation was included simply because it was politically unavoidable. It was necessary for Programme legitimation, but no theory suggested its logical inclusion. At base it was a design in co-optation. This programme would entail no risks, for Washington or for the mayors.

The community response to Model Cities is understandable only in the context of the Community Action Programme. While the social architects in Washington had one strategic model of social change, the target 'citizens' had their own. Neighbourhood residents had learned well from their struggles over programme control in community action. The attempt to restore social reform to the established guardians of the poor banged up against determined, battle-scared community veterans in nearly every city which initiated a Model Cities programme. These citizens were reinforced by many OEO reformist administrators who, noting President Johnson's shift of support from community action to Model Cities, migrated to the new programme where they injected a healthy dose of 'militancy' into the sedate objectives of the programme. The conflicts which erupted were as bitter as any in the Community Action Programme. The outcomes of these struggles over citizen autonomy speak to the power of participation as a learned skill. Citizens in all the Model Cities programmes in western United States, which had originally relegated citizen groups to a purely advisory role, had somehow managed to wrest *de facto* veto power over programme decision-making within one year after the initial funding. In every case where the Model Cities neighbourhood was black, neighbourhood residents had won numerical dominance in the governing coalition (Moguluf, 1969). In other Model Cities programmes on a national scale, there was an interesting process of 'reverse co-optation' or radicalization in which agency experts lent out to Model Cities emerged as committed advocates of the poor. Because of the success of community participants in forcing their way into positions of influence, the Model Cities programmes which eventually emerged were usually the product of lengthy conflict and bargaining and turned out to be more responsive to neighbourhood residents than the programme authors ever intended. Had it not been for the unbending commitment by Washington to established local authority, Model Cities might have continued the community action rebellion.

In his eleven-city study, Kaplan (1970) found two key factors which explained much of the course of the Model Cities experience. In cities where residents remained relatively unorganized and lacked leadership which could speak authoritatively for their constituents, the established city agencies dominated programme development. Where citizens were organized and tensions were not so high as to make collaboration risky, a co-operative process emerged. But where city officials confronted serious tensions and well-organized neighborhood groups, the latter dominated Model Cities planning from the outset. Much depended, in short, upon the risks perceived by City Hall and the capability and skill of citizen groups in carrying out their demands.

Despite the success of neighbourhood residents in winning a role in the control of its programmes, many of the problems which pervaded Community Action lingered on in Model Cities. Participation levels on the whole remained abysmally low. The more middle-class elements of neighbourhoods continued to dominate citizen participation structures. Communication between elected neighbourhood members of resident boards with their own constituents was often weak and sporadic. In the view of one City Demonstration Agency director, inadequate representation apparently convinced many neighbourhood residents that those they elected were a scant improvement on traditional political authorities.

On the other hand, there have been significant accomplishments. Some cities, such as Cambridge and Boston, Massachusetts and Dayton, Ohio, delegated substantial power to neighbourhood groups. In those cities and others, the community action experience confirmed that participation, once initiated, tends to mushroom and to become self-sustaining. Once involved, neighbourhood participants demand a larger and larger role in planning local projects. Second, Model Cities also provided an important avenue of social mobility for neighbourhood leadership talent. Third, the programme encouraged city governments to engage in comprehensive planning, to co-ordinate local services, and to strengthen the effectiveness of delivery systems.

The overall approach of Model Cities remained generally conservative in the years following its inception. With City Hall riding hard on the design of local programmes, there was, on the whole, relatively little experimentation. The programme soon expanded the number of demonstration cities to 150, de-emphasized social redistribution, and simultaneously tightened the control by mayors and city governments. As a result the programme gained in political acceptability. Only the defection of a conservative Republican saved the programme from termination in 1967. The following year the administration requested $650 million and received less than half ($300 million). In fiscal year 1969, Congress appropriated over twice that amount ($600 million). This support remained relatively stable over the next several years, with very little Congressional opposition. By fiscal year 1971, 98 per cent of the Senate Democrats and 100 per cent of the Senate Republicans, along with 99 per cent of the House Democrats and 95 per cent of the House Republicans, followed suit. Support among city mayors was no less enthusiastic. Model Cities had uncovered the route to political success.

What Went Wrong?

The beginning of this chapter asks what went wrong with federal intervention into participation during the decade of the 1960s. A fully satisfying answer to this question is beyond the scope of this discussion, but answers to two important questions would provide at least a partial explanation. First, what types of problems were associated with central intervention into participation in urban social problems? Second, was the participation paradigm adequate for the adopted strategy of social change?

The two examples of central intervention, despite the marked contrasts, show several important similarities. They shared, for example, a liberal faith in social reform through planning and central intervention. There is an assumption that by exposing the existence of a social problem, by highlighting the fate of those who suffer from it, by harnessing people of good will for its solution, and by demonstrating that such reform can indeed be achieved, widespread social innovation will follow. Such a view, of course, is a monument to liberal thinking, to a belief in reform through orderly and rational planning. Shared values and good will are assumed; leadership from the central government is the vital need. To begin then, there were erroneous bases to the philosophical framework which ultimately sabotaged central intervention of social change. A less benign view of social institutions and power relationships would have served the architects of change in better stead.

The programmes were also similar in their degree of commitment. Both harnessed rather paltry sums (Community Action, $500 million; Model Cities, $900 million) for rather grandiose objectives. Such a pool of resources, far less than the budget of a single city, could scarcely produce the impacts envisioned unless one assumes a ready propagation of imitators of the original demonstration models. Both programmes (and especially Community Action) were, in their objective to induce far-reaching changes in a limited number of carefully selected 'models', examples of social redistributive policies. But since social redistribution predictably generates controversy and political conflict, these programmes were immediately beset by vociferous local and national oppostion. Both were, in fact, nearly cancelled within two years of their inception.

The route to programme survival, summarized in Figure 12.3, involved first a

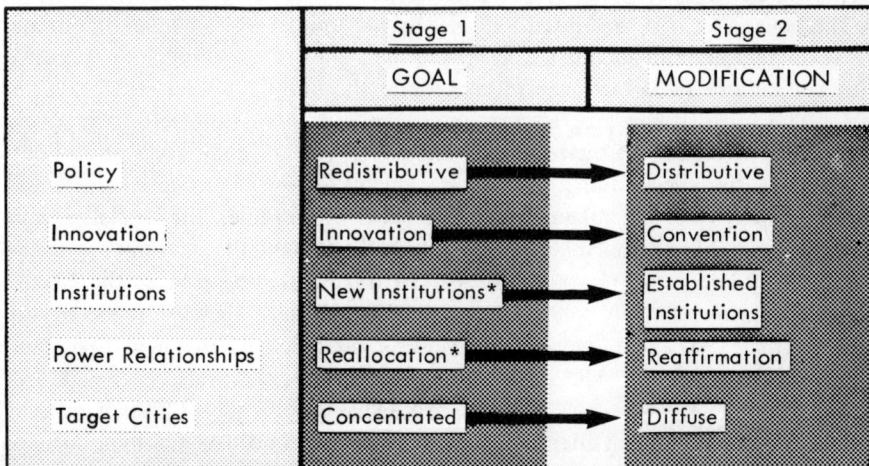

*applicable only to the Community Action Programme

Figure 12.3 Model 3: programme metamorphosis for survival

dilution of the 'change' component of the programmes themselves to placate traditional political authorities. Consequently, Community Action Programme directors de-emphasized its more controversial elements, replaced the more reformist of its regional personnel, and ceased to bypass City Hall. Second, both programmes surrendered on the 'demonstration' strategy of concentrated funds applied to selected cities. To win political support in Congress, the administration spread its money thinner over a much larger number of cities. Model Cities and Community Action Programme 'target cities' eventually increased to over twice the number originally intended. Inevitably, the resources were insufficient in any city to deliver the scale of social reform originally intended and a greater portion of total programme funds flowed to existing agencies and institutions. Survival paid the price of social change. Central intervention slipped from a programme of social redistribution to one of distribution. Meanwhile, at the base of the programme, the intended recipients were sold out.

This survival formula points up the dilemma confronting central intervention into the present state of widespread citizen non-participation. Participation is not just another social good or service to be bartered, provided at one time, withdrawn at another. It involves first and foremost a prevailing set of power relationships. Mobilizing participation involves activating a group which currently holds little power and whose very lack of power is a prerequisite for the hegemony of power by established elites. Central intervention into this state of affairs requires a clear conception of social change, a committed constituency of support, a tenacious adherence to the goal at the price of other objections, and a high ability to tolerate conflict and opposition. But the centre is itself the making of the political elites at its base; it is the outcome of a set of power relationships. It is, in fact, logically both part of the problem as well as a prospective instrument of change. This dilemma suggests the difficulty of centrally induced changes of any significant proportions in areas of chronic non-participation in American society.

The surrender of well-intentioned national administrations to traditional power-holders and bureaucrats is apparent in the results of the decade of experience with community participation efforts. Despite the brave promises which accompanied the birth of the programmes, in the end the poor were left to scramble among themselves for the scraps which remained as federal funding was phased out. In Model Cities, despite marginal improvements in social services, social and physical blights remain blatantly undisturbed. Meanwhile, the social service bureaucracy – those colonial institutions which the Community Action Programme had squarely in its sights – have shown remarkable staying power; the 'vested interests' remain relatively unchallenged. In fact, central intervention has been a boon to their existence; they gradually absorbed much of the new funds and aggrandized their power. The impact on local government has also been minimal. No local power structure has fallen, no mayor has lost his job or even significant political power, no radical changes in the distribution of influence or benefits have occurred. And since it is no less difficult or more rewarding for the poor to participate in American society, little has changed in the slums of American cities.

This raises the question of the adequacy of the participation paradigm(s) employed by the central authority. Such a paradigm presumably would embrace both (a) a model of how and why citizen participation does or does not occur, and (b) a model which links this participation to the operation of the political system. While CAP gave careful consideration to the culture of poverty and Model Cities recognized the ineffectiveness of extant programmes in reaching the residents of slums, neither programme embodied a clearly conceived view of why poor people and/or neighbourhood residents did not participate in social institutions or how the programmes intended (assuming they did) to rectify this need. But some tacit assumptions do appear to underlie both efforts.

Clearly both viewed participation as a means to an end and not an end in itself. Community action sought, through participation, to reform unresponsive service institutions and to generate a continuing demand for new resources as a means of eradicating poverty. Model Cities required participation for programme legitimacy, for proper responsiveness in service programmes, and for easing implementation. There was also a conviction that opportunities established by the new programmes would, especially if buttressed by technical and financial assistance, lead to increased participation by the 'target' populations. This means would be reasonably efficient, so that the 'participation factor' could accomplish this stated (or implicit) objective with a 'reasonable' expenditure of time and funds. Finally, the programmes also assumed, as already pointed out, a fairly benign, if traditional, political environment — a consensual system of values in which government played the honest broker role for competing interests and in which planned social change and institutional reform were attainable.

But this paradigm of participation is not only limited but also seriously flawed. Increased participation properly conceived cannot be solely a device of manipulating people to achieve other desired social ends. There must always be an ends goal as well. As long as they are defined solely in the category of means, the time-frame will always be short-term and the impact incremental whereas the need is long-term and strategic. But a conception of participation as an end in itself involves very fundamental questions because it relates to the entire operation of democracy. A programme designed to increase participation acknowledges at least implicitly that the political system — or better, the political culture — is not doing its job. To be genuine, an approach to participation with an ends goal must be open-ended because it recognizes that the participants must be involved at all stages, that goals must be left open. Pranger (1968) distinguishes between the *participator* and the *participant* to indicate the difference between an active and vital role in decision-making and one which is passive and marginal, where the citizen is simply attached to an on-going process. But an emphasis upon the former, as the early history of Community Action attests, is at minimum uncertain and at maximum potentially revolutionary for the existing power holders. The *participant* role, the assumption of Model Cities, is safer, because uncertainty is minimized; the lid is carefully kept on participation. Programme legitimation and citizen co-optation are the central objectives. The history of conflict in the Community Action Programme and Model Cities is very much connected with the issue of participation as ends and means, of *participators* and *participants*. While federal programmes stressed throughout the means function, the neighbourhood residents pursued the ends function.

The planners of community action suffered most, however, from their inadequate conception of what was needed to produce *participators* among the urban poor. Apparently they believed that new opportunities to participate in indigenous neighbourhood organizations would lead to widespread grass-roots participation. This would be consistent with the outline of 'opportunity' theory. But this rather simple view, when added to the pluralist conception of a consensual political order in which social planning could provide orderly and basic social reform, resulted in a paradigm hopelessly inadequate to the task. Increased participation in this paradigm would lead to collaborative planning, a joint effort by established institutions and new participants to solve common problems.

The first need was a behavioural model which explained how potentially active citizens became chronic non-participants in the first place. Such a model would recognize at minimum that participation is a learned phenomenon, that it is a trait of the mature individual. The political culture socializes some individuals into a role in which they allow elites to make decisions for them and others into the role of active participants. Each of these acquired roles, therefore, is the outcome of a large cumulative process. The socializing agents are not only the political system, but the place of work, family, schools and peer groups as well. Liberation from this role requires positive experiences, but for the poor most encounters with a political system biased against them are unsuccessful. Since effective participation is a learned skill, the more the individual refrains from participation, the less he is able to participate when the opportunity arises. Eventually the individual becomes fatalistic, convinced of his powerlessness, alienated from authority. The ultimate has happened; he enslaves himself.

Effective intervention in this situation is not a question of the techniques which are so chic these days in the programmes designed by 'CP' experts. Breakthroughs in the non-participatory life style require an intense effort, truly a pedagogy of the oppressed (Friere, 1970), focused squarely on the determinants. That Community Action achieved any success is perhaps because it recognized that 'powerlessness' was an important attribute of non-participation and sought to combat it in a variety of ways, primarily through self-help and through indigenous neighbourhood organization. But, by and large, neither the Community Action Programme nor Model Cities intended to strike at these depths, nor did they have a theory to show the way.

The paradigm was no more successful in relating participation to the operation of the political system. Given the assumptions of a pluralist polity with consensual values, the administration was neither anticipating nor prepared for the storm of controversy which erupted. The notion of 'countervailing power', so radical sounding in its rhetoric, never sought more than a healthy dose of reform in established institutions, a partnership of the poor and the bureaucrat, a pluralization of the elite structure. Model Cities intended less; it sought carefully to limit citizen participation. A more adequate political model would have recognized that non-participation by those on the 'bottom' of the political system links tightly with asymmetrical power relationships (Almond & Verba, 1965; Walker, 1966). Poor people, once activated, can be expected to do more than reform delivery systems; they may well begin demanding a full share in society's benefits, challenging democracy's 'rules of the game' which are stacked against them. Nor would this model assume that bureaucrats would happily surrender a measure of their power over programme designs and operations to 'non-professionals' or 'clients'.

Failures both in the role of central interventions and the underlying participation paradigms suggest some broad lessons for future efforts for more participatory planning and political institutions.

Some Lessons

Several generalizations emerge from this brief evaluation of central intervention into participation in America:

1. While policy-makers, planners and bureaucrats tend to see participation primarily as a means for achieving other ends — programme legitimation, better designed services, greater ease of implementation — citizens tend to view participation as an end in itself. Participation programmes which emphasize only a means function without considering an ends responsibility may well be viewed by citizens as essentially manipulative and co-optive. Moreover, many conflicts which appear as disagreements over procedures or policy really involve this more basic question of purpose.
2. Beneath every participation programme lurks a particular social theory, paradigm or at least a set of assumptions concerning the need for intervention and the connection of participation to the operation of the political system and the creation of social change. This theory or paradigm should be made explicit and thoroughly examined. It may well suggest that the intervenor is logically part of the problem.
3. In urban America, chronic non-participation by those at the 'bottom' or 'periphery' of society is a prerequisite for the power of political elites and the system of political biases which support them. Active participation by those who habitually are inert has fundamental implications, then, for the current operation of the political system. Almost inevitably it will threaten reallocation of power from existing elites or bureaucrats and perhaps even the political 'rules of the game'. As a result, conflict with elites is the almost inevitable result of any effective and lasting participation of these groups.
4. Participation programmes which conceive their task as one of utilizing various techniques to provide additional opportunities for 'all interested parties' but which fail to confront the behavioural and systemic obstacles currently limiting broad participation, will succeed largely with those who are already active participants. In effect thay will continue the 'closure of the political universe' of which Marcuse speaks (Marcuse, 1964).
5. Central intervention for socially redistributive policies, such as participation by the poor involves, will usually be forced over a period of time to dilute

its emphasis upon change and become distributive, in content if not intent, in order to survive.

6. Participation once established is not easily controlled or manipulated. As a learned and cumulative activity, participation once begun tends to snowball, to become self-sustaining. As participants accumulate participatory skills and self-confidence, they tend to demand progressively larger roles in governance. Once larger roles have been won, there is generally an unwillingness to return to less authority. Participation, in short, is not something which can be 'given' and 'withdrawn'. It resides in the citizen alone.

7. Established governmental and private agencies have remarkable staying power in the face of challenges or demands exerted by citizen participants. These agencies are often successful in absorbing, co-opting, or discrediting short-run challenges over the long run.

References

Aleshire, Robert A., 1972. 'Power to the People: An Assessment of the Community Action and Model Cities Experience', *Public Administration Review*, September, 428–443.

Alinsky, Saul, 1965. 'The War on Poverty – Political Pornography', *Journal of Social Issues*, 41–47.

Almond, G. A. & S. Verba, 1965. *The Civic Culture*, Boston: Little, Brown & Co.

Boone, Richard W., 1972. 'Reflections on Citizen Participation and the Economic Opportunity Act', *Public Administration Review*, September, 444–456.

Clark, Kenneth B. & Jeannette Hopkins, 1968. *A Relevant War Against Poverty* New York: Harper & Row.

Cloward, Richard A. & Lloyd Ohlin, 1960. *Delinquency and Opportunity*, New York: Free Press.

Friere, Paulo, 1970. *Pedagogy of the Oppressed*, New York: Herder & Herder.

Harrington, Michael, 1962. *The Other America: Poverty in the United States*, New York: Macmillan.

Kaplan, Marshall, 1970. *The Model Citizens Program*, New York: Praeger.

Kravitz, Sanford L., 1969. 'The Community Action Program – Past, Present and its Future', in James L. Sundquist (ed.), *On Fighting Poverty*, New York: Basic Books.

Marcuse, Herbert, 1964. *One-Dimensional Man*, Boston: Beacon Press.

Mogulof, Melvin, 1969. 'Coalition to Adversary: Citizen Participation in Three Federal Programs', *Journal of the American Institute of Planners*, 225–232.

Pranger, Robert, 1968. *The Eclipse of Citizenship*, New York: Holt, Rinehart & Winston.

Ripley, Randall, B., 1972. *The Politics of Economic and Human Resource Development*, Indianapolis: Bobbs-Merrill.

Rose, Stephan M., 1972. *The Betrayal of the Poor*, Cambridge, Mass.: Schenkman.

Strange, John H., 1972. 'The Impact of Citizen Participation on Public Administration', *Public Administration Review*, September, 457–470.

Urban Data Service, 1970. *Citizen Participation in Model Cities*, Washington, D.C.: The International City Managers Association.

Walker, Jack L., 1966. 'A Critique of the Elitist Theory of Democracy', *American Political Science Review*, June, 285–295.

13

The Politician's View: The Perspective of a Member of the House of Commons in the U.K.

JOHN P. MACKINTOSH

Though members of parliament are supposed to operate largely at the national level, on most planning questions they usually become involved as constituency M.P.s and are expected to fight for any groups or interests that are deeply concerned in a case. Indeed, some M.P.s become so caught up in certain planning disputes that their own credibility seems to be involved. Mr. Stoddart, the M.P. for West Edinburgh, was clearly shaken by the outcome of the Turnhouse Airport Inquiry when his colleague, the Secretary of State for Scotland, turned down the Reporter's finding against a new runway. Similarly, Mr. David Steel at one time thought that the retention of his seat in the central Borders depended on his capacity to convince the authorities that the Edinburgh – Carlisle railway line should not be closed. In both cases, the M.P.s survived adverse decisions on these local questions but this does not detract from the importance they attached to these issues at the height of the controversies.

What, then, does the M.P. learn from his involvement in planning cases? The lessons may vary, but certain fundamental points do appear for any one interested in generalizing about his and other M.P.s experiences.

Firstly, there is no clear-cut alternative of planned decisions or unplanned happenings; the latter are simply the result of a variety of private plans. The public authorities may have plans, but so have speculative builders, the industries in the area and the existing owners of the land. The contrast is not between some planning and no planning but between different plans drawn up by different people with varying degrees of completeness and dissimilar objectives.

Secondly, it is a mistake to suggest that the choice between a public authority's plan and the proposals of private interests is the same as choice between coercion and freedom. A plan, when approved by the Secretary of State, may have the force of law but there are recognized methods of seeking to amend such plans. On the other hand, if the public authorities will not seek a compulsory purchase order and the private owner will not sell the land, nothing can be done and the private person or public authority wanting to use the land has as little choice as if it were a legal prohibition.

Thirdly, despite current fashions, it is not self-evident that certain parties to a dispute normally have right on their side. For example, among some people, the mention of professional planners conjures up a picture of men quite remote from the community deciding to impose major changes to please their own personal whims. But in many cases, the planners are pressing points which have been put to them by the elected representatives of the public. For other people, 'developer' is a dirty word, yet many developers provide a real service to the community, which might not be rendered by any public authority if they decided to pull out. In some cases, the developers are the only effective planners. For instance, it seems clear that the expansion of Edinburgh will take place in the western outskirts which are now included in the new District of Edinburgh but were not within the former city boundary. No effective plans for this area were made by the previous local authorities nor have the new authorities which took over in 1975 been able to produce any detailed proposals so that in the intervening period of two or more years any planning has had to be done by the developers.

Finally, plans of the kind authorized by the 1947 Town and Country Planning Act are only one among a number of methods of controlling or influencing what happens. Local authorities may designate industrial sites but industry may refuse to go there. Firms may acquire old industrial premises in order to use them for new purposes or political pressure may be brought to bear on the local authority, so that while plans do influence what happens, they are not necessarily totally effective and they cannot alter some deep-seated social trends. All the planning that Scotland can muster, for example, has not reversed the downward spiral of poor housing conditions, lack of new industrial investment and general decline in west central Scotland.

Bearing all these points in mind, the lesson is that no M.P. (or anyone else) should accept a plan or take a side in a planning dispute unless he has looked at the actual objectives embodied in the plan and assessed the alternatives in terms of local social conditions and of the desirable priorities for an area. And even if he supports a plan or his side wins in a dispute, it is important to remember that this is not the same as achieving the objectives sought by the planners or the parties to the dispute. Victory only means that these goals may not be inhibited or hampered by contrary decisions or prohibitions.

In short, the M.P. faces the same problem as anyone else of trying to weigh a mixture of technical possibilities, a series of value judgments about the desirable pattern of a society, the wishes of local groups as against regional and national interests and the frequent conflict between the short and the long term. The difference between the position of the M.P. (which also applies to his party and to both the opposition and the government) and that of the average citizen is that the politician has probably made some commitments on long-term issues for which he will be held accountable and these may counterbalance local pressures. For example, Scottish M.P.s of various shades of opinion have forecast an easier economic position when North Sea Oil comes ashore so that while they may support this or that objection to the siting of a refinery or some other necessary installation, they are conscious that all such installations cannot be opposed.

Moreover, it is not acceptable in Westminster to say 'it is a necessary monstrosity but it should be built in your constituency rather than in mine'. An example occurred recently in the South of Scotland when the Electricity Board wanted to acquire sites for four new power stations. Those M.P.s with local amenity groups objecting to particular locations were rightly asked to decide first 'do you agree with the Board's projections of demand in the 1980s?'. If these were even roughly right, then the issue was not whether to have new power stations or not but given that they had to be built (and nothing riles voters more than power cuts), which were the most suitable sites?

Not only does a politician encounter this clash between the local and the national interest and between the short term and the long term, he is also acutely conscious of different scales of values among those concerned in his own constituency. To continue with the example of the new power station, local residents will be up in arms over desecration of the landscape and, if it is to be a nuclear station, over possible dangers from radiation. But the neighbouring town council may be delighted and demanding his support on the grounds that in a depopulating area, much-needed jobs will be provided in building the power station and a permanent skilled force will be employed in operating it.

As is only too obvious, the parties to conflicts do not easily fall into two categories of 'goodies' and 'baddies' nor is there always a clear division between public and private interests. A small local authority may be in dispute with a regional authority over the latter's proposal that the small town be designated a holiday resort when the inhabitants want to try and attract some industry other than the tourist trade. A major authority may be drawing a line for a new trunk road and the smaller authorities which will no longer be on the main thoroughfare may protest that this will kill their garages, petrol pumps and restaurants. Conflict can also be between private interests, a familiar one in the south of Scotland being between the proprietor who wants to convert a field into a caravan park and his neighbours who object on grounds of amenity and nuisance. In this case, a further factor comes in. Some of the interests involved are difficult to organize and, therefore, perhaps count for less than they should. Most citizens now go on holidays and more and more people use camp and caravan sites. Thus there is an overall pressure for more well-laid-out and equipped sites yet the same campers and caravanners, in their capacity as local residents, are much more easy to organize and vociferous in their claim that holiday facilities are desirable, but not near their own homes. The M.P. is also conscious that residents have votes and know him and his actions while summer visitors live elsewhere and will not dream of attributing any discomfort they may experience during their holiday to the local M.P.

In addition to this range of experience with actual plans and cases arising from them, the M.P., as someone involved in the machinery of government, is very conscious of how the machinery itself works, whether it makes his task easier or harder and whether public criticism is focusing on the methods of making and amending plans and of settling disputes as well as on the actual outcome in particular cases.

Recently there has been some dissatisfaction with the machinery and the criticisms are numerous and come from a wide variety of sources. Perhaps the most common criticism is over delays. For individual citizens, planning departments seem to take an inordinate time in dealing with small requests to put in dormer windows or build a garage. In the bigger schemes, speed may be of the essence with an industrialist trying to get into a new market or to beat a rival with a new product and, in this case, delay may lead to the investment going elsewhere. At the moment, Britain as a nation has a great interest in getting North Sea oil ashore as rapidly as possible. Sometimes, the delays can turn a whole project sour. The Tweedbank project in the Central Borders began — in terms of a formal application for planning permission — in 1967 and was only settled in 1973, the passage of seven years meaning that the original period of great interest in regional development had largely passed.

This criticism is so general that different groups involved in the planning process, and in particular in the procedure over appeals, tend to pass the blame on to others involved in the various stages. For instance, planners say of the appeals procedure that it is not their part, the making of the plan or the submission of evidence at an inquiry that takes time, it is the delays in finding a Reporter, setting up the inquiry and, above all, the time taken between the presentation of the Report and the Secretary of State's decision. The civil servants tend to blame what they call 'poor management' and 'poor Reporters or Reports' so that they have to wait while the proper procedures are established, and they also claim that they are forced to take time to collect and submit essential evidence to the Secretary of State which is not subsequently brought out at the inquiry.

The complaint of 'poor management' goes wider than being merely part of the argument over delays. It is alleged that there are far too few trained planners (and therefore, perhaps, an inadequate percentage of really able planners); that virtually no Scottish lawyers specialize in planning law and, as a result of both these shortages, many mistakes are made. For example, many requests for ·planning permission are processed and eventually granted when they need not have been made at all in the terms laid out in the various Acts. Again, part of the delay at Tweedbank was due to legal errors. This whole situation is made worse by the recent sudden increase in the pressures on the machinery. Planning applications in Scotland used to run ar 20,000 to 22,000 a year but two years ago they rose to 32,000 or 33,000. Similarly, the number of appeals went up from 130 or 140 a year to 600 and even if there is some decline, the officials concerned do not expect the number to fall below 300 in the foreseeable future.

There are more specific complaints about the way the procedure deals with two kinds of cases, those singled out being the very minor applications at one end of the scale and the massive complex developments at the other. On the minor applications, it is argued that the procedures are too elaborate. If, when an area is scheduled for a certain kind of development, an application in accordance with this established pattern is made, and provided that there are no objections, then detailed scrutiny could be waived. At the other end of the scale, some industrial developers are bitter about the fact that each appeal reaches a decision only about that particular site. The company concerned assembles its case and goes through the long and expensive process of answering objections and putting its arguments at an inquiry. The application may then be turned down on the grounds that sites B, C or D would perhaps be more suitable but this is no guarantee that an application for one of these alternatives will not meet objections, lead to an inquiry and then in its turn be rejected because sites C, D and E were held to be less damaging to the environment.

Tied up with the objections to these specific types of case and with the allegations of delay and poor management, is the question of costs. These lengthy hearings can be terribly expensive. The Drumbuie Hearing is likely to cost one of the parties, the National Trust, £30,000 and the whole inquiry may cost around £150,000. Two points are made about this. One is that the process is too expensive in any case; that the costs are disproportionate to the results; and the second is that while this level of expensive legal expertise may be worth having, the cost prevents certain poorer groups and many individuals from presenting their views. At present, bodies like the National Trust, the Countryside Commission, the Landowners' Federation and the various amenity societies receive many appeals from private citizens to take up cases and they have to discriminate not only on the merits of the cases but also on the grounds of costs. Clearly, private individuals could not afford the kind of costs involved in the Drumbuie Hearing. It is possible for the Secretary of State to agree that the Crown should meet part or the whole of objectors' costs but, in the case of the proposed new runway at Turnhouse Airport, he refused to meet all the costs though the Reporter had found in favour of the objectors. It can be argued that it is odd that the Crown will give legal aid to criminals but not to citizens who have committed no offence but want to protect their property, the local environment or the life of a local community. On the other hand, to offer legal aid to all objectors could invite something like a filibuster in certain cases. If there is no automatic aid, this leaves the difficulty of deciding which objectors are 'genuine' and introduces an element of doubt which will certainly deter the poorer would-be complainants.

There are, however, much deeper objections to the current procedures for judging the validity of cases put up by the opponents to planning applications and equally strong defences of the mechanism, and the clash between the two positions goes to the heart of many of the oldest problems of political theory and of political institutions. The specific issue round which the argument centres is whether objections to proposed developments are mainly matters of law and of an individual's rights or whether they are matters of policy; involved with this is the question of whether the current procedure tilts the balance unduly in favour of either the opponents or the proponents. Extra edge is given to the argument because the two sides also reflect the broad division of opinion between proponents and opponents of change and between those in favour of growth and those who have come to the conclusion that growth is of dubious value or is even positively harmful.

According to the critical school of thought, which is strong in the civil service and among those responsible for achieving long-term social and economic goals, the present process is the result of what they call the 'Franks Tribunal Neurosis'. They are referring to the aftermath of the Crichel Down affair in 1954 when the Franks Committee insisted that all inquiries and tribunals should be as like courts of law as possible, with the minimum of government interference in the resulting quasi-judicial processes. Their point is that, as a result, the government is inhibited from putting the broader policy considerations before inquiries. To do so would be to plead one side of the case when the Secretary of State was also the final judge, thus compromising his role as a court of last appeal. Also, they would argue that while such a procedure inhibited the chief agency concerned with long-term policy, namely the government, it encouraged opponents. All whose property rights were affected appeared in strength at the inquiry while the general public, who would benefit by the change, could not be easily organized; they were too diffuse to constitute an interest and with both the government and 'the silent majority' unable or unwilling to present their cases, all the publicity and public sympathy went to the objectors.

This school of thought also stressed that it was misleading to appoint senior lawyers as reporters and to behave as if the inquiry were a court of law since this suggested that the Reporter could isolate objective, legal reasons for finding in favour of one party or another. In reality, the Reporter's judgement was a matter of his own values and social priorities, except that he would have no personal responsibility for the long-term objectives to which governments are usually committed and whose chief beneficiaries are the public in general.

Finally, this school of thought would point out that because certain widespread interests were not represented at a hearing and because some Reporters failed to consider the long-term policy objectives accepted by the political parties, the Secretary of State had to reject the Report. This, though — they would allege — right under the circumstances, casts discredit on the system as there is a presumption that the findings of a system of review, if it is working properly, ought to be accepted. Otherwise there is no point in going through the elaborate and expensive process of an appeal.

Those in favour of the present system, who would merely wish to see the procedure strengthened and to reinforce the presumption that the opinion of the Reporter should not be overturned, make the opposite case. They argue that the proponents of a scheme have too much in their favour. Both government and developers have the resources to draw up elaborate plans while objectors have to face a huge cost and cannot easily provide alternatives to the proposed plans. Yet the hearing may not turn on the merits of the suggested development but on the existence of preferable sites. To revert to the power station case, how can objectors conduct trial bores and challenge the Board's evidence that only a certain few sites have the rock base capable of bearing the weight of a nuclear power station? On this line of argument the objectors have no obligation to produce alternatives. Their task is simply to demonstrate the unsatisfactory aspects of the existing plans.

They would emphasize that the cost of being represented excludes many potential objectors. Some have also said that the onus of proof is wrong and that the mere title of 'objector' suggests a shrill and selfish individual pitting his personal property rights and well-being against the laudable desire of the mass of the community for progress. It should, on this view, be up to the developer or public authority to prove its case for disturbing the peace of private persons. It is those wanting change who should be labelled as 'objectors' in the sense that they want to break the existing calm of contented communities.

Finally, this approach would accept that any appeals going before Reporters were being submitted to a quasi-judicial process. Only if this process were maintained could powerful interests be forced to answer questions put by independent lawyers of more than equivalent social status and ability than the civil servants and developers on the other side. But if it were accepted that this was a quasi-legal proceeding and both sides had had full freedom to present their case with full publicity in the media and much public discussion, then the final judgement by the Reporter should not be overturned. Indeed, for this to happen makes a mockery of the entire procedure, and this is the product of a fundamental error in equity which is to permit the Secretary of State to be the final court of appeal in cases in which he or his subordinates have often been involved as one of the parties to the dispute.

Before going any further with the description of the rival pressures on the M.P., it is possible to come to some conclusions about the merits of these two lines of argument. First, and most fundamental, planning disputes are not the same as legal cases and the task of the Reporter is in many ways quite distinct from that of a judge. A judge's task is to ascertain the facts and apply the law. For the Reporter, there is no law. His decision has to be a mixture of considerations including equity, policy and a number of value judgements about aesthetics and the environment. Moreover, the idea that the reporter should be totally independent has misleading overtones. It suggests that there is a valid independent resolution of a planning dispute when, in fact, a planning dispute is about the best way of implementing a policy. Sometimes the merits of the policy itself get drawn into the dispute. Into the siting of an airport, there comes the question of whether more air travel and more airports are in any case desirable. But both this and the siting of the airport are matters of policy and in reaching a decision there are no absolute rights and wrongs. There is a value in holding an inquiry over a proposed location but it only creates confusion and bitterness if it is suggested that an inquiry can come to one proper, legal conclusion like a court of law.

What then is the value of such an inquiry? It is to act as an aid to the Minister in making a reasonable ultimate judgement on a policy issue for which he and his government will be responsible at the next election. It is also to permit local objectors to hear the case of the proponents, to allow them to put their points of view and to cross-examine all those involved and to make sure that the experts have done their homework and have conducted the necessary investigations and assembled all the relevant facts. The essential difference between the position of the Reporter and the Minister is that the Reporter is not culpable if in x years time there is not enough electric power, or there is intolerable airport congestion or there are too few doctors because a new power station, airport or training hospital was not built. It is the government, quite properly, which will bear the responsibilty. In this situation, planning disputes are not single cases where legal processes can establish the one true result. They are aids to the Minister in verifying the ends and determining the means of conducting certain policies.

This does not imply, however, that there should be any detraction from the process of conducting inquiries and hearing appeals. Indeed, these processes could be improved in order to achieve the objectives set out here. Firstly, it is of great help to the public and the Minister to have the forecasts of those proposing the changes carefully probed with the help of outside expert witnesses. Secondly, the arguments for the particular proposals put forward in order to implement policies based on the forecasts must be scrutinized in detail. To do this, the use of high-level, legally-trained advocates is a great help as this means using men who are used to cross-examining witnesses and these men are at least the equals in social status and self-confidence of those they are examining. It is also probably better that the Reporter should be an independent person rather than a professional inspector paid as a civil servant, as this makes it clear that the inquiry is being conducted by someone outside the governmental machine. But there is no reason why the proponents, if they are the government, should be inhibited from stating their case. Indeed, it is essential that this case should be heard and, if the government is clear that an overall policy must be pursued, it should say so. The Secretary of State should send his officials with a brief that the government will not contemplate power shortages in six year's time and that, therefore, x new power stations must be built, the argument then being not over whether to have any such stations but over which are the least unsatisfactory sites. If it is clear that the whole exercise is part of a policy decision and an aid to the government in using the best means of implementing that decision, then the careful rehearsal by the government of its case and the ultimate decision by the Secretary of State both fall into place as essential elements in the process.

Some further changes could help speed the process and reduce the sense of frustration felt by some participants. More staff are needed in the government departments dealing with planning. The group of lawyers and prominent persons available as Reporters should be enlarged. All expert information to be led at inquiries should be shown to the parties concerned and the costs of all serious objectors should be met if they have not adequate means – that is if they are private persons.

In December 1973, the Secretary of State for the Environment and the Secretary of State for Wales appointed Mr. George Dobry to consider whether the development control system adequately met current needs, bearing in mind the reorganization of local government with planning split into structure and local plans. In his Interim Report, published in January 1974, Mr. Dobry states (without any evidence) that 'the British system of planning and planning control is the best in the world'. He also says it is 'over-criticized, over-worked, under-guided and under-appreciated'. Mr. Dobry was not asked to look at the situation in Scotland, but his remarks are relevant. The new system of local government in Scotland divides planning between the nine regions and the forty-seven districts (it is the only major function to be split in this way). The regions are to be responsible for structure plans and the districts for local plans. The latter are the successors of the present plans drawn up under the 1947 Town and Country Planning Act. The precise nature, number and rationale of structure plans is quite unclear. The whole case for the new regions was based on the claim that they were sensible units for strategic planning of the major local government functions yet, astonishingly, each region is not to have a single structure plan. What factors, functional or demographic, are to determine the approriate areas for structure plans within the regions remains obscure. In addition, at the regional level there are to be 'regional reports' which set out plans or guidelines for each region on housing or education and they may combine these in some cases.

This is relevant to Mr. Dobry's interim proposals which do not suggest any serious departure from the present system. In a welter of minor recommendations for more discussion and collaboration between planners, developers and objectors, the only significant line of thought is that the more detailed applications for minor changes should be speedily granted if they do not conflict with the general lines of local plans and that architectural and aesthetic objections should not be pressed. It might be possible, in this category of case, to take appeals from officials' decisions either to the chairman or to a subcommittee of the local planning committee as the elected representatives of the public at the local level. A second line of thought which, though not made explicit by Mr. Dobry, follows from his emphasis on policy guidelines, relates to larger inquiries dealing with major developments of significance for a whole region or for the country in general. The point here is that if it is government policy to have a third London airport, then this should be stated in evidence by the official spokesmen and the inquiry, like the Roskill Commission, should be charged not just with examining the objections to one specific proposal but with looking at other possibilities and coming up with a preferred solution. The final decision, once again, would have to lie with the Minister.

If there is, therefore, a real distinction between regional reports and structure plans on the one hand and local plans on the other, it makes sense to devise different methods of procedure for each category, the object being to clarify the policy content in decisions, ensure a proper hearing for applicants and complainants and a more rapid method of reaching a decision. All this appeals to anyone who has had responsibility not just for keeping people happy and fairly treated but also for ensuring that the wider desires of the community for development — and such desires do exist and will exist as long as some are enjoying a much easier life than others — are not unduly thwarted.

All this leads into the series of points made in the various reports about public participation in the process of preparing plans as well as the provision of adequate opportunities for objection. Most of the ideas were drawn together by the Skeffington Report in 1969. It dealt mainly with information and recommended that the public should be told when it was decided to prepare a plan and that a programme of consultation and a timetable for the various stages should also be published. If the authority considered a series of alternatives, these should be explained, the public's comments invited and a pause observed to allow for reactions. Then when one of the alternatives was chosen, reasons should be given for this decision and another chance for objections to be made. 'Community development officers should be appointed to secure the involvement of those people who do not join organizations', the people should be encouraged to take a positive part and be told what their representations have achieved and why some recommendations have not been accepted before the final Report is confirmed.

All this has its merits but it can also do considerable damage and harm relations between the public and the authorities concerned if the basic conditions on which participation takes place are not made clear. For example, objectors may easily assume that public opinion is vocal opinion; that is that they represent the public, but this is not true. Interests are always stronger than mere opinion. Representing opinion puts a premium on the organizable. Producers are always easier to organize than consumers, the receivers of subsidies shout louder than the taxpayer, and so on. Secondly, great damage may be done if those prepared to make the effort to participate are allowed to think that they are part of the decision-making process. If all the property-owners in a holiday area say 'no caravan park here' and the local authority still decides to go ahead and build one, they may feel that they have been wickedly cheated.

Participation has its value but only if these muddles are avoided and the public are clear about precisely what is meant by this idea, what it is supposed to achieve and how far it can go. First, it must be said that the opponents of schemes are almost always easier to organize and more vocal than the proponents. Indeed, the latter may not exist. The objections to new towns are alive and active but no one can speak for the would-be inhabitants of towns not yet built. Lord Cockburn, when he wrote his essay on the best way of destroying Edinburgh, his great tirade against the railway companies building their stations at each end of Princes Street and putting a line through the Gardens, could not have guessed that amenity groups 130 years later, pursuing the same cause, would be extolling the self-same railways and holding up the desecration he condemned as a great triumph of sensible planning. There may be no time gap in such contradictions. The same people who want shops full of goods in the pedestrian precincts do not want lorries to deliver and remove these goods.

So it must be made clear to all who participate that they represent only a section of public opinion. Who represents the rest? The answer is the elected representatives at district, regional and national level because only they are actually responsible if the wrong decisions are taken and the wrong balance is achieved. If the traffic in Edinburgh grinds to a halt in a few years, no one is going to sack the presidents of the various amenity societies who may have stopped the necessary transport developments. The purpose of participation must be reiterated. It is to give interested parties a chance to state their case. It is to keep all planners and officials up to the mark and to force them to look at all other possibilities and explain their preferences. It is to open up the full range of issues for the elected representatives who must take the final decision.

Even when this limited but important role for participation is made clear, there are still dangers. The first is of intolerable delays. These need not arise if the public are kept steadily informed and if the planners are able and confident. But there can be appalling results if a sensible proposal is objected to with vehemence and then the planners take fright and settle for worse alternatives after endless inquiries, simply because this saves them from the strongest opposition. (One cannot help fearing that this is what happened over the third London airport.) Secondly, a full programme of participation can seriously spoil relations between the public and the local authorities even when the best decision is taken, if the local media decide to play up only the case of certain objectors. Perhaps because the objectors are there on the ground and the beneficiaries are too dispersed, it is thought that supporting objectors sells more newspapers than backing new proposals. In any case, attacking officials is more fun than defending them. So the outcome may be to stop valuable developments, to demoralize officials or, if they proceed, to lead to strained relations. This does not mean that participation should be avoided; it has great merits and can be a real help but care must be taken to avoid these pitfalls.

In Britain, part of the problem lies in the current psychology of the public and particularly of those sections of the public who set the prevailing intellectual atmosphere. It is not too much to say that there is a general distaste for change. Middle-class people, despite inflation and the trade unions, have a very comfortable life so why alter or build anything? Yet it is clear that if their standards are to be shared by the rest of the community, there will have to be new houses, larger sewage schemes, more holiday spaces, modern schools, more universities: in short, many distasteful developments. Apart from these class considerations, people in Britain have widespread doubts about change, as can be seen by the defensive, not to say, hostile reaction in many quarters to the discovery of North Sea oil as compared with the confidence and positive enthusiasm evinced by the Norwegians. Among those interested in aesthetic standards, there is little confidence in our new architecture; old buildings are almost always bound to be preferable and one senses the real surprise evinced over the rare new building which is not a monstrosity.

Finally, the central theme of this paper, the ultimate responsibility of elected representatives for policy decisions affecting the long-term standards of the community, is bound to be unpopular because these same elected representatives have been conspicuously unable to solve the main political and economic problems facing Britain in the last twenty years. A lack of trust in our representative institutions goes hand in hand with a lack of confidence in our architects and our planners and a conviction that when in doubt – and who is not in doubt? –it is better to do nothing.

Yet this is not the answer. Change cannot be prevented and therefore it is always best to try and grasp the problem and provide right solutions, even in a period when there is such a marked lack of national self-confidence.

14
Postscript

J. T. COPPOCK

The studies included in this volume are only a sample of the many investigations of public participation which have been undertaken in recent years, but they do illustrate various aspects of the process and some of the major problems which attempts to achieve a greater measure of public participation pose. In particular, they clearly show that public participation is a complex concept and that the issues are rarely clear-cut.

Underlying the debate about the role and contribution of public participation is a more fundamental debate about representative and participatory democracy, though in practice the antithesis between decisions taken on behalf of the people by elected representatives and decisions made by the people themselves is a false one; for they represent extremes on a continuum rather than clear-cut alternatives. Nor is public participation new, for representative democracy has always required some input from constituents, and there is a long tradition of attempts to influence policies and decisions on major issues by public discussion. In general, the difficulties which led to demands for greater and more effective public participation arise from the sheer size and complexity of modern society and of the issues which face it. Ironically, we now seem to be approaching a point when advances in electronics will make it technically possible to have direct participation by all members of the community, who could listen, debate and vote by means of appropriate terminals in their own homes. There have already been experiments along these lines in North America where those watching a televised discussion have been asked to switch electrical appliances on and off so that changes in consumption of current can provide an indication of the level of support for different propositions. Such a possibility, though not immediate, poses in acute form the question as to whether greater public participation is necessary, desirable and feasible, and whether, if it is implemented, it leads to better decisions and to a lessening of the alienation between governors and governed.

It is important to see these demands for greater participation in perspective. The concept of government by representatives of all the people, which has been somewhat tarnished in recent decades by the emergence of strong political ideologies and by voting systems which allow the election of those who do not have an absolute majority, has itself been interpreted in two different ways, as the devising and implementation of policies which the people want or which governments think are good for people. Yet whichever philosophy is accepted, representatives have themselves sought to provide channels of communication with their constituents, not only through the mail box, but also through regular 'surgeries' and public meetings in their constituencies. In recent decades, various pressure groups have been formed to influence the voting of individual members and the decisions and policies of governments, though they have rarely been as powerful and as formalized as the political lobbies in the United States. More recently, the mass media, in addition to their long-established role in airing and discussing issues of public importance, have increasingly provided opportunities for direct inputs by members of the public, particularly through radio and television programmes in which listeners and viewers can telephone their comments and questions directly to officials and elected members for immediate answer. Lastly, there is the great multiplication of public opinion polls, in which the opinions of representative samples of the public are sought on a wide range of issues.

There is similarly a long tradition of public inquiry in which members of the public, generally through professional organizations or societies and occasionally as individuals, have had the opportunity to make their views known. Royal Commissions, Commissions or Committees of Inquiry, Select Committees and the like have provided well-established channels for the making of public statements of opinion on desirable courses of action; and while these opportunities are frequently restricted to those who are invited, general invitations have sometimes been issued to anyone who in sufficiently interested to submit a memorandum or brief. In the United Kingdom, at least, there have been increasing numbers of public inquiries in the period since the Second World War, particularly in the context of land-use planning and of the growing concern with the environment, as in the Edinburgh airport inquiry which is discussed in Chapter 4.

Despite the existence of such channels, there have been repeated claims that the public is not adequately consulted, and it is certainly true that much of the input from members of the community is largely hidden from public view, as with the widespread consultation which public servants commonly undertake when some course of action or some new policy has been proposed, and measures are increasingly designed to improve the opportunities for discussion and consultation – such as the publication of green papers or discussion documents and the holding of public meetings or the mounting of exhibitions. New legislation increasingly contains provisions for public consultation and, at least in public statements, governments recognize the desirability of promoting it; yet public dissatisfaction remains. Is it simply that the machinery for consultation is not properly used, are there major deficiencies, or is the concept of public participation misconceived, seeking a level of interest and understanding which the public is neither willing nor able to provide? How far is it true to say that, if there were good planning, there would be no need for public participation, as the public's wishes would have been taken fully into account in the planning process? Clearly there is a need for further evaluation both of existing machinery and of alternative methods of consultation.

Examination of the many experiments in public participation does suggest that, in general, the level of interest is very variable and tends to be scale-dependent. At the local level, where individuals can see their interests directly affected by greater noise, obnoxious fumes, a decline in the value of their property and the like, they often take a keen interest. At the regional level, however, as in the evaluation of structure plans or regional strategies, a much smaller proportion of the public likely to be affected takes an interest, possibly because the issues are too remote and the difficulties of identifying the likely effects on individual citizens too great. It does not take a great feat of imagination for the citizen to visualize the effect of a motorway cutting across his garden, whereas a general rise in the level of pollution (which might have no readily observable visual effects) is much more difficult to envisage and requires a feat of imagination. At the national (and, *a fortiori*, at the international) scale, the expressed level of interest declines and the effort of imagination increases.

Yet scale is obviously not the only factor. Many of the issues, especially those which arise in planning and in environmental matters generally, are highly complex, and it has been argued that they are beyond the capacity of the individual to grasp, at least beyond the local scale. Indeed, it may well be that many are beyond the grasp of those who must make the decisions, and Mutch suggests in Chapter 4 that councillors involved in the Edinburgh Airport controversy did not appreciate the nature of the evidence being presented to them. In any case, there are many aspects of the human environment on which it is not possible, on present knowledge, to make firm pronouncements, particularly about the probable consequences of proposed policies. The level of understanding can, of course, be improved by education, and a great deal of effort is being devoted to presenting issues in ways in which they can be grasped by members of the public, for example by film montage of, say, the existing landscape and alternative types of roads, by the construction of scale models and by the use of cathode ray tube displays for interactive three-dimensional graphics. Yet considerable simplification may often be necessary for comprehension and this may give a false picture of the issues involved. Experts frequently chafe at the gross over-simplification and dramatization of issues which are characteristic of radio and, more especially, television programmes on serious issues designed to interest even the relatively small minority of the population which has the initiative to watch them.

Knowledge and understanding are, of course, inextricably linked, and Schatzow notes in Chapter 10 how even a high level of interest is accompanied by a low level of knowledge and comprehension. Information is of critical importance, whether about the very existence of an issue, its nature and seriousness, about the courses of action that are feasible or about the likely consequences. Of course, no information may exist, a frequent occurrence in environmental problems; no one may have thought of collecting it or it may be too difficult or costly to obtain. Alternatively, information may exist, but is not used because no one outside the agency responsible is aware of its existence, or it is not in a suitable form, or it is regarded as too confidential or too technical to comprehend, or officials are unwilling to release it for a variety of reasons associated with their views of their roles and of the public. Information may be deliberately withheld or provided too late for it to be of value in order to limit the effectiveness of public protest, possibly because those who control it see themselves threatened. There appear to be differences between countries in this respect which would merit examination. Thus, governments and public servants in Great Britain have always been more secretive and less willing to disclose information than their counterparts in the United States, where such information is regarded as being in the public domain. The role of information in public participation clearly warrants further investigation.

Public participation involves both members of the public and officials and representatives but it is frequently seen as a challenge by those in authority. Politicians regard themselves as the proper channel for making the public's views known and claim that they know what the public wants. Both politicians and officials fear that public participation may simply be a means whereby unrepresentative groups impose their views on the public at large, a risk which is strengthened by the general apathy of the public. Such occurrences are common in trade unions, where small but dedicated minorities can easily seize power, and, to a lesser extent, in the political parties themselves, and experience with the operation of the National Environmental Policy Act in the United States, where the courts have been widely used by environmental groups to frustrate developments to which they are opposed, may strengthen this fear. The official may see participation as a challenge both to his expertise and to his conception of his job, as it has been shaped by his experience, by his training and by tradition; this may partly explain the hostile reaction when those who object can muster equal expertise. Officials may genuinely feel that they know best, that they have the public interest at heart, and that existing procedures provide ample opportunity for all who are interested to make their views known. They fear that the delays which consultation may impose may be excessive and may not result in any significant improvement in what is finally decided. Alternatively, both officials and politicians may simply be too busy to be aware of weaknesses in the machinery or of the inadequacy of the investigations on which policies have been formulated. Further research could usefully be undertaken on the ways in which the professional background and training of officials affect their attitudes towards public participation.

It is, of course, misleading to talk about the public and the public interest as if these were homogeneous and easily defined, for while a majority opinion can be identified through the ballot box, whether in elections or in referenda, there are many publics, with different interests, different motives and different levels of concern and understanding. It may be asked whether the public at large does and should have an interest in all public issues; whether the public knows what it wants and is capable of articulating its wishes; and whether silence is not a legitimate expression of opinion. If there is an adequate level of trust between elected representatives and officials on the one hand and members of the public on the other, most of the latter may be willing to leave the decisions to those in authority; but if such trust is lacking, and this seems to be the common experience, there will be increasing alienation between the public and those responsible for government.

The election of representatives can decide only the general character of administrations, not individual issues; and unless the whole population is to be consulted directly on every major issue, no single method of public participation can provide adequate opportunities for all those with legitimate interests to make their views known.

If there is to be greater and more effective full participation, it must take a variety of forms which will be suitable for different purposes and have weaknesses and strengths which need to be assessed. All methods of public participation involve a cost, both directly in specific expenditure on the holding of meetings, the preparation, distribution and analysis of questionnaires and the like, and indirectly as opportunity costs in relation to the time of officials and ministers, and as costs that may result from delays in making decisions. There may, of course, be corresponding benefits, for example, in savings through the avoidance of conflict and the need for public inquiries; there may also be gains in higher levels of satisfaction, in the consideration of a wider range of alternatives and possibly in better final decisions, though none of these can easily be quantified. Characteristically, such public inputs will come from a variety of sources, and this poses the question as to how inputs of different kinds can be related. Letters, votes at meetings, the results of surveys and the like must be equated in some way, a dilemma which Hendee and his colleagues have tried to resolve by their formulation of CODINVOLVE, as described in Chapter 7. There are other dilemmas posed by differences in the strength of feeling; does a majority of marginal preferences always outweigh a minority with passionately held views? Here, too, there is a need for further research.

Public participation is not, of course, an end in itself, though to some enthusiasts it seems to have become a way of life. Its purpose is to influence decisions which will generally be political in nature and require the expressed views of sections of the public to be weighed against the cost, the alternative claims on resources, the advantages of avoiding conflict and the like. It seems unlikely that it will ever be possible to know exactly what goes on in the smoke-filled committee rooms in which, convention has it, political decisions are made, but it is at least reasonable to expect some response from decision-makers to such inputs in which they either accept the views put forward or provide the reasons for their rejection. It is certainly possible to attempt to monitor the outcome, particularly with a view to establishing how far the decision, as implemented, proved acceptable to the public and whether any objections which were discounted were subsequently shown to be justified.

In an age in which authority is being questioned more and more it seems likely that members of the public will increasingly demand that their voices be heard. It will help the process of consultation if governments provide clear and unambiguous statements of their intentions, are seen to be willing to consider a range of options (though this need not preclude an expression of preference), give adequate time for members of the public (who cannot command the resources or expertise of government) to consider the issues, and readily make relevant information available.

It will also help to avoid a sense of alienation if the role that consultation or participation is expected to play is made explicit so that members of the public do not expect more than government is willing to concede.

Public participation is an evolving concept which it is easy for politicians to accept in theory, but difficult to implement in practice. The forms it takes will be determined by the ways in which politicians and officials view their respective roles and the effectiveness with which they perform them, and by the level of public interest and the willingness of members of the public at large to devote time and energy both to inderstanding the issues and to participating in discussions. Lessons can, of course, be learnt from experience, methods can be refined and improved, and research can help to make participation more effective; yet it may well be that the output of public participation is not its most important aspect. Its chief role may well be educational both for the public, in helping its members to become better citizens and to understand more adequately the true nature of the problems facing society, and for elected members and officials, in shaping their thinking and encouraging them to examine their assumptions and preconceptions and to consider a wider range of alternatives than they might otherwise do. Better informed citizens and more open-minded governments may thus help to reduce the sense of alienation which seems to have been the main stimulus to demands for more participation.

Biographical Notes

J. T. COPPOCK is Ogilvie Professor of Geography at the University of Edinburgh, Scotland, and Director of the Tourism and Recreation Research Unit. He is also Chairman of the Steering Committee of the School of the Built Environment at the University of Edinburgh. He is the author of numerous books and articles on rural resources management, tourism and recreation, and on the development of information systems for planning and policy-making. He has been an advisor to various government agencies in the United Kingdom and Canada on policies relating to resources management and recreation. From 1971 to 1972 he was specialist Adviser to the Select Committee on Scottish Affairs in its investigation of land resource use in Scotland.

NORMAN DENNIS is Reader in the Department of Social Studies, University of Newcastle upon Tyne, England. His recent participant-observation research has been of municipal government as a full-time local government officer, then as a citizen participant, followed by a period as an elected councillor. The first two studies published as a result of this work (*People and Planning* and *Public Participation and Planners' Blight*) were of municipal housing provision. The third deals with the whole range of municipal decisions affecting a particular locality during the three-year period of his elective office. He is principally concerned with the formal and informal techniques available to and used or neglected by diverse groups of paid officials, elected representatives and citizens to bring about the effects they aim at achieving, freedom from democratic or other control.

W. A. HAMPTON is Senior Lecturer in Extramural Studies at the University of Sheffield, England. His main research interests are in local government politics and in public involvement in the provision of local authority services. He has written *Democracy and Community* (Oxford University Press, 1970) and many articles for academic and professional journals Dr. Hampton has lectured widely both in the United Kingdom and abroad on English local government reform, community involvement and various aspects of social service and town planning provision. Between 1973 and 1976 he acted as Research Co-ordinator to the Linked Research Project into Public Participation in Structure Planning sponsored by the Department of the Environment.

JOHN C. HENDEE is an officer in the Division of Legal Affairs, U.S. Forest Service, Washington, D.C. Until recently he was Recreation Research Project Leader for the U.S. Forest Service, Pacific Northwest Forest and Range Experiment Station, and Affiliate-Associate Professor of Forest Resources, University of Washington.

His main professional interests are the application of social research methods, concepts and techniques to resource management. He has written many articles from his research on outdoor recreation, wilderness, wildlife and public involvement. In 1974 he received an American Motors 'Conservationist of the Year Award' for his work 'applying social research methods to help solve people problems in resource management'. Dr. Hendee recently led a task force review of Forest Service public involvement and, as a member of an international committee, helped write a new North American Wildlife Policy. Dr. Hendee received his Ph.D. from the University of Washington.

HELEN INGRAM is Associate Professor of Political Science and Director of the Institute of Government Research at the University of Arizona. Her research interests relate principally to policy-making in resources development and environmental management. Recently she has been engaged on an interdisciplinary study of environmental assessment and energy resources decisionmaking relating to Lake Powell, a new lake in an arid land. Prior to her present appointment, Dr. Ingram was Staff Political Scientist for the National Water Commission and Assistant Professor of Political Science at the University of New Mexico. She is Associate Editor for political science and public administration for the *Natural Resources Journal*.

ROGER E. KASPERSON is Professor of Government and Geography at Clark University in Worcester, Massachusetts, U.S. Prior to his present appointment he served on the faculties of Michigan State University and the University of Connecticut, and has lectured at universities elsewhere in other parts of the United States, Canada and other countries. He has written widely in the fields of political geography and environmental politics. Recently, he finished a study of the diffusion of water re-use systems in American cities. His current research interest is a study of safety policy-making in the American nuclear energy programme.

JOHN P. MACKINTOSH is Member of Parliament for Berwick and East Lothian. Formerly Professor of Politics at Strathclyde University, he has been Visiting Professor of Government at Birkbeck College, London. He has written widely in the fields of political science and government, and has been Joint Editor of the *Political Quarterly* since 1975. He has been a member of several House of Commons Select Committees, including those on Procedure, Agriculture and Scottish Affairs. Dr. Mackintosh is a Member of the Chatham House Research Committee and a Fellow of the Royal Historical Society.

WILLIAM E. S. MUTCH is Senior Lecturer at the Department of Forestry and Natural Resources at the University of Edinburgh, Scotland. His writings and principal research interests are concerned with the economics of land use and with the allocation and management of renewable natural resources. Dr. Mutch's teaching relates to various aspects of urban, rural and regional planning. Prior to his present appointment, he worked at the University of Oxford and in government service in Nigeria. For several years he has been active in community affairs in his home area at Edinburgh; he was a committee member of the Cramond Association when plans were released for the reconstruction of

Edinburgh Airport, and an executive member of the Runway Joint Committee. Currently he is President of the Cramond Association.

TIMOTHY O'RIORDAN is a Reader in the School of Environmental Sciences at the University of East Anglia, Norwich, England. His research interests include the case analysis of environmental policy issues and the evaluation of public preferences for environmental amenity. His publications include two books on the analysis of environmental policy questions plus numerous articles and chapters on cognition, behaviour, decision-making and environmental ideologies. He has undertaken several research projects on public-involvement in decision-making, both in connection with resources management and city planning. Prior to his appointment in England, Dr. O'Riordan taught at Canadian and American universities and spent most of an academic year in New Zealand.

STEVEN SCHATZOW is a lawyer in Washington, D.C. Formerly he was Senior Research and Policy Officer and Legal Consultant for the Ministry of State for Urban Affairs, Ottawa, Canada. Among his major research interests are decision-making processes and particularly the interaction of public, media, business, professionals and government to produce societal decisions. From 1971 to 1975 he was co-organizer of a number of environmental policy studies, notably an in-depth analysis of the rise and fall of the environmental issue in Canada. His interest in public participation stems from his involvement as a Washington poverty lawyer in trying to gain 'maximum feasible participation' for his clients in federal programmes.

W. R. DERRICK SEWELL is Professor of Geography at the University of Victoria, Victoria, B.C., Canada. Prior to his present appointment he was on the faculty of the University of Chicago, and formerly an economist with the Canadian Government. A specialist in problems relating to resources development and environmental management, Dr. Sewell has written more than a dozen books and monographs, and over a hundred articles in scholarly journals. He is a consultant on water and energy matters to governments in Canada, the United States, France, and Hungary, as well as to the United Nations. His recent research has focused upon institutional innovations in water management in the United Kingdom, France and Canada, and on the role of the public in planning and policy-making.

MARGARET SINCLAIR is pursuing an advanced degree at the University of Toronto. She was a Resources Research Officer for the Department of the Environment at Burlington, Ontario, Canada. Her position at the Canada Centre for Inland Waters involved research relating to social planning and the influence of attitudes and behaviour on the use of the environment. She has undertaken various attitude and perception studies of water-related issues. More recently, her interests have focused on public participation in environmental management, and she has worked on a study of the role of 'conserver-oriented' attitudes in improving environmental quality.

J. M. THOMSON has been Head of the European Intercity Transport Study at the OECD, Paris, since 1973, before which he worked as transport economist at the Road Research Laboratory and was Research Fellow in Transport at the London School of Economics (1965–1973). He has worked extensively in the field of transport economics and has undertaken consultancy work in various parts of the world. He has been editor of the *Journal of Transport Economics and Policy* since its foundation in 1966. As Chairman of the London Amenity and Transport Association between 1967 and 1973 he took a leading part in public participation in the planning of London, in particular in the discussions on and public inquiry into the Greater London Development Plan. In addition to numerous professional publications he has published *Motorways in London* (1969) and prepared *Transport Strategy in London* (1970).

SCOTT J. ULLERY is Research Associate in the Institute of Government Research at the University of Arizona. Concentrating principally upon political theory, he has collaborated with Dr. Ingram on a number of research projects concerning resources management. He is currently working on the Lake Powell research project.

COLIN J. B. WOOD is Assistant Professor of Geography at the University of Victoria, Victoria, B.C., Canada. His research interests focus principally upon the fields of economic and cultural geography and particularly upon resources management issues. He has published a number of monographs and articles on innovation diffusion and simulation gaming, and conflict resolution in resources development. His recent studies have concerned the changing role of the public in planning and policy-making. In addition to teaching at the University of Victoria, Dr. Wood has lectured at the University of British Columbia and the University College of Swansea. He has also been a consultant to the government of British Columbia.

Index